Is Capitalism Forever?

by

NELSON GIST

ISBN:1539676323
ISBN-13:9781539676324

****

In dedication to a world in struggle against the forces of private property

****

"Some men see things as they are and ask why. Others dream things that never were and ask why not."

George Bernard Shaw

CONTENTS

INTRODUCTION

My political awareness began while I was in college during the 1960s. The Vietnam War was raging. Hundreds of human beings were dying daily, both Americans and Vietnamese. The death tolls were being reported nightly on the television, and people of all persuasions were shocked by the carnage which seemed to have no end. Our government and President Johnson were stubbornly resolved to win a war that could not be won. We could see that America was on the wrong side of history and justice. The devastation of civilian lives and the massacres of villages were particularly troubling. The war was being driven mostly by the blind ideology and paranoia of the anti-Communist sentiment which had been whipped up in the 50s under McCarthyism. The driving force behind the war was the "domino theory," that told us Communism was going to take over the world. At home the Civil Rights Movement reflected the awareness that the Civil War had not ended discrimination. There was still a deep-rooted prejudice in the South which had resulted in 100 years of Jim Crow laws. In the South slavery had only taken on a new form. There was a close relationship between the Civil Rights Movement and the anti-Vietnam War Movement. Martin Luther King had become aware of common grounds between the two movements shortly before his assassination. Both were a struggle against "white supremacy" and racial hatred. Both movements were a struggle against Capitalism, which seeks to divide people by race at home while exploiting foreign markets abroad.

Although today the struggle for civil rights contin-

1

ues, the 1964 enactment of the Civil Rights Act was a real victory. Most Americans knew that the Civil Rights Movement was a righteous cause, but it took several years before the majority of Americans supported the anti-war movement. By the late 1960s soldiers were revolting: lobbing hand grenades into the tents of their superiors and deserting in record numbers. Young civilian men were fleeing to Canada and other places to avoid the draft. The demonstrations against the war were growing. The increasing death tolls on the nightly news report were rising and sickening everyone. By the time the war ended, there had been approximately 60,000 American troops killed. There were over 1 million North Vietnamese troops killed, 600,000 wounded and over 2 million civilian deaths of the Vietnamese people. Despite those numbers we lost the war. The people of Vietnam were clearly willing to sacrifice whatever was needed to maintain their independence. History and justice were on their side. Before we were finally run out of the country in a humiliating defeat, thousands of our American troops had died wondering, as did the nation at home, what the hell we were doing there.

Our nation, at first, was split between generations and within families. In time, the splits were less, and there were fewer counter-demonstrations. A significant portion of the country was in the streets and on the campuses protesting against the war. The upheaval destroyed at least two presidents: Johnson and Nixon. Part of Johnson's downfall was his stubborn pursuit of the war. For Nixon, his war-related Watergate cover-up brought about his disgrace. The hawks supporting the war said we were invited into Vietnam but, as revealed in the "Pentagon Papers," we had overthrown the South

Vietnamese Government and set up a puppet government in order to get the invitation. The Kennedy assassination may also have been related to the war. It was
rumored that Kennedy wanted to disengage from the
war in the early stages. Kennedy's position went
against the corporate/military establishment. Even
President Eisenhower, who initially sent American military advisors to Vietnam, warned the nation of the military establishment. The war alienated a good portion of
a whole generation of young people, myself among
them. The 1960s and 1970s were truly an era of political and social upheaval in America that shook the foundations of American democracy.

As the war dragged on into the 1970s a friend of
mine put a copy of *The Communist Manifesto* in my
hands. Reading it felt like someone turning on a light
inside my head. I finally began to realize not only that
the war was wrong, but why it was happening. The
cause of the war was Capitalism. It was a corporate-
driven war for resources, new markets and cheap labor.
It was based in a deep-rooted fear among the Capitalists
in America that Socialism/Communism would spread,
and that public rather than private property would become the basis of the world's economic system. Private
enterprise and the accumulation of wealth cannot exist
under public property. The corporations like Dow
Chemical, DuPont, the armament industry and others
were profiteering off the war and the politicians were
their cheering section. It was the politics of fear, much
like what we see today. At the same time, there were a
growing number of politicians who were speaking out
against the war who were influenced by the demonstrations. They were beginning to respond to the social unrest that was threatening the credibility of the American

establishment. The Vietnam War changed my life. The war and my growing knowledge of Marxism destroyed my trust in government and helped me to see the role of the private economic system, the corporate world, in its dominance over the political system.

Within a decade after the end of the war, the U.S. became trading partners with Vietnam, in spite of their Communist Party government. As terrible a blood bath as the senseless Vietnam War was, and as much social unrest as it caused in this country, it was not as long-lasting a mistake as the invasion of Iraq. After 9/11, the Iraq invasion upset the whole balance of power in the Mideast, began an immigration crisis around the Mediterranean, and was a shot of adrenaline in the arm of terrorism. The effects of Iraq will plague the world for decades. We certainly haven't seen the last of these wars yet, as the driving force of Capitalist imperialism has a mind of its own. Our invasion of Iraq clearly showed that we did not learn the lessons of Vietnam. The current roll back of the gains of the Civil Rights Movement, and the slow progress in racial equality, also show that the 1964 Civil Rights bill did not end racial discrimination.

By the early seventies, I had decided to struggle against Capitalism in the factories and in the communities and to try to educate people as I went along. I wanted to spread the word on the nature of Capitalism, fight for change and build a revolutionary movement. I had become a self-proclaimed independent Marxist. I read the historical works of Marx/Engels and Lenin and participated in many study groups. I came to believe that none of the so-called Communist countries were really Communist. I also believe that the critique of Capitalism developed by Karl Marx and Frederick Engels, is a major achievement in human thought. In my opinion, it deserves to be counted with Darwin's theory of evolution and Einstein's theory of relativity. My Marxist view of Capitalism over the years has been continuously reconfirmed by observing the world and its changes in light of the theory and its predictions. My insight into how Capitalism works has progressively grown over time. Gradually, society is sensing that the system of Capitalism is at the root of our social, political and economic injustices, that it is more than just sellout politicians. The embracing of Socialism, however, is another question and is progressing much more slowly in this country. This is because of the enormous amount of Capitalist propaganda which white washes the nature of Capitalism while at the same time shunning any objective analysis of Socialism. As Americans observe and learn more about what Capitalism is and how it drives the economic and social problems of their lives, then Socialism will gradually be viewed in a more favorable light. As a whole, society will have to initiate an honest inquiry into the differences between Capitalism and Socialism.

In writing this book I am attempting to articulate my cumulative knowledge and raise the class consciousness of the reader. By raising the *class consciousness,* I mean to bring people to realize that their lives are shaped by their relation to the forces of economic production. Class is a common thread that runs through us all. It can override the differences in income levels, culture, nationality, religious affiliation, gender, and sexual orientation. As the working class, we are locked in political/economic struggle against the owning class, whether we are aware of it or not. The cooperative struggle for important reforms, as impermanent as

5

these reforms may be, raises one's class consciousness. This awareness, combined with the inevitable decline in the economic conditions of Capitalism, will eventually bring the working class to realize the necessity for a more systemic, revolutionary change.

The struggle against Capitalism has proven to be more effective through direct action than through the ballot box. Many times this direct action requires peaceful civil disobedience. The stories of my work experiences all involve direct action. That's what a political activist is: a person who doesn't rely on the limited electoral system, union bureaucrats and politicians to fight against common injustices. An activist takes direct action on their own and encourages others to do the same. The larger the numbers of people struggling together through direct action, the more effective it is. It's the practical application of the slogan "the people united will never be defeated." So, in addition to my long term goals of political revolution, I have participated in and sometimes led the day-in, day-out struggles on the job and in the communities against the immediate injustices in the Capitalist system. Direct action is at the heart of the struggle for reforms under Capitalism, as well as the revolutionary struggle to eliminate Capitalism. People who learn to struggle together will create a culture of solidarity and common goals. Today, the struggle is for reforms but eventually the struggle will be for revolutionary systemic changes. People united in direct action have always been more successful. The electoral process is becoming more and more ineffective as the contradictions between the classes intensify. This doesn't mean we should stop voting. It just means we cannot rely on voting alone.

Many times in the American history of class struggle, the privileged class has given in to meaningful demands of the people resulting in positive reforms. These major reforms, such as the eight hour work day, Social Security, labor unions, civil rights, women's suffrage, LGBT rights, child labor laws, and ending the Vietnam War, were all won through direct action and, often, civil disobedience. Then in a few years or decades, the system's "benefactors," the wealthy, through the use of their controlled politicians and the courts, reverse or set back the earlier reforms. The struggle starts over again in an endless cycle. We also continue the endless involvement in economically-driven wars which become progressively more devastating. This is why the eventual end of the Capitalist system will be necessary for lasting change. As the material conditions for people worsen, it will become clear that big systemic changes will be necessary. These changes will at least curtail the extent of private property or, ideally, eliminate it altogether.

The recent Occupy Movement in America, with their 24/7 encampments of free speech, was challenging Capitalism in their reference to the 1% versus the 99%. Their statements recognize the class nature of society. The Occupy Movement represented a "dress rehearsal" for a renewed class struggle. The current era of unrest was encouraged by the 2008 economic collapse and its continuing effects on our citizens. Since the Occupy Movement, the demonstrations and civil unrest have spread throughout society and have taken on a grass roots nature, confronting many political, economic and social issues.

So what is Capitalism? During the early stages of the Industrial Revolution in the 18th century, Adam Smith and others defined Capitalism as the free market which follows the law of supply and demand. It supposedly brings the needed products to the consumer and, as demand increases, the prices come down and the consumers obtain what they need at an affordable price. The ideology was that Capitalism would benefit everybody, even the poor. This is a very simplistic, and idealistic view of Capitalism. It focuses on people as consumers, and centers mostly on the distribution of products and market forces. It doesn't recognize any of the social implications of Capitalism. It does not speak to the relationship of working people to the forces of production and how this affects the income and living standards of 99% of society. This view of Capitalism is just wishful thinking of what Capitalist economists would like Capitalism to be. Alternatively, this view is what those economists would like the middle and working class to believe. It is a subtle form of brainwashing that encourages the view that Capitalism is good for us all. It avoids the glaring facts that the "free market" creates numerous inequalities, stress, broken families, homelessness, divisions between nationalities, discrimination, foreign wars: the list is endless.

Now to the more scientific and objective definition of Capitalism as described by Karl Marx and Frederick Engels in the 19th century: **Marxism defines Capitalism as an economic system where the means of production are owned by a very small percentage of society while most of society possess nothing and are left with no alternative but to sell their labor to the owners of the means of production. "The means of production" are the factories, the equipment, the land, the raw materials, the buildings, the technology, the tools and the capital; essentially everything that is necessary to facilitate the manufacturing and**

**service *industries, except, of course, the labor pow-
er. The workers, owning only their labor power, become just another commodity to the Capitalists and
lose their human dignity. Capitalism therefore presents a contradiction between the <u>private</u> ownership
of the means of production and the <u>socialized</u> nature
of the workforce.***

Thus the Marxist definition of Capitalism views the
social and economic world the way it really is: a world
that is destined for economic struggle between two very
different classes with different interests. That is to say a
world with a handful of owners in contradiction to the
masses of workers who must work for the owners in
order to survive. These two classes have very different
interests. The owners strive for economically affluent
lives and building riches, while the masses of working
people struggle for adequate food, housing, medical
care and if possible a better education. It is the property class verses the property-less class, the haves versus
the have-nots.

Capitalism has not yet run its course, but for quite
some time now we have been in the advanced stages of
Capitalism referred to as Imperialism, or monopoly
Capitalism. The huge corporate entities are becoming
bigger, more powerful, fewer in number, and the competition between them is fierce. The distribution of
wealth in this country has moved upward and away
from working people at an enormous rate. The United
States now has the most unequal distribution of wealth
of any country in the world and the opportunity for social mobility is near the bottom of the world's nations.
The increasingly fierce competition between international, monopolized companies has resulted in increasing pressure on the working class by the system to

9

squeeze more and more profits out of us. This means fewer benefits and lower wages and decreases in our standards of living. It means cut backs in government social programs for working people, and more corporate welfare and lower taxes on the rich as the corporate state uses its influence on politicians. This is part of the inevitable progression of Capitalism which requires a continuous *increase* of profits in order to survive. This trend is far more than just the booms and busts, or the ups and downs created by market fluctuations.

So as conditions in the world and in America grow steadily worse for working people, fewer people are being fooled. More people are seeing through the cloud of deception, and political understanding is growing in America, although very slowly. I remember over 30 years ago how some people would cringe at the mention of the word Capitalism as if to even mention it was unpatriotic. In 2012 the most googled words were "Capitalism" and "Socialism." This recent interest in Capitalism and Socialism is a direct result of the economic crisis and the growing political curiosity of the public. Since the 2008 recession, the economic conditions of working people have not rebounded to pre-2008 conditions and people are questioning the systemic nature of their hardships. "The times they are a-changing" and anti-Capitalist signs are becoming more common in the current marches of protest. People are beginning to see that there is a difference between our *political system* of Constitutional Democracy with a public approach to the interests of all people and the *economic system* of Capitalism favoring narrow individual interests through the use of private property laws. The two systems are in conflict with each other and it is the *economic system* that has become the more powerful of the two. This growing influence of the economic system on the political system, which I call the *corporate state,* has nearly rendered the democratic political system useless. Since the most recent "great recession" where the country witnessed the near total collapse of Capitalism, people have seen the ongoing effects of the collapse in a permanent blow to the middle class and in increased suffering of all working people. It's getting harder for the politicians, the pundits and the media to appease people, because the material conditions for working people have worsened and people can no longer maintain the standard of living they had in previous years. The people at the bottom of the working class, minorities and poor whites, who have always suffered more economically, are today worse off than ever and are the basis of many demonstrations and growing civil unrest. The living conditions of working people have a record of recovering somewhat from the lows of these Capitalist down cycles, but the overall trend has been downward for several generations. It looks like the current generation of people reaching adulthood are facing an increasingly uncertain, if not a bleak future.

Therefore, I am a proud, unapologetic Marxist. I refer to myself as a Marxist because I do not view the so-called Communist parties of the world to be following the philosophy of Karl Marx. Most people think of Russia and China when they hear the word Communist. I see both of these countries as deeply engrained in Capitalist economics. (More on this in Chapter One: "The History of the Communist State").

My story is a condemnation, or an indictment, of the system of Capitalism. The political views that follow are totally from the perspective of anti-Capitalism, anti-private property, and anti-Republican Party politics. The political spin *for* the free market, private property and right wing politics are in abundance everywhere and will get no sympathetic consideration here. The distortion and simplistic handling of Capitalism in American literature is part of my motivation in writing a book that boldly and brazenly analyzes political economy. This can only be done from the perspective of a committed advocate for Socialism, such as myself. My political view is not an immediate call for revolution or an armed insurrection. Exactly how the fall of Capitalism will come about will be determined by the future generations and the concrete conditions at that time, and it will have to be a democratic decision of the majority of the people. Today, the role of Socialists is to educate people on the cause of their political, economic and social inequities, which is private property as represented by Capitalism.

The idea of individual ownership, central to the issue of private property, promotes and encourages individual selfishness in contrast to the ethics of sharing. When the ownership of wealth reaches the level of the "1%" billionaires, the selfishness turns to outright greed. It is true that differences in human values are partly responsible; some people are more driven towards self-interest than others. These are differences in human values that will have to be dealt with in any society. But the laws of private property under Capitalism encourage this selfishness on a wide scale, and eventually create a society where the more aggressive few wind up on the top owning and controlling all of society. My story is a call for direct action in the struggle for reforms, to raise the class consciousness of people and the awareness that an eventual revolution is inevitable.

Part of this consciousness-raising agenda is to combat the American Capitalist propaganda that inundates society and creates a cloud of deception on the true nature of Capitalism and Socialism. (A more in-depth analysis of Capitalist propaganda is covered in Chapter Seventeen).

I have been told that I have a lot of practical experience and political insights to share. Telling a story verbally and putting it in writing are two different things. I am not a professional writer and written composition is not my forte. But I will do my best. Let the reader be the judge as to whether you can relate to my enthusiasm and arguments for Socialism and against private property. I have read my share of books and I know the importance of holding the reader's attention. If you are a person with political curiosity, the content in itself may be enough to hold your interest. On the other hand, if you are not particularly politically curious my lack of writing skills may distract from my message. Regardless of your perspective, I feel there is some valuable information here that will make you at least a little more informed on economics and political struggle as well as exposing you to a leftist point of view. I have tried to make my narrative interesting. I have also tried to express my political views so that they address commonly held beliefs and experiences of the American people. I don't expect to convince anyone of my beliefs in one exposure. But if I am successful in sparking an interest in you to do more research, or get politically involved, I will have succeeded in my goal to educate and motivate. In the long run, the increasingly negative conditions in the lives of Americans, created by Capitalism, will open people's minds to the necessity of systemic change. I apologize in advance for my unpolished writing skills and implore you to listen to the message and tolerate the imperfections of the messenger.

CHAPTER ONE

The History of the Communist State

A part of the struggle against political, economic and social injustice involves political discussions with other people centering on the causes of the many injustices in American society. If the person is an activist, their previous experiences with direct action helps them to understand the systemic nature of the injustices they have struggled against. They are more open to considering private property and Capitalism as the cause of so many of society's problems. The current political understanding of people and their openness to the concept of Socialism and public property will for the most part depend on other factors, such as their level of education, their ethnicity, the nature of their livelihood (how they make a living), their class background, the current economic conditions in their lives and where they live. But very few who suspect that Capitalism is the problem understand Capitalism as defined by Marx in the introduction. When people come to appreciate that the individual ownership of the means of production is *made possible through private property laws* and consider the ramifications of this throughout society, then the concept of Capitalism takes on a whole new meaning. But when you start advocating public property and Socialism and discussions of Communism, the discussion will meet much stiffer resistance amongst most Americans. Most people have strong negative, biased notions about Socialism or Communism. This is because the owner class, through their institutions, the media and their influence through our politicians, have a powerful effect over the political opinions of the American public. This influence has been defined as everything from brainwashing to Capitalist propaganda. It's a form of political advertising. Every nation has this political spin process which always represents the views of the class in power. In the United States, the class in power is the wealthy Capitalist class and the message is anti-Communist and anti-Socialism. Likewise, the message is pro-free market and praising the rights of private property as a benefit to all people when in actuality these concepts serve, almost exclusively, the sole interests of the accumulators of capital: the very wealthy. The ideology of a Communist or Socialist economic system is a threat to this same wealthy, owning class. The threat of terrorism may be a threat to social order and civilization, but Socialism is a bigger threat to the rich, ruling class. Socialism is not a threat to the rest of us. We have been brought up to view Communism/Socialism as threatening because of the decades of propaganda. The degree of resistance among individuals to open minded discussions about Socialism or Communism can be influenced early in life in your family, where political mindsets of parents filter down to young children during their formative years. The degree of individualism and self-interest, widely accepted in a Capitalist society, can be a strong influence on how people view Socialism, which appeals more to the interest and wellbeing of the community as a whole. If a person is getting along fine or is more economically affluent, they are less likely to be open to Socialist ideas even though financial disaster may be right around the corner. On the other hand, if a person is, like most of us, living paycheck to paycheck then they *could* be more open to alternative economic systems that offer more stability in their lives. The economic status of people, however, is not always a clear indicator of how people might view Socialism, because there are wealthier people with strong concerns for other, less fortunate people regardless of their own comfortable economic situation. There are poor people, as well, who are opinionated against the Socialism / Communism alternative especially those with low educational levels. There are poor and working class rural Americans that hold to traditional Capitalist values as a result of their isolation from urban life where most of Americans now reside and where the failures of Capitalism are more pronounced. So anti-Capitalist/Socialist propaganda is very ingrained in American society and reaches across all economic and demographic classes.

Regardless of the material condition of the individual, most Americans, in my experience, have resistance, to one degree or another to the Communist/Socialist option, in spite of the increasing failures of American Capitalism. The past failed attempts to form a Communist society, such as Russia, China and to a lesser extent even Cuba, have added to this resistance. But the American propaganda to undermine any positive aspects of these earlier attempts and demonize the concept of Socialism is the main cause responsible for the negative views of Americans towards Socialism and/or Communism. By writing these off as a possible alternative, solely on the basis that it has been tried and failed, leaves no options. It's like handcuffing yourself to a sinking ship. I openly admit that so far the few attempts have not succeeded. This does not mean that Marxist philosophy is wrong. It just means that the leadership of the Socialist or Communist parties have lost sight of and abandoned Marxist principles. But it's more than just Communist parties gone astray that has given Socialism a bad name in the minds of Americans. It's the propaganda and overt action by our government. Vietnam was a campaign against Communist ideology and an action taken in support of the much preached *domino theory*. This stated that Communism was going to take over the world and had to be stopped in Vietnam. The Cold War that went on for decades with the previous Soviet Union was all about this same idea of combating the spread of Communism which threatened the "free market" and the American way of life. The propaganda against Communism preceded Vietnam when, during the 1950s and the era of *McCarthyism*, the U.S. Senate hearings jailed Hollywood writers for not participating in the witch hunts for Communist Americans and others for exercising their freedom of speech. Earlier still, the Communist/Socialist movement in America surfaced during the 1930s in response to the total world collapse of Capitalism during the "Great Depression." Even before the latter movement the IWW (International Workers of the World, "the Wobblies") had preached Socialist ideas in response to previous conditions of Capitalism in the 19th and early 20th century. The Wobblies, who wanted to take over the means of production, were viciously attacked, by the federal government. There were many cases of murder, or imprisonment where torture continued. The Communist movement of the 1930s influenced the "New Deal" of Roosevelt, which gave us Social Security and Unions. The subsequent McCarthyism created a nation of fear where Americans were too intimidated to speak freely and afraid of being accused of being a Communist or Social-

ist. This was the phenomenon of Communist "Red Baiting" which lingers to this day and adds to the resistance
of some Americans to openly talk about and consider
Socialism or Communism as an alternative to Capitalism. Today worldwide Capitalism through its financial
institutions, and government political influence under-
mines any attempts for governments to implement any
forms of public ownership. All countries are forced into
the world free markets in order to survive. This is the
"Capitalist encirclement" that Lenin talked about, which
started with the first attempt at Communism in Russia
and the world Capitalist community conspiring to make
sure that the Russian experiment failed.

So now I try to convince you, the reader, that the
idea of Socialism and, ideally, Communism is righteous.
I'm telling you that Capitalism is the real problem: both
economically and morally. Convincing people is an up-
hill battle. But I try because I believe it to be the truth,
and I have hopes for a better and different America.
The American public is more ingrained in the anti-
Communist, anti-Socialist mindset than in any other
western country, all of which have either active Socialist
parties or more social programs than we have in the
United States. So some of you will agree with some or
most of what I'm saying, and others may agree with
very little. It may turn on a light in your mind like reading Marxist literature did to me over 40 years ago. Others may be prompted to read further, and still others
may get disgusted and burn the book. I cannot address
the different levels of class consciousness that I would
in a one-on-one conversation. All I can do is just pour it
all out there and let readers, of different levels of political understanding consider it in parts. If I convince anyone that Capitalism and private property has to be dis-

carded I will have accomplished my main objective. But if some aspect of my philosophy or argument makes you question any part of your current beliefs, that in itself, could be the beginning of a positive change and a personal accomplishment from my perspective.

For most of us the learning process is more than just reading about Marxist theory. The theory, as in my case, can turn on the light, but then putting theory into practice is necessary to continue the learning curve. In the long haul, it will be your material conditions, your economic situation, and your shrinking living standards or the living conditions of your children, as our economic system progressively declines, that will open your mind out of necessity. Your material conditions also consist of where you live and with whom you break bread and with whom you work and play. If you are part of the declining middle class with a comfort zone that is still above a day-to-day existence level of income then, in addition to reading and studying the theory, you will need to physically step outside your comfort zone to see through experience how others are struggling to even subsist. Or, as standards of living regress, you may be forced out of your previous and privileged comfort zone. Very few people can come to realize the truth of Marxism if they live in an ivory tower. You need to seek out and expose yourself to the bottom half of society, to verify through exposure and experience the ugly truth about Capitalism and how it inadequately provides for the majority of people. People need to experience firsthand or through personal contact with the people on the picket lines; or witness on ground level the atrocities conducted by out-of-control and many times racist police officers in their treatment of the less fortunate. You need to live in a neighborhood where bars on your windows are necessary to a safe night's sleep. You need to experience the speed up of a production line, or witness the pressure of employers who push you to produce more. An entry level job at Walmart alone might change many of your previously held prejudices. Have you ever talked to a homeless person? They are just like everyone else, your brother, your sister or daughter, although sometimes just a little rougher around the edges, reflective of their unfortunate situation. Homelessness can strike anyone, anywhere and at any time and the phenomenon is growing. Life under Capitalism is a tenuous situation and it can be a real jungle according to who you are and where you live. *As your material conditions decline and your daily environment changes or you just learn a little about how the other half lives, then the Marxist theory put forward in this book will resonate with you.* I personally made a decision to take my Marxist theory into the inner city and do community work and become politically active on the job in the factories. I made friends and lived in the same multi-ethnic neighborhoods. I experienced how the other half lives and became a part of the inner city society where the overwhelming majority of Americans live. It was during these years that I verified over and over again the social economic theory that I embrace to this day. The point I am trying to make is that it will, in most cases, take more than just reading and understanding the theory to convince you that Capitalism is the problem and Socialism is the only solution. You have to live it, and experience real life situations. You can seek it out by leaving your comfort zone and initiating contact with the masses, or you can wait until economic disaster hits and your comfort zone is destroyed. Because once you suspect that Capitalism is the problem, it will take real life experiences with people outside your familiar world to really internalize the true nature of Capitalist America. You are what you eat. If you eat bagels every day you could turn into a giant bagel. Marxism says, in so many words, that your class consciousness, your political and social views, are formed through the material conditions of your life. Building confidence in Marxist philosophy takes studying the theory, putting the theory into practice, and then taking the experience back and reflecting on the theory. So try to do volunteer work in a soup kitchen, or distribute Christmas presents to the poor neighborhoods. There are many ways you can expand your learning process. Reaching out to other people, and talking and listening to them will open you up to things you never could visualize back in your own world. Go to an inner-city demonstration and communicate with protestors and the community. Even if you are in the upper half of the population in regards to the standard of living in today's economy, you can still reflect on the growing decline in financial security of even the so-called middle class. That's because things are getting worse for all economic levels except for the very rich. But no matter what I say, or how conditions in your life may change, there will always be a few people who will never get to the point of accepting Capitalism as the problem. There will always be a certain percentage who will bury their heads in the sand, even when the buildings come tumbling down. I am not even trying to appeal to this politically backward element in society. I have in mind moderate to left-leaning individuals who consider themselves progressive, or at least open minded. This book may also resonate for some right wing, anti-government people who have been confused with all of the conspiracy theories. Some may be working class people who are already experiencing the growing hardships of Capitalist society. Others may be more affluent people who are still clinging to relatively comfortable lives. This latter group have the luxury of the comfort zone that I refer to, and that shields them from the conditions plaguing the bottom half of society. I truly believe that this protective shield for some people, mostly white, is disappearing along with the middle class. These people can wait until their material conditions deteriorate or they can start reaching out to the less fortunate people that they or their children will eventually be a part of, as the shift in wealth continues its upward trend. My goal, as it has been throughout life, is to bring all of these open minded people to see the need for eliminating Capitalism and building Socialism. My body clock is running down, so I choose to record my profoundest thoughts and experiences in hopes that my words will continue to do this work when I am gone. If nothing else, and I am never able to put a copy of this book in the hands of anyone other than a few friends and family members, then so be it. My objective is to just get it out there. I put forward a candid, straight forward and unrestrained criticism of Capitalism and right wing politics. The struggle against Capitalism has been the main driving force in my life, second only to surviving under Capitalism. The difference in my approach, compared to other writings on political economy, is that it is an appeal based on the certainty and passion of my beliefs. Other books on Socialism, private property, public property and the pitfalls of Capitalism define and record history but, in general, seek middle ground and strive not to offend traditional beliefs, institutions and patriotic mindsets. They are written by professional people who seek at most to tweak the system and fear being marginalized from mainstream journalism by criticizing our class society in a brazen, tell-it-like-it-is manner, in the way I do. They are afraid to step outside the box in their political/economic prose and indeed, most don't even think outside the box. I'm not privileged, professional or even middle class. I am just a working class person who was fortunate enough to receive a formal education. I have a penchant to question, and ask why, while most people just accept society and play the game. I have a deep understanding of Capitalist and Socialist theory and practice. I am also driven by a passion for defending the underdog. The underdog is the 99% of the non-owning population of the country. This book is clearly an argument for the Marxist position and an indictment against Capitalism and private property. I do not present extensive arguments in favor of Capitalism or seek some ideological compromise between the systems of Capitalism and Socialism. I do not believe that a compromise would do justice. Nor do I examine the many conspiracy theories that speak to the problems in society and political corruption, most of which are created in the interests of Capitalism to confuse the issues. There is plenty of that in American culture, which adds to the confusion and makes my endeavor more difficult. I go straight to what I believe is the heart of the problem. It's either the people owning and controlling the resources of economic activity (public property) with the benefits going to all of us, or a few individuals owning these resources and controlling economic activity in their interests only (private property). I see that nearly all the social, political and personal problems in America are a result of an economic system which creates inequality. The one system is Capitalism and the other system is Socialism / Communism. There are no other alternatives. If 80% of the country was public property and 20% was private property, the continued existence of private property laws would leave the gates open to the greedy few who could use the ownership rights to recreate an unequal society and the struggle against class oppression would continue.

Having reviewed the nature of some of the mainstream political views which are generally bent against the ideology of Communism/Socialism in America, let's now turn to the central theme of this chapter: "The History of the Communist State." Have the attempts at Communism or Socialism in state governments around the world been given an objective analysis? Is Marxist theory really a tried and failed ideology, as posited by our Capitalist influenced political representatives and media? Well, I will start out by saying that _there has never been a Communist country or state._ Communism is an ideological, hopeful society a way off in the future. After a revolution and the overthrow or complete collapse of the Capitalist economic system, a new governing body is installed. Marx called this the "dictatorship of the proletariat." This new dictatorship supposedly replaces the old "dictatorship of the bourgeoisie" or in more common language the dictatorship of the ruling class. This term of "dictatorship," whether referring to the dictatorship of the proletariat or the dictatorship of the bourgeoisie, is an unfortunate and inappropriate term. Even in America today, where our government is clearly representing the interest of the _bourgeoisie_ (or wealthy), it is not a _dictatorship._ A new government after revolutionary change which is set up to promote working class interests would not and should not be a dictatorship, either. This new government or political body begins to reorganize society in the interest of the vast majority of the people, as opposed to the old government who represented the interests of the wealthy or the 1%. This new government is the beginning of a protracted Socialist revolution and the building of Socialism and must be, at least as democratic in nature, as was originally intended by the founders of our American Constitution. Its task is to work towards a more equitable distribution of the wealth of the country. This wealth has been skewed terribly out of proportion to the very wealthy. A new government would need to eliminate immediately some of the most grievous situations left over from the old Capitalist economic system. Its primary method to accomplish the end goal, of a classless society, is to replace private property with public property. But it would also have to be the "watchdog" against attempts to undermine or reinstate private property rights by the remnants of greed left over from the old system of Capitalism. I suppose that this strong and assertive new government, or watchdog, is what Marx was visualizing when he used the term "dictatorship of the proletariat." But the choice of the term and subsequent diversion from Socialist principles by Stalin who truly became a *dictator* and imposed overt human suffering and Orwellian measures on his people following the Russian Revolution has giving the pure and righteous concept of real Socialism a long lasting bad rap.

So how would this new government, dedicated to the interests of working people, function in practice? Initially, this may involve limiting the amount of private property that any individual or entity can possess; by gradually nationalizing industry which will be run by the people to produce the goods that we all need instead of products sold around the world for profit; by imposing heavy regulation on the privately owned industries and enterprises to reduce the amount of exploitation of the employees and consumers and to gradually eliminate these private industries; by instituting and enforcing a livable wage for everyone while limiting the excessive wages now taken by CEO's. So this new government immediately addresses the major problems like homelessness, mass incarceration, starvation, the poor, and immediately institutes healthcare for everyone, which will involve the rapid elimination of free-market, for profit healthcare. At the same time, this new government must be a watchdog, not a dictatorship, for the reemergence of greedy individuals and practices from the old regime. But have no doubt, these benefactors of the old regime who refuse to accept the change and attempt to undermine the new society will be dealt with as firmly as is necessary and, in the most severe cases, could be incarcerated. Capitalist laws have a way of protecting the CEO's and their wealthy benefactors from selfish, greedy acts and they never go to jail. But under a Socialist government not subject to private property laws, these white collar criminals would have no blanket protection. During the transition from private property to public property the opportunity will still exist for manipulative people to use the private property laws to stop the transition and reinstate the former Capitalist system. Because as long as private property laws exist, even minimally, the building of Socialism can be undermined and reversed. The long term goal is to eventually eliminate private property completely and to win over all the people to the Communist principle: *"to each according to their need and from each according to their ability."* This means that everyone, every family will receive what they need, which will vary, and everyone will give, or work, according to their ability. No one will go without life's essentials, even if they can't work. This protracted change will take many decades and sets the stage of Socialism. It will demand a firm and honest government that is absolutely dedicated to the interest of all working people. Under Socialism, everyone who can work will be working. There will be work for everyone because there will be plenty of things to be done that were neglected, as unprofitable, under Capitalism. Eventually, this building of Socialism and public property will gain more and more support. There will be some immediate changes to address the most pressing problems of the old system and others that will be more gradual. You can't just pull the rug out from centuries old systems of private ownership immediately, and outlaw all private property in a single sweep, or you would have chaos and anarchy. Hopefully, after many decades of Socialist progress and public ownership people will come to appreciate the advantage of community and sharing the wealth. Individual selfishness will disappear along with the privileged and oppressive class that we all have had to struggle against. This will be a society where no one will seek to be rich and no one will go without the basic needs of life. Surpluses in the production of wealth beyond the basic needs will be shared equally. Then, this philosophical state of Communism will become a reality. It will take decades, if not centuries, to obtain if it is even possible. It might be a utopian pie in the sky because there may always be some who will want more than others, even if they don't need it. There will also be many attempts to reverse course and undermine the movement away from private property. But that is what

<u>Communism is and I think we can all agree there has
never been a Communist state.</u> There may be parties or
governments who refer to themselves, or are referred
to as, Communist parties. But they really are not truly
Communist parties, because today they are not even
building Socialism or Communism. They are too eager
to embrace private ownership and world Capitalist
markets. Some astute political observers (not me) have
referred to Russia and China as *"Comrade Capitalism,"*
which implies Communism in name but is Capitalism in
essence. They gradually move towards free market, for-
profit businesses, and solicit foreign Capitalist investments into their countries. These policies are not Marxist philosophy which guides the building of Socialism.
So the <u>idea</u> of Communism is a good idea. But history
has shown that building Communism or even Socialism
is a challenge which only begins with the overthrow of
the old regime. Communism is sharing, not selfishness
and it favors community rather than individual interests.

So for all practical purposes the goals of Socialists,
or Marxists, is to get rid of Capitalism and build Socialism. We uphold Communist principles, but a Socialist
state is the practical and immediate goal once people
have had all they can take of Capitalism and its rule of
private ownership. Even if it never gets to the utopian
state of Communism, a Socialist state will be a huge and
qualitative improvement from what we have now for
the vast majority of society.

Russia and China have been held up by the "free
market" world as examples of Communism having
failed. But neither country was ever a Communist state.
What they failed at was building Socialism after their
respective revolutions. Both countries have so called

Communist parties who have sold out and become a ruling class in themselves. Both countries started out on
the right footing. China's revolutionary struggle was
against Japanese occupation which was very repressive.
In Russia, it was the Russian Tsar: a wealthy monarchy
that was ruthless and had the wealth of the country
consolidated in fewer hands than the ruling class in
America today. So both of these revolutions were a positive step from the viewpoint of improvement over past
societies. The problem arose almost immediately in
Russia with Stalin. Stalin had his hands full with Capitalist encirclement, but rather than using a democratic
approach to changing society, Stalin became a ruthless
dictator in his attempt to force Communist ideology upon the people. Instead of concentrating on the building
of Socialism in Russia in the interest of the Russian people, which was Lenin's goal, Stalin begin forcing his rule
on eastern Europe and building an empire (the Soviet
Union). The Soviet Union eventually became no better
than U. S. Imperialism or British Colonialism, all three of
which are examples of Capitalist economics. The ruling
Communist party no more practiced Socialism or Communism than did Western Europe with its Socialist programs. The Communist party became the ruling class in
Russia with corruption, and their lifestyles were far in
excess of the working people.

Eventually Russian leadership embraced free market concepts and the Communist party evolved into
what has been referred to as _State Capitalism_. The party
itself eventually directed the investments and exploits
around the world and within the country as they embraced the profit driven free market. Generally speaking, the power in Russia and China is more concentrated
than in the United States. In the United States we have

more of a *Corporate State* where the economic system of large corporations and the wealthy exert control over the political system. In Russia, as in China, the Communist party is both the political and economic systems rolled into one. They have consolidated political power with no interfering democratic processes. But these *comrade Capitalists* in the Communist parties do not follow public, or Socialist principles. Instead, they pursue free market Capitalism, like the rest of the world. The political and economic systems in Russia and China have become one and the same. It is state run Capitalism, or "State Capitalism." Russia and China can act more swiftly in domestic and international economic policies than the United States. They do not have the restraints of Constitutional Democracy. In the United States, we have the Corporate State which (representing our economic system) has to exercise control over our political system and *occasionally* meets some resistance. So the domestic and international economic interests of private property cannot move as quickly in the U.S. as in China or Russia. But the more powerful that America's *corporate state* becomes in its influence and control over our democratic political system of "Constitutional Democracy" the closer *we* get to state run Capitalism. But whether it's the "Corporate State" in the United States or "State Capitalism" in Russia and China, all three countries are practicing Capitalism in one form or another.

During the Great Depression the Soviet Union, had not yet turned to the free market and it was about the only country in the world that was not affected by the Great Depression as it spread throughout the Capitalist world. The failure of Russia to obtain Socialism was in part a problem of leadership. But the power of worldwide Capitalism led by the U.S. and Britain and their success in undermining the Russian attempt to establish Socialism played a major role in the failure of this first real attempt at Socialism. This *Capitalist encirclement* continues today in Cuba, Venezuela and anywhere the masses of people try to obtain economic power through public ownership. Today China and Russia have pretty much embraced private industry and the world-wide markets of private property Capitalism. This was not so in the early stages, right after their respective revolutions. Russia and China still have publicly run enterprises but they are moving rapidly, especially China, to privately held companies both from domestic Capitalists at home and from the foreign investment of capital from around the world.

Capitalist encirclement is still a major factor in Cuba and Venezuela. With the probable lifting of embargoes to Cuba, we will certainly see Cuba moving more rapidly into the unavoidable clutches of world Capitalism. Recent statistics from Cuba (2015) show that since some of the private property law restrictions have been relaxed in the last few years there is already a change in the distribution of income occurring. Even before the recent Obama decision to open diplomatic relations with Cuba, they have been sliding back in the direction of a free-for-all market that subjected the people to exploitation under the old U.S. backed Batista regime prior to the Castro revolution. So we live in a Capitalist world that is ever-increasing in scale and intensity. Countries simply can't survive without irons in the free market fires. It has proven impossible for one struggling Socialist country to survive in a world of Capitalist controlled markets, embargoes and international financial institutions such as the World Bank, the International Monetary Fund, the European Union and the overwhelming influence of U.S. Imperialism. Socialist leaning countries are politically and economically isolated by powerful Western governments and their international financial cartels. It's like the hippie commune experiments in the United States in the 60s and 70s. Some were successful for a while but a complete subsistence level of life without some reliance on the outside establishment proved unsustainable. Not to speak of the conflicts with private property owners in the areas where these communes existed. Countries are no different. A Socialist experiment in any single country soon finds itself surrounded and isolated by world Capitalism. These forces of private property want Socialism to fail and will do anything to undermine it, by means of propaganda, financial isolation, or outright invasions and occupations. Cuba is a perfect example of this. Cuba, under the U.S.-backed Batista dictatorship, prior to Fidel Castro, had turned Havana into a tourist destination and a rest and recreation port for the U. S. Navy. Havana flourished with casinos, prostitution, hotels and small businesses catering to decadent Western life styles. The rest of the country was rural and poor and the U.S. controlled the Cuban sugar crop and denied the country the option to develop more diversified agriculture or a more balanced economy in general. Essentially, the United States turned Cuba into a "banana republic" of sugar and stifled its ability for a diversified economy and self-determination. Right after the Cuban revolution and fall of the U.S. puppet Batista, Castro reached out to the U.S. to open diplomatic relations. President Eisenhower with his anti-Communist fervor rebuked the offer and instead initiated the embargo. Later, President Kennedy unwisely tried to forcibly take back Cuba with the ill-advised "Bay of Pigs" invasion which failed miserably. The embargo has worked against Cuba's struggling Socialist economy for over 50 years. It looks today that, out of necessity, Cuba is slowly sliding back into the free market. But for the last 50 years, in spite of the embargo, Cuba has been better off for the average citizen than under the American backed Batista regime. Every citizen gets a free college education, everyone has free medical care and a small stipend or income. American citizens have moved to Cuba to continue their education and I know of an American woman who lived there for several years and became a doctor. She is now returning to practice medicine in the U. S. She would never have been able to afford such an education in the United States. But all we hear about Cuba is the people who fled the Castro regime, many of whom were the affluent, small business Cubans who benefited from the Batista dictatorship. We also hear about things like the old cars and the absence of many of the foods we have here in the U.S. This is the direct result of the U.S. embargo. Certainly the Castro regime has imposed many restraints on civil liberties but so much of these undemocratic actions have been futile reactions to political interference and non-cooperative policies imposed on Cuba by the United States. Rather than respecting the revolutionary change in the direction of Cuba, which had huge support from the majority of Cubans, the U.S. adopted a sour grapes attitude over the loss of their dictator Batiste. This is much the same as the overthrow of the "Shah" in Iran. We also don't hear much about a free college education for every citizen and government provided healthcare. We don't hear about it much in the U.S. because we have failed terribly in providing affordable education and healthcare for our own citizens.

The American news media know this and play their role by not addressing the positive aspects of Cuban society. There are always two sides to every issue. A good side and a downside, and all we have heard about Cuba for the last 50 years is the downside. Sometimes media propaganda is direct misinformation, and at other times it takes the form of silence and ignoring the very real advantages that citizens of these struggling Socialist experiments have achieved over citizens of the United States. As the United States under the Obama administration is now normalizing relations with Cuba, the lifting of the 50 year embargo will soon follow. The lifting of the embargo will immediately benefit the Cuban people. But it will also open the country to American economic influence within the country. So the last holdout for truly Socialist ideals will soon be joining the rest of the world community in private property Capitalism.

Initially, when Socialist leaning countries turn to the free market there is a period of growth which usually includes a middle class to one extent or the other. As private property takes hold, the social programs come under attack and a majority of citizens begin to lose the government provided benefits they had under a Socialist society. At the same time, affluence grows for some citizens and riches for an even smaller number of citizens. But eventually the inherent nature of Capitalism takes hold. The middle class stops growing and, with it, economic affluence. As the greed of the growing wealthy class takes hold, working people come under attack and the class struggle begins. It looks like the whole world will soon be in the economic camp of Capitalism. It pretty much has been anyway. There will be differences depending on the political systems: Democracy in its different forms, dictatorships both secular and theocratic. The economic system that calls the shots on how people live will be private property through the vehicle of Capitalist economics. As we have seen in Western European Capitalist countries, as well as in the United States, the 1% will take aim on all the social programs to privatize them or eliminate them. Eventually world-wide monopoly Capitalism will reach fruition and living standards will go down for all but the very few: the 1%, the ruling class, the benefactors of private property. We are starting to see the early signs of this decline in China. The coming out party is the shrinking of the middle class that sprung up almost overnight. The class struggle is beginning and with the austerity of the "so-called" Communist party the struggle will be brutal. In the United States, the decline of the middle class is more than in the early stages. American citizens have been losing their middle class status for decades and we all know it.

So know this, there is no Communist State anywhere in the world and never has been. Three cheers for Cuba: the most valiant attempt so far. It's hard to change the world's economic system when the old system hasn't run its course yet. Capitalism has certainly not yet run its course. World Capitalism is becoming more powerful and more abusive. So these early attempts were just that: early attempts. But have no doubt, Capitalism will run its course and the idea of Socialism/Communism will be waiting because there is no other alternative besides anarchy and the collapse of all social order, or even a return to Tribalism. It may be another century or more before the conditions of worldwide Capitalism bring the masses to revolt. No one knows when this will happen. In the meantime, we need to educate ourselves on the nature of the beast and stop fighting each other so we can concentrate on the real enemy of all of us: World Capitalism!

CHAPTER TWO

Is There a Trend Towards
Socialism in the United States?

There used to be a very popular slogan of the more conservative "right wing" politicians in the United States that warned we are moving towards Socialism. I haven't heard it as much lately in part because the conservatives, mostly Republicans, have found plenty of other confusing issues with which to label their political opponents, particularly around election times. But it is still sometimes used as a mild form of red baiting and also implies a lack of patriotism on the part of their targeted opponents; calling progressives unpatriotic for not embracing the free market principals of the Capitalist economic system in America. As Americans slowly get a clearer understanding of the difference between Capitalism and Socialism (being private property vs. public property) these confusing accusations against liberal to moderate candidates become less effective. They probably still do hold water with many voters. Most of the accusations of "growing Socialism" in America refer to the few existing _safety net programs_ such as Social Security, Medicare, food stamps, welfare and, most recently, the Affordable Care Act. It is an attempt by the right wing to associate these programs with the engrained American stigma against Communism or Socialism and secure votes using the politics of fear and confusion. The goal of the right wing is to eliminate the existing programs and prevent any new social programs from being initiated. Politicians who protect the social programs and advocate for more safety nets, like the Affordable Care Act, are not Socialists. The liberal or progressive politicians who support these programs are dedicated to Capitalism, but their form of Capitalism follows the Keynes school of Capitalist economics more practiced in Western Europe, where it is referred to as "Democratic Socialism" and is in contrast to American laissez-faire Capitalism. Bernie Sanders is an American Politician who refers to himself as a Democratic Socialist. When asked about the difference between his views and Socialism he correctly responds that it is a huge difference. The Keynes supporters like Bernie Sanders realize the need for government involvement in the economic activities of Capitalism. The laissez-faire advocates, on the other hand, believe in unbridled Capitalism and hold that the free market, without any government regulation or economic stimulation, will speak to the needs of all the people. The predominant trend in American Capitalism since around the 1980s (with Ronald Reagan's trickledown and deregulated economics) has been laissez-faire Capitalism which has failed working people by departing from the "New Deal" Keynes form of Capitalism implemented during the Great Depression. So no, there is not even the slightest hint of a trend towards real Socialism in American. With the exception of the Affordable Care Act there is no trend towards Democratic Socialism either. However the growing open mindedness of the American people towards concepts like Socialism and Communism has been increasing over the decades, especially with the new millennial generation who were the main contingent supporting the Bernie Sanders campaign. They are not at all hesitant to embrace the fact that Sanders is a proclaimed Democratic Socialist even though some may not clearly understand the difference between Socialism and Democratic Socialism. But this growing open mindedness towards Socialism/Communism in the population is not characteristic of our politicians regardless of their generation. It is the boomer generation and older generations who have been conditioned to resist concepts like Socialism and Communism. We were subjected to the Capitalist propaganda of the anti-Communist witch hunts of the 1950s and the Viet Nam War domino theory that Communism was taking over the world, as well as decades of the ideological Cold War. This growing change in the mindset of Americans is why we don't hear, as frequently, the red baiting by Republicans with slogans like "moving towards Socialism." It has become a far less effective method of attack on the left by the right. In the first place, America is not moving towards even Democratic Socialism. Second, the "moving towards Socialism" attacks no longer resonate because people are far more concerned with the failure of Capitalism and its effect on the economic conditions of their lives. There was a period when right wing politicians even portrayed the term "liberal" as negative and un-American. Today Americans are more concerned with right wing, over the top, neo-Conservatism which has deadlocked the legislative process into a hopeless state of Republican led-obstructionism. The Barry Goldwater conservatism of the 1960s would be somewhere to the left of center in today's Republican Party. The extreme nature of the current Republican Party appeals only to the fringes of society; the single issue voters, the racially biased and the uneducated or misinformed voters. The 2016 rise of the disgusting Donald Trump as the leading candidate in the Republican primary has been depicted by traditional Republicans as an unacceptable "change" to the party. In reality, Donald Trump is the result of decades of a growing extremism in the values of Republican Party politics.

Western Europe has a lot more Socialist programs but they are still within the confines of a Capitalist system. Many of these programs have been under attack in recent years as monopoly Capitalism becomes more powerful and relentless in its move towards privatization and its attempts to eliminate the tax burden on corporations resulting in reduced social programs. The Western European countries practicing "Democratic Socialism" are still Capitalist economies with the laws of private property firmly in control. In the United States an example of a Socialist program is the veteran's healthcare program. It is the only "single payer" health care plan in the United States. The veteran's program steps back from the private, for-profit health care system by using government owned and run facilities with government employees. Even our Social Security program doesn't qualify as an example of Socialism. It is a direct payment of benefit dollars to recipients at or about the age of 65 out of contributions from employees and free market employers. A Socialist program would be available to everyone over 65 regardless of their work history and based on need alone. But Social Security recipients must work for the free enterprise system which does not guarantee full employment. The amount of your Social Security check also depends on the level of your average earnings so it discriminates against women who are paid significantly less than men. If everyone, regardless of work history or ability to work were eligible for a Social Security check at 65 then the Social Security program would truly be a Socialist program, although still within the Capitalist free market economy and subject to its restrictions and short-comings. There are other groups, such as teachers, who don't work under the Social Security System and are ineligible for any Social Security benefits. There are also badly wounded combat veterans who were disabled at an early age and never able to work and earn the necessary points for the Social Security retirement benefits. In talking to a veteran's benefits person the other day I was told that I would be surprised at the number of veterans who have no Social Security benefits. All they have, if they're fortunate, is service related disability income. Many are involved in a long term battle to even get these benefits. This leaves them out there in the cold with food stamps, and looking for a ride to the veteran's hospital facility nearest them. So don't be fooled into thinking that Social Security is an example of Socialism. There are just too many people who are not covered under the program and discriminated against by the free-market designed program. A truly Socialist program would be a guaranteed income program for every retired American with no exceptions.

Looking at Medicare, it is easier to see the free market nature of the program. It is not a single payer program like in Britain, Canada and most of the western world, where the hospitals and clinics are owned and run by the state. In those countries the doctors are government employees, and it is available to any citizen regardless of age. The only qualification is the particular need of the individual. So these government run programs stand in stark contrast to the actual Medicare system and other private healthcare plans in the United States. But they are still not Socialism! They are social programs that are run by the government within the overall economic system of Capitalism, similar to veteran's healthcare in the United States. All of the healthcare programs in the United States, with the exception of the Veteran's Healthcare System, are run by and in the interest of the free market for profit. The doctors are non-government, private providers struggling to make a living under Capitalism like the rest of us. The hospitals are privately owned and operated for profit, which becomes their bottom line far too often. Let's not forget the health insurance companies, who are the completely unnecessary middle men. They dictate to the doctors what they can and cannot do and add nothing to the medical services. In addition, they add 30% or more to the overall cost of every health care dollar. All the Government Medicare program does is dole out tax payer dollars to the free market providers of all of these services. The same people who spread the fears that we are moving towards Socialism accuse the Medicare program of bureaucratic inefficiency and corruption. Actually most of the corruption in Medicare is the private sector stealing from the Medicare program. The hospitals and doctors padding their bills, filing bogus claims, and just basically playing the system, are the corrupt ones. Because of the privately run healthcare system, the United States has the most ineffective health care system in the western world. It is the only one that is not government run, and it is completely owned and operated by the private free market. Certainly we have some of the most modern technical healthcare procedures available here in the United States. But the availability of this medical science depends on who you are and how much money you have!

Veteran's healthcare, although still within the confines of the overall Capitalist system, is the exception. It is a Socialistic *program.* All the hospitals are owned by the government, and the doctors are employed by the government. The best thing of all, in this system, is that the health insurance companies are out of the picture. Doctors are free to perform any procedure they see as necessary and in the interest of the patient. No credit applications or any of the free market restrictions apply. I have been under veteran's healthcare for nearly 15 years and I personally have found it to be absolutely the best healthcare program I've ever had. Like a veteran buddy of mine expressed to me the other day, "they don't hassle you." He has access to other private healthcare plans, but doesn't use them. He prefers the veteran's system. When it comes to expensive invasive procedures, many times the VA will employ the services of the best specialists in the private sector and pay them from the Veteran's budget. There are still no conflicts of interest and no insurance companies. All of the recent scandals around the Veteran's Administration stem from underfunding by a Republican congress that is re-luctant to allocate any money for programs that help the working class. Also, with all the extended wars of the last 10 to 20 years the number of returning injured vet-erans has overrun the system. There are now 19 mil-lion veterans enrolled in the plan. Many are young men who are in need of help right now for their injuries, not someone like myself who only has a need for healthcare in relation to the aging process. From my personal ex-perience I can see how much better a completely gov-ernment run, single payer Socialist program, fares com-pared to the free market plans. I've experienced them all including Kaiser, Blue Cross, and Aetna etc. But there is no trend to duplicate the veteran's healthcare Social-ist model. In fact, the trend is to starve it off financially and drive it, along with Medicare, into the American free market model of healthcare. This is being done by contracting out more and more services to the private sector, instead of expanding the system through the building of new veteran's hospitals and hiring more government health care workers and doctors. The effect of this will be to increase the cost of healthcare and reduce the quality of medical services provided. All Congress wants to do is throw a few dollars at the system and push it slowly into the free market model, rather than spending the money necessary to enlarge the program and accommodate the growing demand. The Veteran's Healthcare program should be the model for all American healthcare instead of the target by conservative politicians for further privatization. Of course that would take money and increased taxes on the rich to accomplish. This is an unlikely prospect in the current political atmosphere which has bowed out to the corporate state. So as far as healthcare goes there is certainly not a trend towards Socialism but rather a continued trend towards free market Capitalism, which refuses to speak to the needs of people.

Much of the conservative rhetoric about the growing trend towards Socialism in this country is a propaganda attack against real Marxist Socialism, which truly threatens Capitalist ideology. Our political leaders and their corporate masters are well aware of a growing revolutionary sentiment in America, even if they refuse to recognize or speak of it publicly. The rhetoric also comes from the traditional conservative belief that regulation of industry and social programs are not the role of the government. Every time the government backs off from its role of providing services it turns a little more business to the private sector and brings in more campaign contributions. Many times these political positions are more practical and self-serving than principled beliefs. About the only thing that too many politicians get out of the Preamble to the Constitution is _to provide for the common defense_. They overlook the part about _insuring the domestic Tranquility and promoting the general Welfare_. Well, we sure are providing for the common defense, aren't we? We are providing for the common defense in every nook and cranny of the world, leaving little (if any) money for Americans at home. It would seem to me that a roof over your head, food and healthcare would be absolutely essential to insuring domestic tranquility and promoting the general welfare. So if the economic system of Capitalism results in homelessness, hunger, and millions of people with no healthcare, then according to our Constitution it would absolutely be the responsibility of government to intervene and insure these basic human rights. Yet conservative politicians, especially Republicans, argue against government programs. Their arguments use catchy phrases involving the "free market," "the private sector," and fear driven accusations of "moving towards Socialism," and "it's not the role of government." This is nothing more than the cold, callus and heartless Republican politics serving the economic interest of the wealthy 1%.

Except for the growing revolutionary sentiment among our youth, and older revolutionaries like myself, there is certainly no trend towards Socialism in the United States. I certainly wish there was, and as a Marxist and student of American politics, I think I would know if there was. We aren't even moving towards Keynes economics. _But what we are moving towards is "Fascism"_: the exact opposite of Socialism or Communism. Fascism is where civil liberties are taken away from the people including privacy rights, free speech, and free movement. Fascism is where there is massive incarceration, widespread surveillance of the community, and police brutality gradually evolving into a complete "police state" with house to house searches. These searches could be looking for terrorists or illegal immigrants. Many times, Fascism takes on the face of racism and, in the case of Hitler's Fascism, outright genocide. Fascism can come about with ruthless dictators but many times it grows out of advanced Capitalism (monopoly Capitalism), or just Capitalism in trouble. In the current situation in the United States, the trend towards Fascism is in part related to the normal progress of monopoly Capitalism. More specifically, Fascism in the U.S. has been given a boost by the Patriot Act and changes to the National Defense Authorization Act (NDAA). The NDAA changes are directed towards U.S. citizens and includes indefinite detention with no legal rights of those accused. These congressional acts which were part of the reactionary response to 9/11 have been an attack on the civil liberties of free speech, due process and privacy rights. So there certainly is no movement towards Socialism or Communism or even a return to the New Deal liberalism in our American political system. The invasion of Iraq, driven by blind revenge over 9/11 and political ignorance, has not only turned the Middle East upside down, rendered terrorism more profound throughout the world and tarnished the reputation of the United States as a world leader, it has also leveled unprecedented attacks upon the civil liberties of law abiding American citizens. This is not Socialism in any way, shape or form. This is nothing more than reactionary Capitalism heading towards Fascism.

CHAPTER THREE

"Walmart"

An Icon of Growing "Monopoly Capitalism"

I've referred to "monopoly Capitalism" but now I would like to elaborate a little more on what I mean and how it differs from earlier Capitalism. Walmart is a good example, but first let's examine what it is and how it comes about. In the early days of Capitalism there was no monopoly Capitalism, only the owners and the workers. The owners were made possible by "private property" laws, and workers had their bodies and labor power as their only asset. Capitalism in general is sometimes defined as the accumulation of capital. The owners start out with ownership of the means of production, including capital, and they make profits off the unpaid wages of the workforce. When I say unpaid wages, I mean exactly what I've said. Labor creates the products, and the value of the products labor produces is far more valuable than the wages paid. The rest of the value, above that paid to the workforce (this "surplus value" referred to by Marx), is confiscated from the workers and all of this value goes to the owners as their profit. But most of the value should go to the workers who created it. It should go to society, not to a handful of the wealthy owning class who created nothing. They just use their capital to start the whole process in the first place, and then oversee the process and count their riches. Through this accepted process of wage reimbursement the workers receive just enough to feed their families and return the next day again to get paid for a small portion of the value they create and again donate the rest, the surplus value, to the owners of the means of production. The process goes on and on. Pretty slick set up, huh? All you need to make money is to already have money. As the process progressed over time more and more profits were accumulated and much of these profits were reinvested in more factories. The companies became huge and the owners became very wealthy and politically powerful. *The need to grow and continually make more profits is a necessity under Capitalism.* That is because of the competition within the various industries. If you don't grow and expand and at the same time remain price competitive you will lose to the competition and drop by the wayside. Companies can't just decide they are large enough now, that they are willing to just level off and maybe share more with the employees and stop expansion. To not continuously grow, expand and make more profits is not an option under Capitalism. Capitalism must continually grow. The drive for more profits and larger profit margins is not an option. Eventually, the domestic market becomes saturated, by any particular industry, with too many producers and sellers and not enough consumers so the larger companies expand overseas for new markets, cheaper labor sources and raw materials. This is the stage of Colonialism or Imperialism or monopoly Capitalism. The same basics of earlier Capitalism are still there (the wage system and surplus value) but just on a larger more intense scale. The competition between monopoly Capitalists drives the intensified attacks on working people for more and more profits. These intensified attacks include: union busting, moving the cost of healthcare onto employees, corporate pressure to stop minimum wage increases, the use of part time workers to replace full time workers, automation aimed at eliminating jobs and many other means aimed at the workforce. These large domestic and international companies begin to dominate their respective markets. The smaller companies within the specific industries who lost out on the competition disappear and every industry will eventually become dominated by only 2 or 3 big players within a certain country and several more large conglomerates on the international scale. Eventually all the companies become international conglomerates with no national loyalty. Today we are well into this stage of monopoly Capitalism. Theoretically, you could wind up with one bank, one grocery outlet, one retail outlet, and one automobile manufacture within each country. It's pretty much like the board game "monopoly" where you start out with a level playing field and everyone is given a certain amount of play money and after many hours one person winds up with it all. Except in real life, everyone is not given money and it's not a level playing field. As Capitalism continues to grow and spread world-wide, companies compete internationally and vie for foreign markets. In the beginning it's American companies versus Japanese or European companies. The competition becomes fierce and wars are fought to re-divide the world up economically, and nation states sometimes disappear. Today the national lines between competing companies are becoming blurred with joint ventures and mergers between American companies and European, Chinese or Japanese companies. Companies build plants in each other's countries and the production process involves parts being produced all over the world and assembled in yet different countries. The old terms "American made", or "Japanese made" have little meaning. This is monopoly Capitalism. Companies getting bigger, fewer in numbers, and more politically and socially powerful. Competition declines except for the large companies battling it out. Within different industries, such as retail, there are fewer places to shop. Eventually all small businesses, so called mom and pop stores, disappear. Karl Marx and Frederick Engels foresaw where the nature of Capitalism would take it and predicted monopoly Capitalism long before it surfaced.

The increasing negative effect of monopoly Capitalism on the working class, nationally and internationally is devastating. The competition between the huge corporations of the world is truly fierce. The working class in the developing countries that don't have rounded diversified economies yet and are subjected to the foreign corporate exploitation of their resources are the most devastated. But this fierce competition comes down on the working class of the developed nations as well. The natural place to increase profits is at the *point of production* where more *surplus value* can be squeezed from the workforce. This means cancelling retirement plans, and eliminating health plans or hiring people part time with no benefits, reducing wages and eliminating jobs altogether through automation. The more the surplus labor force grows with rising unemployment the easier it is to reduce wages. In addition the growing power of huge companies that are left whether it's in manufacturing, banking or oil exploration gives them unlimited influence and leverage over the political system until, as is currently the situation in the United States, the economic system becomes clearly dominate over the political system which is rendered nearly useless. So today we wind up with a "corporate state" form of government. With the establishment of the corporate state and the politicians working *directly* in the interests of this dominant class, Congress no longer responds to the needs of the people and in fact enacts legislation that directly favors the interests of Wall Street and large corporations.

Accordingly, the shift in the wealth of the country moves upward to extreme levels as it is today and the class differences become more profound. Opportunities for good paying jobs disappear and the middle class, which was a short term aberration in the first place, begins to dwindle and eventually disappears. Bernie Sanders is correct in his attacks on Wall Street, the question remains what can he or anybody do about it? The effects of monopoly Capitalism on working people will vary from country to country. The struggling developing countries will suffer the most. Those Capitalist countries who practice "Keynes economics" of government monetary stimulation, more regulation of industry and social programs such as in Europe will fare better for working people at least for a while. But in those countries with more laissez-faire, unbridled Capitalism the working class will suffer more and experience the swiftest changes to their living standards. The United States falls into this latter category. That is why the wealth has shifted more to the rich and social mobility is the lowest in the United States than any industrialized nation. It's sort of like "the bigger they come the harder they fall." Unfortunately, monopoly Capitalism has a long way to go, so you "ain't seen nothing yet!"

Alright, let's talk about Walmart. Walmart has approximately 2 million employees world-wide, creating over $400 billion in annual sales. That $400 billion is the _value of the product created_ by the workforce. That amounts to an average of approximately $200,000 in value created by each employee. The average worker at Walmart works approximately 25 to 30 hours a week (which would be high), and gets paid approximately $9.00 per hour. I know that figure is high, as some of the workers in Asia may not even get $9.00 a day. But $9.00 per hour and 30 hours a week would be $270 a week, times 52 weeks in a year, equals $14,000 per year. Therefore each employee creates $200,000 in value per year and gets paid $14,000 a year. So the surplus value we talked about above is $186,000 per year per employee. Walmart employees only get paid about 7% of the value they create. The owners of Walmart confiscate 93% of the value their employees create. It exemplifies the Marxist description of wage slavery, and "surplus value." Some of you readers may be thinking that these figures are deceiving because Walmart and other companies have a lot of additional expenses. Well that is true, so tweak the numbers a little if you want. Double the value of their work that they get paid for. They still would only get 15% of the value they create, with 85% surplus value going to the Walmart family and major stockholders. But don't tweak the figures too much because any employer, large or small, will tell you that wages are their biggest expense. The point is that workers should be getting the largest portion of the value they create. The opposite is true. The owners always get the "lions share" and workers get the crumbs. The surplus value percentages will vary from company to company, industry to industry but the extent of working people getting ripped off under Capitalism (and the wage system) made possible by private property is generic world-wide. That's where all profits come from: the unpaid wages. Yet the Republicans balk at raising the federal minimum wage to $12 or $15 per hour? Hello! Is anybody in there? The Walmart family wealth of the six heirs alone is equal to the combined wealth of the bottom 42% of Americans. Since the 2008 crises the Walton's family wealth has increased by an additional 22% while wages have gone down for the rest of us. On National Public Radio news yesterday they reported that Walmart is planning to reduce health care benefits for their part time employees. It's not hard to see why the wealth of the country has been shifting upwards in the hands of fewer and fewer wealthy magnates and forcing the 99% closer to poverty. The United States has the biggest disparity in the distribution of wealth than any country in the world!

Yes, Walmart is a perfect example of monopoly Capitalism. Wherever they go they run small retailers out of business. This has been happening for years. Now they're concentrating on some of the giant retailers still hanging in there from past decades, like Sears, J.C. Penny's and K-Mart. They're even challenging the supermarket chains, drug chains and, with the relaxed regulations on banking and Wall Street, they are moving into consumer banking. Walmart's main method for eliminating competition is by concentrating on the "point of production" (the workplace) and intensifying their squeeze on their employees. *They literally treat their employees as trash.* Their employees say the company has no respect for them as human beings. I remember 30 years ago talking to a friend who during the course of a year had worked for both Walmart and K-mart. She said it was a world of difference and that she would never work for Walmart again. Seventy percent of their workforce are women which is not a coincidence, as women are still paid less than men for the same work. The largest sex discrimination lawsuit ever filed was against Walmart. It went all the way to the conservative packed U.S. Supreme Court and the workers lost as almost all worker issues, discrimination issues and civil rights issues are losing nowadays in the conservative court. I know a person working at Walmart today, a middle aged woman who is the most helpful ideal customer service worker you could meet. She has been with Walmart for 3 or 4 years, is part time, as almost all the women are, and she has literally been pleading for more hours work and the company keeps refusing her request. The workforce is made up of part time middle to older age women and the full time managers are mostly young white males. The people who are inventorying and re-stocking the shelves are under tremendous pressure to get their work done in a very limited time (a form of speed-up) and if they don't they get written up and disciplined which, in many cases, amounts to reduced hours. Walmart is a real sweat shop, and one of many huge and powerful companies that make up the growing trend of monopoly Capitalism. The employees have been revolting lately with one day strikes and some really big demonstrations. When you see them out in front of the stores in their green T-shirts, stop and talk to them, they are all very friendly people who love to tell their story. I've been to a couple of their demonstrations in the last few years and in one of the events we all marched through the store in front of their managers and the public. Their main demand is for "RESPECT," which they certainly don't get. Even with all the low wages and little or no benefits it's the treatment and harassment, and lack of respect that is their main complaint. Walmart employees are the largest recipients of food stamps in the country. The company has shifted their cost of doing business onto the tax payers by paying such low wages that most of their workforce is eligible for food stamps and Medicaid. I wish I could be around another 100 years to see what happens once Walmart has driven all the other competitors under, once they have won the monopoly Capitalist battle in their own industry and no competitors are left. I imagine that then they will start treating the customers the same as their employees and that the days of cheap prices will be over with. The pricing policies of all U.S. corporations has always been "whatever the market will bear." Once Walmart stands alone with no competition left at all then they can do whatever they want to and maybe accumulate as much wealth as the bottom 75% of the population.

I have one last remark about Walmart. Like most corporations, when presented with criticisms of their practices they lie and engage in misinformation. In 2014, there was a terrible fire in a garment factory somewhere in Asia. The workers were living on the premises and over a hundred perished in the fire, in part because some of the exit doors had been locked. Walmart denied even knowing that there were Walmart products being produced there. "Oh well," they said, they can't keep track of all the world sites they use to make their products. Within days of the statement the news media, again public radio, discovered that there was a Walmart corporate production manager working in the plant full-time whose job it was to oversee production. Maybe he locked the doors? So it's not just the lack of respect and low wages in regards to the U.S. workforce, it's also the horrific conditions created worldwide by Walmart on the international working class. Like all big companies they will deny and lie about their activities. Usually it is impossible to get to the truth of the crimes committed by major corporations. Don't forget that the big corporations also literally own the news media. Now you know where the chant "workers of the world unite" came from. It came from all workers worldwide having the same enemy: international monopoly Capitalism.

Walmart is only one of the international companies well into the stage of monopoly Capitalism. The growth of monopoly Capitalism still has a long way to go. The need to keep increasing profits and grow or die is in the systemic nature of Capitalism. The jobs that are lost to technology are also gone forever. With growing unemployment due to technology, the value of human labor will decrease and working people will continue to be viewed as just another commodity. This will be accompanied by an increasing lack of respect for workers by companies like Walmart. So the plight of Walmart workers could be the future for all working people in all the different industries. Right now Walmart has more employees than any company in the world. Their reputation of worker abuse is not a positive indicator for the future of working people under monopoly Capitalism. All of the indignities suffered by the working class under the various stages of Capitalism would not be possible without the law of *"private property."* It truly is the creator of class societies, and the intensity of the struggle between the "haves" and the "have nots" will increase as monopoly Capitalism matures.

CHAPTER FOUR

The "Union" Question

The pros and cons of unions have long been a political debate in this country. Ever since the intense political attacks against unions beginning with the Reagan
Administration in the early 1980s, the percentage of union organized jobs in the U.S. has been decreasing. Rolling back wages and employer provided benefits for all
workers are a direct result of this union busting. At one
time, around 30% of American jobs were unionized.
Today that percentage has fallen below 10%.   There
has always been a lot more establishment propaganda
out there *against* unions than there are *for* unions. This
comes back to the social class in power having more influence with their propaganda and opinion swaying.
Certainly the wealthy 1% have much better access to
the media on the union debate, as they do on any subject. What is clear is that no employer, large or small,
really wants a union interfering in any way with their
ability to control the workforce. What is also clear is
that this *"interference"* and oversight is vitally necessary
to and in the interests of the public whose very lives are
dependent on the terms of employment in the workplaces.   Even though union employees are better
trained, more productive and more satisfied with their
jobs, which results in less turn over, etc., employers
would still prefer to have free reign and keep unions
and government out of their affairs. Unfortunately this
unchallenged control (laissez-faire Capitalism) over the
workforce works to the economic disadvantage of employees and encourages arrogant abuse by employers,
as it has with Walmart and many other companies large

and small.

I am from the older, boomer generation so I have witnessed and worked in both union and non-union jobs. These days most of the younger generations have never even experienced unions and many only know how business people and conservative politicians address the question. They criticize unions as special interest entities separate from workers' interests and interfering with the beloved concept of the "free market." Unless younger people of the millennial generation have talked to older workers or done some secondary historical research, they may never hear the union's side of the argument. There are also many boomers who never had the opportunity to work in both union and non-union environments. So brace yourself folks, here comes the argument "for" unions from someone who has experienced both union and non-union employment. It's a no brainer: union jobs win hands down! Today most of the well-paying jobs with benefits that are not requiring extensive higher education are government jobs that are unionized and removed from the private sector profit motive. Not surprisingly, the current political attack on what's left of unions is centered on questioning the right of government workers to organize. Governor Scott Walker of Wisconsin and his attack on unionized government workers comes to mind. As the middle class is gradually disappearing before our eyes and the private sector doesn't pay enough to live on, let alone enough to support a middle class life style, unionized government workers are the largest group of what is left of the middle class.

One negative view point I hear from some working class people, is that government workers *should learn to live like the rest of us.* This is a negative and divisive position that comes out of ignorance and individualism, and even acts against the interest of the people who express it. What we all should be doing is supporting government workers to keep their collective bargaining rights, and struggle to organize our non-union jobs so that all working people can enjoy the benefits and wages that government workers have. Instead we attack the more fortunate workers in a fight to the bottom. What's the matter with some people? Are they so selfish that if they can't have something for themselves then nobody else should either? If everybody thought this way what kind of a society would we have? I have always tried to run my own moral/ethical life by a certain guideline: Before you engage in an action or take a position, and you're questioning yourself whether it is ethically correct or not, ask yourself this question – "What would the world be like if everyone did what I am considering?" In other words if everyone thought or acted in a particular way, what would be the effects on society in general? If the answer is that things in general would be worse for most people, then it's a pretty good indicator that the action is not a good idea. This attitude, "if I can't have it, then nobody can" is one of the many ways where individualism and selfishness too often prevails in a Capitalist society that fosters these values. Because people are suffering economically and at the same time all of this anti-union rhetoric is coming at us, we start feeling sorry for ourselves and looking for someone to blame. It's easier to blame government workers and unions than to embrace unions and struggle against the system that works against all of our interests. Anything that divides us weakens the working class and middle class unity and serves the interests of the ruling elite, whether it's convincing people to blame their problems on minorities, immigrants, government workers or unions.

Years ago I had a discussion with a man after class in a community college. This guy was about 20 years older than I was and the question of unions had come up in class. I was inexperienced and had never been in a union workplace at that time, like most young people today. Anyway this man said "there are always two sides to an issue, but just remember that *unions didn't come about for no reason.*" He had made a point and I began thinking to myself, what were the reasons that caused the union movement? So gradually, through studying labor's history and later in classes that I took in sociology and union relations, I learned more about the past terrible conditions of working people. These conditions created the push for the union organizing drives of the early 20th century in the United States. You can read Marx's "Capital" if you want to know just how bad conditions were for working people during the birth of the Industrial Revolution or you can read Charles Dickens for a good overview. You can go on line with your inquiries or you can talk to any Socialist about the early American struggle of the miners against the Rockefeller family, or the <u>Triangle Shirtwaist Factory fire in New York in 1911,</u> when hundreds of workers (mostly women and children) were locked into a 3 story garment factory and either jumped to their death or were burned alive. The struggle against horrid working conditions and child labor lasted through the nineteenth century and well into the twentieth century, until the union movement turned it around and began to improve conditions.

As recently as the 1980s, President Reagan's Secretary of Labor Donovan tried to re-invent garment sweat shops and child labor in America. Even though his attempts were exposed there still are little sweat shops in Los Angeles abusing desperate immigrants brought to

America through the continuing slave trade. Just like anything else that required major changes or improvements, it took people out in the streets demanding the changes. Socialists played a major role in the union organizing efforts. Working people have much more common grounds with Socialists / Communists than they do with populist libertarians. In the organizing drive of the miners there was a lot of bloodshed during the strikes against workers by the Pinkerton Private Security forces hired by the mining companies. So, there is a lot more to United States history than George Washington chopping down his father's cherry tree and Davy Crockett. It's all out there for you to inquire about. Or you can disregard working class history and add to the phenomenon of uneducated U.S. citizens. The above references to working class history are just the tip of the iceberg regarding the conditions that led up to the union movement in the U.S. Whole books have been written on this subject alone. So if you want to be an informed citizen then take it on yourself to get informed.

Our enemy is not the unions, immigrant workers, or liberal politicians. It's not someone of another nationality, Communism, the Illuminati, the United Nations, Islam, the Consumer Protection Agency or The Affordable Care Act. None of these things are the enemy of working people. The enemy is big money, monopoly Capitalism, the big banks, the IMF or the World Bank, international corporations, Imperialist wars, Walmart, McDonald's and big agribusiness industry who control the food supply and fill our arteries with saturated fats, salt and sugar and make us sick as billions in profits are made. It's the prescription drug companies, the fossil fuel industry, the mortgage industry and Wall Street. It's private property! It's Capitalism that creates all of this oppression, in its many forms, and it sure as hell is not unions! The unions made us strong in the past and can do so again in the future!

All of the above being true, today there is a big difference between the union leadership and the rank and file members. The real strength of unions is that it provides the setting where rank and file members can influence the collective bargaining process as well as use the organization form to take direct action on the job. The power is always with numbers, the power and effectiveness is with the people. That power is greatly enhanced within a union atmosphere as opposed to non-union workplaces, where corporate rule is supreme and no dissension is tolerated. So stop thinking of a union as this powerful special interest organization with a bunch of fat cats at the top as the only benefactors. That definition would more rightfully describe the U. S. Congress than what's left of the existing unions. Campaign financing laws look upon unions as just another special interest organization. Stop for a moment and reflect on who writes these laws. Unions are not special interest entities like religious organizations, corporate industry groups, the National Association of Manufactures, the Chamber of Commerce, etc. Unions are the peoples collective. When unions were strong and influenced better pay, benefits and working conditions, even non-unionized workers benefited because non-union employers had to offer similar conditions of employment to attract workers. Notice I said similar conditions not the same conditions. So if unions are out there fighting for better conditions for the American people, both unionized and non-union, how can they be a special interest group? Are the American people a special interest group? I always thought the American people *were* America.

With few exceptions there has always been a problem with the union hierarchy. There is not a union rank and file member alive, whether Communist, red-neck or otherwise, that won't tell you that if you're trying to struggle with the company, no matter what the issue, that you have to fight your way through the union leadership to even get to the company. But it's still better to have to struggle with the union leadership than to try and approach callous management practices without a union. Socialist leaning union activists used to refer to the union leadership as the "TUB's" for *trade union bureaucrats*. The rare exceptions were active locals like the Molders Union back in the 1970s (discussed in chapter 10). The leadership of the Molders Union local 164 were ready to approach the companies and even organized the rank and file to do so. Not surprisingly, Local 164 had a Socialist leaning President. Unions require ongoing grass roots activism to keep their leaders pointed in the right direction. So why is this? Well, unions are just like any other organization where people who get into power (like politicians) change. They lose touch with their working class base. They start hobnobbing with the company executives, they sometimes get bribes or perks and they learn that in order to keep their privileged lives they need to limit their demands on the companies. Some of the leadership, from the very get, are just smooth talking, opportunistic careerists like so many politicians. Even during negotiations they capitulate to things like no strike clauses, and give the company free reign to replace union employees by contracting out to non-union contractors. More recently, unions have negotiated contracts with a two tiered pay and benefits system where older workers keep their existing benefits with newer workers getting paid less with fewer benefits. But unions usually get workers better wages with automatic raises. Wages are the same for men and women performing the same job. There is some degree of seniority so that the company can't get rid of you when you reach 40 and replace you with a 20 year old. You also have a formal grievance procedure with representation so you can voice your concerns without getting fired. Union jobs are so much better for working people than non-union jobs. But just because there are some crooks in the leadership of many unions is no reason to throw the baby out with the bathwater and buy into the propaganda that unions are special interest organizations who only benefit an upper echelon of leaders. There are many problems that come up in the workplace that union leadership can address. But usually these issues require rank and file pressure on the union leaders to stand up to the company management on issues like discrimination, safety issues and other issues of worker abuse such as speed-ups, forced overtime, and abusive supervisors.

No one can stand up alone against *capital*. If you're organizing in the community, in the streets or in the workplace, you need the strength of people united to-gether. Unions have proven successful in the past as the organizational form for uniting workers on the job. Throughout history they have organized general strikes and supported community struggles as well. Today be-cause a lot of the demands for livable wages are against companies like Walmart, McDonalds and other fast food giants that don't have unions, the workers have orga-nized themselves and taken to the streets without un-ions. These struggles may lead to union organization or they may not. But the principle behind unions is still there; the people have come together, *in union with each other*, in direct action against the financial power of cap-ital. *This concept of "people united" is far more im-portant than the imperfections within the organizational form itself.*

Generally speaking unions today are not as power-ful and effective as decades ago. Corporations have be-come much more dominant than unions in the class struggle. In American Capitalism, money is power and corporate America has unlimited financial resources while unions' financial resources are limited. Today corporate America has become much more aggressive in their attacks on working people. Companies are eliminating and taking back the gains made by working people when unions were stronger. Wages have been rolled back on all of society, not just union jobs. Com-pany retirement plans are being replaced by employee contributions to 401K plans and health care benefits are unavailable to the growing numbers of part time work-ers. As the Capitalist international environment has progressed into monopoly Capitalism the increasing cutthroat competition for hegemony and survival of the powerful world corporations has prompted the attacks on the wages and benefits of all working people includ-ing union workers. The aggressive nature of this com-petition is also responsible for undermining our politi-cal system. So while companies are attacking working people directly on the job, they are also manipulating our politicians to enact legislation in their interests and stifle any legislation in the people's interest. Legislation in the interest of the public would involve increased corporate taxes, environmental restrictions on compa-nies, increased minimum wages, and legislation against so-called *right to work laws*, equal pay for the equal work performed by women, and many other legislative issues that have been road blocked by Congress as they continue to represent corporate interests. Instead, we get historical lower taxes on the wealthy and corpora-tions, government subsidies and bailouts of corporate

America, and repealing of laws that restricted dangerous and speculative practices on Wall Street. I sometimes feel that our politicians have only one purpose in
life and that is to serve the 1%. Certainly that is the
agenda of the current Republican Party. In my view
there is no longer any government in the world that approaches the power of the international corporate giants. This upper hand by corporations over workers,
unions and our political system is the basis of my view
that Americans are living under the reign of a "corporate state".

Let's take a closer look at just one example of corporate America influencing our politicians to the detriment of working people. I am talking about "right to
work laws" or "right to work states." When a particular
state adopts right to work laws it then becomes illegal
to have a union "closed shop." It instead becomes a unionized *open shop*. A closed shop is where everyone
working within a particular workplace must be a dues
paying member of the recognized union. The closed
shop is the traditional format for unions. The closed
shop brings everyone together in purpose and vested
interests through their union dues, creating less divi-
siveness and a stronger unified voice amongst the rank
and file members. The open shops created by "right to
work laws" in some 25 states like Alabama, Texas, Ar-
kansas, Florida and Arizona allows workers to reap the
same rewards achieved through the collective bargaining process but allows them to abstain from paying
their union dues. This creates many animosities among
the workforce and divides the unity of workers from the
very start. The open shop also weakens the bargaining
power of the union negotiators. Of course this is the political intention of right to work states in the first place.
That is, to weaken the unions, resulting in fewer bene-

fits and more profits for the companies.   I personally never worked in an open shop but I am sure I would find it similar to an ordinary non-union work place. The conservative rationale behind right to work legislation is that working people should not have to pay for the right to work with mandatory union dues. The suggestion that the workforce may get more returns out of the collective bargaining process than they pay in union dues goes unaddressed by "right to work" supporters. Besides, don't we all pay for the right to work when we pay our federal and state income taxes? A case could be made that people might get more for their union dues than they get for their taxes. So right to work laws are no more than just part of the "corporate state" propaganda to confuse people and, in the long run, to weaken the strength of unions. This makes it possible for companies to squeeze more profits from the workforce. That's exactly what the right to work laws do. States with "right to work" laws provide lower wages, and fewer benefits and lower standards of living for their citizens than states without right to work laws. In spite of the misleading propaganda about right to work laws they are clearly an attack on working class families and another way of the government subsidizing corporate profits.

Unions have also been weakened by negotiating away the right to strike in exchange for short term concessions from the companies. Not all unions have given up this right but even those who haven't are a lot more hesitant to use this power. There is another piece of misinformation that goes "*nobody wins* in *a strike.*" Well sometimes it seems that nobody wins, but the companies always lose. They lose because every day the business is down they lose profits. All profits come from value created by the employees. So when employees are not on the job no value is created. Yes, without their paychecks workers lose money while out on strike. Sometimes, however, workers get back pay when returning to work and sometimes there are strike fund subsidies for workers provided by the unions. It depends on how long the strike continues and it is different in every situation. But successful strikes can benefit existing workers in the years to come and future generations of workers as well. Sometimes the decision to strike becomes an issue of principal rather than just solely for the immediate gains of the moment. There is also the question of pride amongst workers, even if they don't get all they wanted. The companies are always shaken up by walk outs and employees can hold their heads a little higher when they come back on the job. It sometimes increases the self-respect of workers who are determined to stand up and fight and not take it sitting down any longer even if it might mean a sacrifice. Is there anything wrong with a sacrifice for a righteous cause? In the current political atmosphere many strikes are motivated over stopping companies from taking away current benefits. So all strikes are not workers asking for more, but just struggling to keep what they have, like healthcare benefits. In addition, company management may view future complaints with a little more tolerance in an effort to avoid another walk out. So in many cases the after-effects of a strike can raise spirits. Let's be clear about it though, the decision to strike should not be taken lightly as it does create immediate hardships on families.

Unfortunately, as companies become more stubborn with their intentions of rolling back wages and benefits, the necessity of strikes will increase. It's almost always better to reach an agreement through negotiations, but if the right to strike has already been negotiated away before hand, then the bargaining position of unions has been weakened. In the case where the right to strike has been negotiated away or denied by union leadership there are two alternatives. One is to *"wildcat,"* which is an unauthorized strike. That's what the Molders local 164 did in the 1970s. The other alternative is to organize workers on the job to disrupt the normal flow of business, through slowdowns, sick outs and other peaceful but disruptive tactics. The latter is a tough way to go because it is always under the watchful eye of management and leaves everyone subject to firings. This self-organization of groups of workers on the job around particular issues is wide spread. It can get intense but sometimes can resolve smaller issues quickly. On the job confrontation of issues can be more effective and less risky in an already unionized workplace, especially if the union leadership can provide support. The only other alternative is to bite the bullet and capitulate. But if the issue is serious enough and it goes unaddressed, it creates a boiling pot of stress and resentment where individual acts of violence are always possible.

On a national level, the union leadership in the United States engaged in a huge tactical error. They became imbedded with and dependent on the Democratic Party. Ever since Roosevelt and the New Deal the Democratic Party was known, for a long time, as the working man's party. The international union leadership slowly but surely put all their eggs in one basket. They convinced their members that all they had to do was support Democratic Party candidates. The unions had stepped back from the direct action of the past and the rank and file attitude towards struggle changed. Millions of dollars in union dues were spent on lobbying efforts and campaign contributions to Democratic Party candidates. This united effort between unions and the Democratic Party worked for a while but as the international situation changed and the competitive pressure of monopoly Capitalism continued to grow, companies put more pressure on both political parties. As the unions shrank in size, their financial assets were reduced and they were unable to compete with corporate dollars. The Democratic Party politicians became more dependent on corporate campaign contributions. All of this has had an effect of moving our government further to the right and away from the interests of working people. The Republican Party which was always to the right, moved to the extreme right where it is today and the Democratic Party, which at one time was seen as the working man's party with a liberal agenda, moved to the center right. The growing political power of private property interests has been undermining our political system and weakening the power of unions. The unions' strategy of playing the Capitalist money game in Washington, and seeking support through Democratic candidates had, in the long run, failed them and they had _forgotten how to fight_. The leadership had forgotten that their power was in the combined strength of the workforce through direct action and not in this or that politician. The Democratic Party of today, however, remains the lesser of the evils when compared to the outright attacks on working people by the Republican Party. The Republican Party of "Lincoln" has long vanished from the American scene. It became the party of "Reagan." But the Democrats can no longer be counted on to advance the interests of working people, on the job or in the communities. The conditions in the Capitalist world simply will not allow a return to past economic standards of living through the ballot box alone. People are being forced to struggle through direct action, and they know it.

Most of the reforms which created the middle class in this country (and raised standards of living for everyone) were the result of previous direct actions led by the union movement. Without the union movement we never would have had a middle class in the first place. At the end of the Second World War the United States and its corporations were in complete control of the entire political and economic world. The coffers of U.S. companies were overflowing with super profits, but if it hadn't been for the strong union movement demanding that they share some of their profits with working people, the middle class would never have come into existence. The current practice of the last few decades of taking back previous reforms illustrates the illusive and temporary nature of both reforms and the middle class. The rise and decline of the middle class varies from nation to nation. Today, for example, in the U.S. the middle class is disappearing. China's middle class has been growing and is beginning to level off. Tomorrow China's middle class will begin to shrink. As worldwide monopoly Capitalism progresses, some developing countries may never even experience a middle class. The middle class is not a permanent class like the ruling class and the working class, that were created by the private ownership of the means of production and the public nature of the workforce. So in the long run the struggle will come down to only the rich and the poor, the 1% versus the 99%. The unemployed working class, along with part time and underpaid workers, is a growing social phenomenon. Upward social mobility during the rise of the middle class has been replaced by a clear downward mobility and is accompanied by the consolidation of wealth upward in fewer hands. There is no end in sight to these trends. You can't roll back the clock on the inevitable progression of Capitalism. Because of fierce competition in the modern Capitalist world, corporations will be hard pressed to give back to the working class. The trend will be to take away and squeeze more out of the workforce.

But we cannot give up without a fight, and unions are still the best organizational form available to the class struggle in the workplace. The existing union leadership can be pushed to firm positions, and new unions can be organized. When it comes to improving working conditions, the _union concept_ of workers using their combined strength with or without the formal structure of a legally recognized union remains a powerful tool. We are seeing this more and more among non-union workers from Walmart and the fast food industry taking to the streets with marches and demonstrations, and employees walking off the job. We don't always hear about all of this action going on because the news media usually only covers the sensational aspects, particularly the violence. But the struggle through direct action is growing on the job and in the communities. Some of these actions may result in unionization and others may not, but the important thing is that many workers are not waiting for the long process of unionization and negotiation that are being hindered, in part, by our politicians. People have rightfully become impatient with the increasing lack of stability in their lives, and direct action on all issues including work place issues, homeless issues or police brutality is becoming the alternative to traditional methods of voting. We have lost our trust and patience in the government and private enterprise to correct the growing political and social injustices. This direct action was always what our democratic society was about. We have also forgotten our history of struggle. The process of reforms through voting and legislative action has broken down as the economic system of Capitalism has undermined this traditional political process.

The democratic process guaranteed by the First Amendment in the U.S. Constitution allows for all forms of free speech, and not just expression through the ballot box. Freedom of speech is a constitutional right and a patriotic responsibility. In fact, the history of progress and change in America favors democracy more through direct action which is a form of free speech. It has always been a more effective vehicle of change than the free speech through the electoral process. Today direct action, in the minds of many, has become the only method for necessary change. In the minds of many others it is still looked upon with raised eyebrows and skepticism. But the continuing increase in economic and social injustices will eventually change this latter mindset. Unions, and the union concept, as a form of direct action has played a positive role in the past struggles for economic justice of working class families. As the United States moves into another period of civil unrest and growing economic injustices only time will tell if formal unionization will regain its past position in America or if workers will organize themselves outside of the union structure. In either case, the concept of working people coming together in "*union*" with each other will be the same. It will be citizens choosing to be united in the face of Capitalism's effort to divide us.

CHAPTER FIVE

"Lupe"
The Warehousemen's Union Local 853

After graduating from college in 1969 with a business administration degree and a minor in political science, I went to work for Shell Oil Company as a marketing analyst. A degree in business is the closest thing to majoring in Capitalism. You are exposed to the managerial mindset and familiarized with all of the techniques used by corporate America. I had already become an anti-war advocate while in college and during the course of my business curriculum I had developed a lot of reservations about business values that conflicted with societies' interests. The business community has a very weak sense of social responsibility or empathy towards employees. Once during a discussion in a marketing class, at the time of the Watts riots in the black community in Los Angeles (1965), a discussion came up in class as to whether business advertising had any effect on the looting that went on during the riots. My opinion was yes, because poor people like everyone else are constantly inundated with commercials to buy all of the products that corporate America wants to sell us. The problem is that poor people just don't have the money for all these things. Although advertising didn't cause the riots, once the riots got out of hand people starting looting on a large scale, taking all the things they could never hope to buy. The advertising had created a pent up demand that reached fruition during the riots. We still see this phenomenon today when protests get out of hand. There were maybe one or two other students in the class that agreed with me. So goes the typical mindset of business students, the executives of tomorrow.

Not long after working with Shell Oil Company during the so called "Arab Oil Embargo," the company had a two day conference for employees where we were wined and dined. The purpose was to convince employees that the huge increases in gasoline prices were justified. The U. S. population was expressing strong anti-oil company sentiment because prices had risen sharply in a very short time. This was seen as price gouging by the oil industry. The company was trying to persuade its employees to become spokespeople in defense of these huge increases. But I had already been of the opinion, along with most people in the country, that we (the consumers) were being defrauded and that the Arab Oil Embargo was the excuse for getting the prices way up over two dollars per gallon. The prices never really came down from these historical new levels and only proceeded upwards over the decades. Anyway, I walked out of the conference in the middle of the Vice President's appeal, which was insulting to my intelligence and morally disgusting. Not long after that, I quit my job with Shell Oil. I then worked about another year and one half for a small aerospace contractor that manufactured components for the space program. The problem was that the same products were also being used in the missile defense program for the Viet Nam War. This gnawed at me in the back of my mind. As a contract administrator I negotiated government contracts, a learning experience that later helped me as a union grievance man at U.S. Steel. During my experience as a contract administrator, I had a chance to observe a production line and all the forms of speed up and pressure that were suffered by workers. I had been praised as the best contract administrator the company had ever had. When it came time for annual wage reviews I received a hundred dollar a month pay increase which was the largest raise given anyone. At the same time, the hourly blue collar workers, men and women on the assembly line, received no more than 3 to 5 cents per hour increases, if any. This was a perfect example of how middle management and/or supervisory personnel are rewarded while the bulk of the workforce, were used and abused. The employees that were actually making all the products were being neglected to provide inflated salaries for management and profits for the stockholders. I had a discussion with my boss, the Vice President of Marketing, over the workforce receiving the crumbs while I was receiving a substantial raise. I expressed that this wasn't right. He said that was what Karl Marx thought. At the time I had no idea of Marx's analysis of Capitalism. Within a short time this knowledge would change as my exposure to Marxism was not far off. Between the company's role in the ongoing Viet Nam War and the blatant class divide within the company I quit that job and that was the end of my aspirations for a career in business. I guess the writing was on the wall. I just couldn't get my ethical and moral values to coincide with corporate America. Later, as my understanding of Capitalism grew I understood the basis for these inequalities in society.

Soon after leaving the business world I left the West coast and traveled across the United States, ending up in Boston MA. I got a job as a building maintenance person as I had developed mechanical skills as a teenager. I actually was happier in working with my hands and, because of my family working class background, I just felt more comfortable being around blue collar workers. Their work ethics and values I found refreshing compared to the more affluent classes which dominate the business community. While living and working in Boston I became exposed to leftist ideology and activism. I lived in Cambridge between Harvard and M.I.T., so there was a strong student atmosphere as well. The Irish Republican Army had ties to the community and there were several IRA Irish Pubs with a lot of revolutionary discussions about British Imperialism, which was a hands-on education in international politics. It was in Cambridge that I first got a copy of Marx's Communist Manifesto which helped me to understand the Capitalist nature of the Viet Nam War. It became clear, through the reading of Marxist material and discussions, that the problem of the war and all the rest of inequalities in the country were in one way or another related to the Capitalist economic system, based on private property. The war was far more than just the incorrect political policies of our government.

While in Cambridge, I met my wife to be and my lifelong best friend. We moved back to California together. Jean, unlike myself, had an intellectual family background but was supporting herself in working class hourly jobs as I had most all of my life. Our relationship always assumed we would both need to work and contribute to our financial needs together. We moved to the Bay Area. My intention was to find work, get involved in the class struggle for change and attempt to educate people about the true nature of Socialism and Capitalism. I was 30 years old and considered myself to be a conscious revolutionary with a goal of struggling against Capitalism and building a Socialist/Communist movement. I never thought that the Soviet Union really had a Communist economy, and although there were hopes that China might be able to establish Socialism the free market movement in China ended any hopes for China as well. Through continued study of Marx-

ist/Leninist philosophy, I could see there were no examples of Communism in the world with the possible
exception of Cuba. Russia and China had certainly lost
their direction in building Socialism. So I had become
an independent Marxist and took issue with revolutionary groups who viewed Russia and China as Communist
countries. My wife was a progressive liberal democratic. Although we didn't agree on every issue, we saw eye
to eye on most political issues. Most importantly, like
me, she was working class in mind and body and was a
very supportive other half. I learned from her, especially around women's issues, civil rights and environmental issues. We arrived in the Bay area and had already
decided to rent a place in Oakland. San Francisco was
far too expensive for our earning potential. I got a job
with Montgomery Wards at the 20 acre warehouse in
adjacent San Leandro as a mechanic's helper. I didn't
know that the company was in the Local Teamsters
Warehousemen's Union. All I knew was that I needed
work and I started off at $3.10 per hour (low for the ar-
ea but better than Boston wages). The time period was
around 1973.

The Teamsters, during this period, were noted for
organizing the whole spectrum of the workforce. Unfortunately the only Teamster workers that received the
big bucks were the truckers or drivers. They had been
Jimmy Hoffa's main claim to success in the unionized
community. The rest of the Teamster shops (organized
workplaces) like the warehousemen, the office workers
and other industries played second fiddle to the benefits
of the Teamster drivers. Many of the contracts negotiated by the Teamsters in these other workplaces were
"sweetheart" contracts which had pay levels and benefits more in line with what the employers preferred to
provide rather than what the workforce actually need-

ed. This being the case, these shops were still a notch above non-union shops. The main difference in organized and un-organized workplaces is seniority, which gives some protection against discrimination in layoffs. The other advantage was that no matter how complacent the local union leadership was, the employers knew that on serious issues they would probably have to deal with the union in discussions. In a non-union atmosphere, the attitude you get from management is *"if you don't like it get out."* Even though the non-driver warehousemen held secondary status compared to the Teamster drivers, Jimmy Hoffa was still admired and respected by all Teamsters, at least those working in the warehouses that the drivers frequented. Even though these non-driver Teamsters didn't have the wages and benefits that the drivers did, these workers still respected Hoffa's staunch direct action with the transportation industry, which had been successful. I think that many hoped that eventually other Teamsters would receive the same bold representation the drivers had. The success of Teamster drivers had even influenced unorganized independent drivers who by example had, on occasion, taken direct action of their own.

Anyway, the workers in the Warehousemen's Local Union 853 in Oakland California were up against some arrogant TUBs (trade union bureaucrats). They conducted their union meetings in an extremely non-democratic fashion and would kill motions on the floor that required them to address many of the day-to-day problems of the workforce on the job. On occasion they would bring in "goon squads," which were paid by the leadership to intimidate the dissenting rank and file members. I experienced this in the local during a union leadership election when the leadership positions were actually threatened by certain grassroots candidates.

The goon squad consisted of bikers who were solicited by the Union President to disrupt and intimidate the election process. This is the atmosphere everyone was up against in Local 853, and my first exposure to union activism.

I had been doing my thing by talking to other employees and discussing workplace problems and political issues and encouraging people to go to the union meetings. I wanted them to join the struggle to get the leadership to actually confront the company on the many unanswered issues in the workplace. I had begun to build up a reputation as an aggressive leader of sorts and was making friends and earning respect among the workers. One night after work during a union meeting I found out I was not alone. There was a struggle on the meeting floor where an employee up in front was trying to raise a job related issue with the leadership. The leadership really didn't want to hear it. So they kept ruling the motion "out of order." Then from a few rows behind me I heard a woman's voice questioning the "out of order" ruling of the local president who was chairing the meeting. I turned around to see the woman who was challenging the leadership. She was a slightly built Chicana woman with articulate speech and a steadfast voice, and she was holding a "Roberts' Rules of Order" book in one hand. She was reciting its contents as applied to the situation at hand, and was telling the president that his out of order ruling was improper. There was dialogue between her and the president over the issue. He was not ignorant at all of the "Rules" but was just used to talking over people and only raising issues that the leadership approved of. He would typically make announcements and then adjourn the meeting in short order. Well, that didn't happen this time. Her name was Lupe Salazar and she won the debate with the President: the workers motion made it to the floor and was voted on. There were a lot of frowns on the faces of the other leaders on the podium, especially the secretary treasurer who really is the boss even over the president who chairs the meetings. A precedent had been set, and the struggle had entered a new phase. From that time on, there was a noticeable improvement in the rank and file participation in the meetings. The leadership would still try to stifle discussions and motions, but they would be reminded of the correct procedure. During Lupe's duel with the officials I had tried to assist her when the President interrupted her with a raw male chauvinist voice in an attempt to shut her up. But she held the floor and with my help and that of others (by interrupting the President with "let her talk") she soon finished her successful challenge to the Chair. I am sure that Lupe would not have given up and would have been successful anyway but I am also sure she appreciated the support. After that Lupe and I worked together to make the meetings more democratic.

Lupe Salazar was a Marxist like me, but with more experience in the struggle. I could tell by the way she talked, staying on the subject at hand but also raising little exposés of the economics of Capitalism. Like myself, she was more educated and articulate than the average blue collar working person. Lupe was a Chicana and, when asked, she referred to herself as Chicana. Nowadays Mexican Americans and migrants from South America are referred to as Latinos or Hispanics. Those terms were around in the 70s as well, but were terms used for the more affluent people of Mexican descent. But in the 60s and 70s, when there was a lot of political turmoil in the U.S., the term Chicana, or Chicano, became quite common among working class Mexican Americans who were involved in the civil rights movement, the anti-war movement, and subsequently in all class struggles for economic, political and social justice. Currently, with the increase in political dissent growing, the term is still around in the Mexican American activist community. Last year at a big rally in Los Angeles on "International Workers' Day" I marched next to a contingent of young women who were chanting "Chicana, Chicana." Indeed, Lupe had come out of a civil rights/nationalist movement in East Los Angeles. It was an anti-Viet Nam War movement that addressed the specific concerns of the Mexican community. This made it essentially a nationalist movement. During the Viet Nam War there was an abnormally high number of young Chicano men (as well as African Americans) being drafted and sent to their death on the front lines of the battles. Plenty of young white men were dying as well, but not in the high percentages in relation to their communities that the Mexicans and blacks were dying. These minority servicemen were an endless supply of "cannon fodder" for the Viet Nam War and were disproportionately being sent to the front lines. Whole Mexican communities in East L.A. were being devastated with this subtle form of genocide.

With Lupe, I had made a friend and a priceless contact in the movement. We were successful in reaching out to a lot of workers and increasing their level of political consciousness and we were instrumental in getting a grass roots candidate elected as a business agent (by one vote, can you believe it?) in the Union leadership. Eventually we both moved on from the Teamsters to other political work. Lupe had gotten laid off and I eventually got fired from Montgomery Wards for political activism on the job. When I got fired the local union leadership shed no tears and in fact saw to it that I would never get another permanent job in the Local

853.

I felt I had won Lupe's trust. There is a lot of distrust of white people among minorities and I understand the reasoning behind this. White America has a long history of despicable treatment of African Americans, Native Americans, Chinese, Japanese, and Latinos. Lupe had become an activist in the Chicano national movement against the Viet Nam War. National movements grow out of national awareness and concerns for the oppressive situations particular to certain nationalities. But Lupe's class consciousness had grown to see that all nationalities, including whites, are oppressed as well. She had become a Communist, a Marxist, and she knew that white people were not the enemy. She knew that Capitalism intentionally builds up these prejudices between the races and keeps us divided and less able to unite in the real battle against Capital. Every time I won trust from a minority person, it made me proud. Because of my working relationships with minorities and whites I was able to win the trust of both. I also think I set a good example for white people by struggling for the special issues experienced by minorities. All nationalities have some stereotypical views of each other. But wide spread racism is definitely more prominent by whites against minorities than vice versa. I think some white people view all minorities as a threat. These are the white people who are filled with prejudicial hatred themselves and feel that minorities must feel the same way about them, and this scares them. But what they are really afraid of is themselves. Whites have a protracted history of racism and, more frequently, just self-righteous white arrogance. Minorities are well aware of this arrogant attitude which sometimes leads to overt white supremacy. But this fear held by some white people that minorities are "out to get you" is unfounded paranoia brought about by ignorance and sometimes guilt.

Everyone is exploited under Capitalism, but minorities are more exploited through discrimination because of the color of their skin and national heritage. Minorities have *special* forms of exploitation that have to be spoken to separately. During my years of activism, I regularly fought against the special instances of racial discrimination, but I was always fighting for the working class as a whole. This included all nationalities. I saved the jobs of several workers in the steel industry and also got several workers promoted.

The principal of divide and conquer has been historically used by the 1 percent to keep the nationalities skeptical of, and sometimes openly opposing, each other. The ruling elite knows that without racial divisions people will eventually figure out who their real enemy is. It is the job of Communists to help them understand that Capitalism is the enemy of all working people. But the status quo establishment does everything they can to encourage racial divisions within the working class. This division of the races is probably the single most common tactic for keeping the wealthy status quo in power. Without this division, working people would be far more united and stronger in the struggle for our common interests. I think that the decades ahead will eventually eliminate the racial division. Already the millennial generation is more color blind and less prejudiced than many people of my generation were. This is a very encouraging social phenomenon that will make it much more difficult for the owners of the means of production and advocates for private property to keep us divided along racial lines. Although it's sometimes hard to see the change happening, there is a growing light at the end of the tunnel.

During the Civil Rights movement, the FBI was used to foster racial divisions in an attempt to undermine the movement. FBI Agents infiltrated the already overtly racist KKK and encouraged their violent acts of lynchings, burning down black churches, and attacking civil rights demonstrations. The FBIs intention was to divide the growing unity between whites and blacks, such as the "freedom riders." The FBI has always played a negative role in the struggle against Capital. They also leveled vigorous attacks on the "Black Panthers" in Oakland, CA. which grew out of defending the black community against police brutality. They have, with their undercover agents, provoked violence within peaceful demonstrations in an attempt to discredit protestors and their righteous issues that strike at the heart of Capitalism. Today, they still use the tactic of blackmail against innocent people and their families to coerce them to cooperate with their criminal investigations which include, but are not limited to, political activists. The old phrase from the John Birch Society, an extreme right wing reactionary group of the past, was "if your mommy is a commie then you have to turn her in." The FBI was the organization to whom you could rat on your mommy. Today, along with the FBI, the NSA (National Security Agency) would be a good place to go and rat on your mommy as a terrorist. In its movement towards a Fascist society, the NSA has denounced even non-violent demonstrators as potential terrorists just as the FBI accused anti-war demonstrators as Communists or Communist sympathizers. We have moved from "red baiting" to include "terrorist baiting." But the ideological beliefs of Communists who attack the concept of private property strike more at the heart of the wealthy/owning class than terrorism. Terrorism is a threat to civilization and the safety of all humanity, but

Marxism or Communism is a direct threat to a particular class of people who benefit under Capitalism. The owners of the means of production can still manage their privileged lives under terrorist attacks but the call for eliminating *private property* by Marxist, Socialists and Communists will always be their main concern. Terrorism may continue to be a permanent aspect of world violence, but as the Capitalist crisis broadens and people begin to consider the Socialist/Communist alterative, expect a renewed round of "red baiting."

The role of the "state" is to serve the interest of the class in power. The "state" is the courts, the legislative body, the executive branch and law enforcement. Law enforcement includes the FBI, NSA, the U.S. attorney general's office, local police forces and sometimes the military. Law enforcement is committed to enforcing the "laws of *private property*" and the vast majority of the working class really don't own any private property. Minorities and poor whites are at the bottom of this property-less class. That is why minorities and poor whites are targeted for police action and, subsequently, police brutality. So the police action against black communities is primarily a class issue. But racism amongst mostly white police departments is a factor and adds to the frequency and intensity of the beatings and murders of scores of unarmed blacks and other minorities. Private property laws create the poor working class and then pit the enforcers of the laws against this property-less class. At the same time, law enforcement responds to protecting the wealth and property of the owning class and the disappearing middle class who still have some financial wealth to protect. So the unemployed, the homeless, the renters in the poor neighborhoods and inner cities along with the protestors for social and economic justice become the target of all law enforcement.

After losing my job at Montgomery Wards I still had union membership and worked out of the union hall as a day laborer, usually getting the least desirable job assignments from the union leadership for whom I had caused so many headaches. This was part of the discrimination I suffered, even as a white person, for my political activity. The normal politics of the workplace would be to assign all of these rotten jobs to minorities. Lupe also worked out of the "hall" and occasionally we went on the same assignments. I had some unbelievable assignments such as steam cleaning out the inside of margarine tanks in the dark with a rope tied to me so if I passed out they could pull me out, to cleaning out the hardened cement from the inside of cement trucks with a jack hammer. My friendship with Lupe continued over the years. She had a lot of knowledge of the political activity in the Bay Area and I got very active in community activism working in coalitions around national and local political issues, while at the same time remaining active on the job. Much of my community work was on my own as I remained independent, but I also worked with Lupe around the issues of affirmative action and the Alan Bakke Decision (chapter 7) which was the beginning of the takeaway of affirmative action programs for minorities under the guise of "reverse discrimination." On this issue Lupe and I went around and spoke to black churches in the Oakland area, informing them of these systemic attacks on the hard earned gains of the Civil Rights movement. So much that was gained by civil rights legislation has been rolled back. A current example that comes to my mind is the voter I.D. laws around the country that discriminate against minorities and, in many cases, remove them from the voting process altogether. This is reminiscent of Jim Crow laws after the end of slavery.

So that ends my story of working with Lupe and my struggle in Local Teamster Warehousemen's Union 853. Times change and people move around. Lupe and her family left the Bay area as I did in time. But wherever she is I hope she is well and provided for, and that her daughters will follow in her footsteps or at least respect her beliefs and honor the commitment she made to the betterment of society. She had a wonderful little family and a hard working husband. She was smart and concerned about others and dedicated to the struggle against American Capitalism. I only know that she helped me grow more in my political consciousness, especially around the national question, than anyone I have ever met. May the universe shine on you, Lupe, wherever you are.

CHAPTER SIX

Thinking Back

THE 2008 PRESIDENTIAL CAMPAIGN

I remember in the Obama/McCain presidential campaign of 2008 when the McCain supporter "Joe the plumber" was attacking the Obama plan to tax the rich more and redistribute some money for social programs. Because of the Republican Party resistance in Congress to taxing the rich, this plan never materialized, but the issue was key to the problem of the consolidation of wealth in the hands of a small yet powerful class. Joe said, "I don't want my wealth redistributed." Sorry Joe, but your wealth is already being redistributed. The wealth of the country is being redistributed right now and has been for a long time. It's being redistributed upward from working people to the super rich through tax policies, government bailouts, reduced wages and benefits, foreclosures and resale of properties, government subsidies to corporate America and many other ways. The concentration of wealth in the hands of a few is higher in America than in any country in the world and it has continued to get much worse since the 2008 campaign. We need to redistribute some of the wealth back into the hands of working people through significant pay increases, changes in the tax code and through government programs that provide social services for working people instead of corporate welfare. The issue was raised during this 2008 campaign and now, in the 2016 Campaign, it has become even more profound. It served as the main political platform for Democratic

Presidential hopeful Bernie Sanders.

As important an issue as the growing unequal distribution of wealth was in 2008, it took a backseat to the immediate concern of the American public for the shameful lack of adequate healthcare to a growing number of Americans. So the main issue in the country at the time of the 2008 campaign was the issue of healthcare. It reminds me of a defining moment in the Obama/McCain presidential debates of the 2008 campaign when the lack of healthcare was addressed on national television. The question was asked of both candidates whether healthcare was a "right" or a "privilege." Obama without hesitation answered that healthcare was a right. McCain stammered briefly at the bluntness of the question then clearly answered that healthcare was a privilege. Really? Really, McCain? Really, Republicans? Really, Libertarians? Do you actually believe that? Is there anything in the world of morality, Christian ethics, civil liberties and humanitarian needs that is absolutely more essential to the preservation of life in this world of hard knocks than *food, shelter and medical attention* when you need it? If our economic system of Capitalism can't provide these three amenities to every citizen in the country then it is absolutely the role, and the mandate of our constitution, through our government, to insure their availability or provide for them directly. Any country, whether Capitalist, Socialist, or dictatorship which cannot or will not see to it that these three basic necessities are provided for is a failed state. The Preamble to the U.S. Constitution states: *"that in order to form a more perfect union, establish Justice, insure domestic tranquility, provide for the common defense, and promote the general welfare, etc.* How can you have domestic tranquility, establish justice and promote the general welfare without food, shelter and medical attention? Of course healthcare is a right. It's a right under our constitution and it's a basic human right. From that point on, it was all downhill for the McCain campaign. The one thing that Obama's presidency will be positively remembered for was his "Affordable Care Act" which has been negatively referred to as Obama care by Republicans. The Affordable Care Act is the first major government program in nearly 50 years reflecting the vital needs of working class citizens. Despite the Republican Party's continuing criticism of the Affordable Care Act, it is overwhelmingly popular with the American people. Only 4 years after the Affordable Care Act was signed into law, healthcare was no longer on the short list of the public's political priorities, where before it was at the top of the list. This fact alone speaks to approval of the Affordable Care Act by the vast majority of Americans. The Affordable Care Act had appeased the national concern over a broken healthcare   system.   Previous   discussions   about healthcare reform had centered on government run, single payer programs as in Canada or in Western Europe. Although these healthcare systems, being socialized, government run programs, provide better health care and are all-inclusive and more cost- effective, the challenge to removing health care from the free market was an unrealistic political demand in 2008. It seems like it still is unrealistic in 2016. That is why the Affordable Care Act was a wise compromise and why it had the support from the corporate world in contrast to their political opposition against socialized healthcare. It kept all the private hospitals, doctors, and drug manufacturers secure in a free market system. The health insurance companies loved it, because it expanded the free market model with the mandatory requirement that everyone must have coverage. The expansion of

Medicaid within the Affordable Care Act was an additional boost to the health insurance industry. To the Capitalist world in general it was far preferable to employer sponsored healthcare, or a government run program. Employer-sponsored healthcare programs put a financial burden on employers and affect the bottom line of profits. Likewise a government socialized program would require higher taxes on corporations to pay for the program, which would also affect profits. Nearly all of the Capitalist world, other than the U.S., have embraced the government run Socialist model as being more efficient in bringing better and more cost-effective healthcare to most citizens. But in America the *corporate state*, in its control over the political system, has been able to keep the free market model alive, with the government subsidizing the profits of a most lucrative healthcare industry. So corporate America jumped at the chance to go with Obama's program and put further discussion of socialized medicine on hold. Even though the ACA was a continuation of the limited coverage and higher patient cost free market system, the expansion in coverage to millions of Americans and the needed improvements such as eliminating the pre-existing conditions restriction have been a long time coming.

Therefore the demands for additional healthcare reform are no longer at the top of the list of domestic issues in America. But the growing movement of all wealth upward has continued to worsen. It has now become the main economic concern of the Democratic Party and the nation in general. It is even coming to the attention of traditional status quo economists. In the 2016 election year, Bernie Sanders, a "*Democratic Socialist*" and a contender for the presidency, focused on this issue in the democratic primaries. But the Republican politicians seem oblivious to the problem. They are all engrossed in the issue of terrorism and anti-immigrant rhetoric with a blind eye to what is happening to working people and the disappearing middle class. The preoccupation with terrorism is, in part, an effort to divert the conversation away from Wall Street not paying its fair share of taxes. The attacks on immigrants are a continued effort to prevent the American people from uniting against the status quo. So what's new with _party_ politics? Not much!

A REFLECTION ON RONALD REAGAN

I remember when Ronald Reagan ran for president. I was working in the steel industry at a mill in northern California. The steel workers in the union were all excited about Reagan and his charisma. Our local union leaders were trying to discourage this enthusiasm because they knew he was anti-union with no empathy or understanding of poor and working people. But you couldn't sway them and many voted for him. Ronald Reagan's popularity was driven by his charisma which he had developed through many years as an actor in Hollywood. Most politicians are, by necessity, actors on one level or another. They are the sales people who peddle the goods of their party philosophies whether Republican or Democrat, and are usually not intellectual deep thinkers themselves. Ronald Reagan excelled at this charisma. Many Democrats were mesmerized by Reagan and voted for the messenger with disregard for the message which was certainly not reflective of the Democratic Party philosophy.

This was the beginning of the conservative element

in the Democratic Party which eventually (1995) led to the Blue Dog Democrats Caucus in Congress. Reagan's election marked the turn of the Democratic Party away from the New Deal of Roosevelt. The Air Traffic Controllers Union (PATCO) endorsed Reagan. The year after Reagan's election (1981) 13,000 air traffic controllers went out on strike over long hours, fatigue and safety issues. The strike was spreading with support from other federal employees. The Reagan administration jailed and then fired them all. Reagan did more damage to working people than any president in my lifetime. He moved the whole country to the right. I had seen the harm Reagan had done in California as a two term governor, and knew that he was much worse than any candidate in recent history. In his endeavor to cut back on social programs as Governor of California, he had closed down mental health facilities and many men and women in need of compassion and professional help were forced onto the streets. This was the beginning of the homeless population in California.

There was a struggle within the revolutionary movement during his run for president as to whether to get involved in the election campaign against Reagan. My view was that he was terribly contemptuous of minorities, the poor, and all working people and that his policies would be uniquely disastrous. Many people in the movement said that all candidates were the same and that it was wrong to encourage people to get involved in the electoral process which was a hopeless path, and that revolution was the only solution. In the 60s and 70s many lefties thought that the revolution was right around the corner and there are many who feel the same today. It's almost like the Christian hope that Jesus' return is very close. My view regarding Reagan's bid for the presidency was to expose him for his extreme political views and vote against him. Afterwards continue with revolutionary work, which includes motivating people towards direct action in the struggle for reforms, and educating people to the systemic nature of their problems. Just because you need a Socialist revolution to really solve the problem doesn't mean that you don't struggle within the existing confines of Capitalist politics for reforms and against attacks on the rights of working people. The revolution may be a hundred or more years away and you have to use all means of struggle in the moment as best you can. The voting system in the United States is far from true democracy. In a presidential election, the "electoral college" aspect of the voting process brings oversight from the status quo and the popular vote does not always hold. The Gore/Bush outcome proved that, with Gore getting more of the popular vote but Bush getting the presidency. In my opinion Bush should never have come to power. What a different world we might have now had Gore been President. The ballot box is still a useful, although limited, tool. If more people had been convinced Gore was the lesser of the evils and more had voted for him, then the election would not have been as close and not as easily manipulated. I had a falling out with many of my political friends over the Reagan issue. I am as much convinced of the need to replace Capitalism as any political activist with Socialist beliefs. But fighting for reforms and against attacks on social programs is vital to the struggle against capital and voting is still a part of the struggle. Voting is not a right that we want to give up simply because of its relative ineffectiveness. That being said, direct action will be at the forefront of the struggle and, as history has shown, it will continue to be the most effective way for bringing about meaningful change. Many of my workplace experiences as an activist were aimed at uniting people to take direct action against all injustices on and off the job.

Returning to Ronald Reagan: He and Nancy Reagan talked a lot about the importance of the family, but he dealt a major blow to the family unit in America with his attacks against organized labor. He successfully rolled back wages for everyone and made it necessary for both parents to work and leave the children at home alone. We are still feeling the effects of that today. Most working class families today still require two incomes. Reagan's attack on organized labor hurt all working people, including those working on non-union jobs. So you might want to reflect on Reagan the next time you go to the polls. There is still a lot of Reagan philosophy out there within both political parties. Voting, in my opinion, doesn't offer a lot of potential for noticeable improvement. But sometimes voting for the wrong candidate can make things far worse.

George W. Bush's invasion of Iraq may have been the biggest blunder in U. S. foreign policy in the history of the United States, but Ronald Reagan's domestic policy set the tempo for attacks against working and middle class people like none before him. We are still living the effects of his political philosophy today, 30 years later. Reagan's main political positions, which are still imbedded in the Republican Party are: The _deregulation_ of all commercial/business activities and the idea of "_trickle down_" economics. Both falsely imply that what is good for the corporate world is good for the people. His position of deregulation and the subsequent legislative enactments of deregulation ultimately contributed to the 2008 collapse (see the "free market" section of chapter 17). His position of "trickle down" gives to the wealthy and corporate establishment in the forms of tax cuts and loop holes, bailouts, and many other corporate welfare laws with the belief that these subsidies to companies will create more jobs. The policy is still widely preached by Republicans today despite the facts showing that the money doesn't trickle down. It is a false premise of Capitalist economic theory.

A point I would like to make is that these ideas of Ronald Reagan didn't just pop out of Ronald Reagan's head. Reagan was a great salesman, but not a deep thinker. The ideas came from the private sector, the corporate state, big business, Wall Street, and the interests of the 1% (the controlling families who oversee the corporate world). With the growing pressure of international competition under monopoly Capitalism, the big players are turning to all measures they can to steel more profits from the pockets of working people. By the 1980s the corporate interests had tired of all the costly benefits of the New Deal - unions, middle class benefits on the job, the war on poverty, affordable higher education etc. It was time to roll back the clock again on the reforms that had already been won. Even though Reagan was the perfect political pawn to represent the interest of the "owning class," to one degree or another, any of the hand screened candidates at the time (early 1980s) would have responded to the current needs of the corporate state to get tough with working people. Even Obama, who today is viewed as a liberal among the Republican neo-conservative majority, is far too chummy with the corporate world. After 8 years in office he still has not been able to get any tax increases on the wealthy or close any corporate tax loop holes. To be fair, he has had his hands full just blocking further attempts at cut backs to existing social programs from the party of privilege, and the same Republicans have rejected anything he has proposed. I feel that Obama being African American is a big part of the unprecedented refusal of the Republicans to cooperate with a Democratic President. It wouldn't be the first time that racism raised its ugly head in Republican politics. We are back to Capitalism again as the culprit. The economic system of private property is undermining and controlling the democratic political system. The oversight of the election procedure and inserting racism into the legislative process have both served the status quo. There are early signs that the Democratic Party is struggling to return to their former liberal roots. If this happens, it could provide some welcome relief to the growing armies of unemployed and underemployed Americans. To squeeze more money from the wealthy to provide for this relief will be much harder than in the earlier days of Capitalism, but not impossible. But the long term reality of Capitalism being unable to provide for the needs of people will remain the same.

Nancy Reagan recently died, about 10 years after the death of Ronald Reagan. Much was said during the funeral about the way she stood behind her man and how they were committed to each other in a circle that even their children could not penetrate. The media talked a lot about the role Nancy played in protecting her man from the harmful influences of some of the people around her husband. The news media downplayed the influential role she played in Ronald Reagan's political views. But Nancy was every bit as influential on President Reagan's political thought as Eleanor Roosevelt was on her husband. Eleanor was just more up front with her politics, whereas Nancy Reagan was more behind the scenes. Back in the 60s and 70s when Reagan was building his political legend, many critics of Reagan were aware of the role Nancy played in the political thought of her husband. Reagan was, among other things, known as the "Teflon" president because no criticisms of his presidency seemed to stick. I think that today, long after his death, this "Teflon" protection still lingers in the form of denying that the Republican icon of the century could have been anything other than his own authentic man. Ronald Reagan had the good looks, the charisma, and the acting ability to have been a convincing spokesman for any cause he chose to undertake. He certainly would not have been the first man to have been completely swayed by love for a woman, which he surely had for Nancy. So the subtle question will always be out there as to what extent Ronald Reagan was an instrument of Nancy Reagan's political passions. The fact that Ronald Reagan was a Roosevelt New Deal democrat before he met Nancy will continue to make me realize the extent to which Nancy Reagan was his political guru.

I view Ronald Reagan's presidency as the beginning of a rapid decline in the middle class and working class aspirations and conditions. The tone and pattern he set in American politics is continuing today. Currently, there are signs that the liberal wing of the Democratic Party is struggling to regain control of the Party. If the hope that the Democratic Party reclaiming its roots is to materialize, it will require the driving force of the people in direct action both in support of liberal/progressive candidates and in continuing to mobilize around the candidates once elected. The door that squeaks the loudest gets the oil. This is the "revolution" that Bernie Sanders talks about.

The Bay Area in the 1970s

Direct action politics in the 70s and early 80s made the Bay Area one of the main hot beds of activity. The Bay Area has a long history of community and union activists, and a left leaning population handed down through generations of families. The Vietnam War and the Civil Rights movements had created many politically conscious activists. The Marxist groups were numerous, as well as many individual Marxists like myself. There were many coalitions between all levels of politically progressive people, including but not limited to Marxists. There were church groups like "Catholic Charities" that were building coalitions and welcomed anyone who would unite to lead and help build movements around specific issues. The black churches were all direct action oriented. The anti-Bakke decision coalition we talk about in the next chapter was another example. The J.P. Stevens boycott committee was another. Most of the Revolutionary groups are no longer around, which is not surprising after many decades.

I remember one, *so-called* communist organization, named the Revolutionary Communist Party or RCP. They were terrible and their understanding of Marxist philosophy was non-existent. They would disrupt events that they were not involved in and would picket events organized by others. They were very sectarian. Wherever they went you could expect the strong possibility that they would go too far and initiate violence. They really never organized anything and were noted for going to grassroots events under the false pretense of supporting the struggle. Inevitably they would force their way into the limelight and take over and portray themselves as the "leaders of the revolutionary struggle." Their essence, if not their motive, was to give Communism/Socialism a bad name. The honest Communists knew they were anything but Communists and many of the Communists I knew thought they were just an FBI front group who were attempting to alienate the people from Marxist ideology and turn them against Socialism.　Whether or not they were an FBI front group with this conscious objective, in practice that is exactly what they were doing: alienating everyone.　The reason I mention this negative example of phony Communism is because the RCP is still out there today, doing their thing.　In 2013, I went to Anaheim CA. to support a community struggle against police killings of Latino youth.　It was a completely spontaneous community uprising of neighborhood people and local churches.　During the last year, there had been 7 or 8 unarmed Mexican American youth murdered by the mostly white police force.　They were unarmed and shot in the back when running from the police, shot while in handcuffs and one was shot while trapped and hiding under a car. I went there by myself to support the struggle.　I saw some people I knew from the Los Angeles and San Diego "Occupy" chapters.　Unfortunately I also saw the RCP with an oversize banner, mixed in with other protestors and passing out their literature.　When the chanting and picketing in front of the Anaheim Police Station had subsided, the community organized speakers went to the microphones and were addressing the public.　Most all the speakers were family members of the murdered youth and some were local church leaders.　Not long after the speeches had started, the RCP waited for their chance, eventually making their way to the podium uninvited, and took over the show.　They ranted on about how they were leading the revolution.　This event and struggle wasn't even a conscious struggle for revolution. They were soon isolated and persuaded to leave the podium by the community organizers and the crowd.　I thought about this later, as I couldn't believe that of all the Communist groups from the past the RCP, the most destructive and divisive group with their political heads, clearly in need of Marxist counseling, still existed.

The tactic of dividing the working class movement typifies FBI involvement. Whether the FBI practiced a hands off approach to the RCP or was actively involved in their leadership thru undercover work is purely speculative. But here the RCP were, still engaging in destructive behavior while many honest revolutionary groups had disappeared. To this day, I have strong distrust for the FBI. They have played negative roles of disinformation and inciting violence at demonstrations to discredit movements for decades, from the anti-war movement, the Civil Rights movement and any struggle that threatens the status quo. The FBI's involvement with the KKK to undermine the Civil Rights movement in the 60s highlighted their negative influence on a righteous movement. They have historically used the unlawful tactic of personal "blackmail" with innocent citizens if they don't cooperate completely with ongoing investigations. Blackmail was used extensively by J. Edgar Hoover, who would blackmail even congressman to get what he wanted. This illegal tactic of blackmail has served as a template for FBI activity ever since. To top it off they are, on certain levels, linked with organized crime in unprincipled relationships. I have had some personal knowledge of FBI agents in cooperative relationships with an Italian Mafia family boss. The case of Whitey Bulger, with the Irish Mafia in Boston, is another known example, gone public, of this unprincipled FBI/Mafia relationship. Bulger was allowed to escape prosecution and run his "winter hill gang" unrestricted by the FBI while serving as an informant against rival gangs. Their role in society has been far more than just the "good guys" out to protect you as many Hollywood and television portrayals would have you believe.

During these years of political struggle in the San Francisco/Oakland area (60s and 70s) perhaps the most glaring fiasco to discredit the Communist/revolutionary movement was the arrival of the SLA, the Symbionese Liberation Army. Unlike my purely speculative view of the FBI's role regarding the RCP, their involvement with the SLA was more substantiated. Some of you might remember the SLA's slogan, "Death to the Fascist insects that prey upon the blood of the people." Such an articulate and appealing slogan, isn't it? Not! This is where the allegedly brain-washed heiress to the Randolph Hearst fortune, Patty Hearst, joined this so called revolutionary group that began killing people and robbing banks all around California. Really!? Communist bank robbers? The SLA would talk about the working class and occasionally were referred to as Communists by the press, when actually they were no more than criminals or terrorists. Of course, the Hearst family owned the syndicated Hearst Newspapers, which gave them some direct access to how the press was interpreting the SLA's politics as Socialist/Communist. There always was a high level of political understanding in the Bay area and most of the activists and all of the left leaning groups knew the SLA were not truly revolutionaries, and certainly not Communists. The key element associating them with the FBI and other police organizations was in the leader of the SLA. His name was Donald De-Freeze. He had a long history of firearms possession and robberies with past incarcerations. At one point he was released from jail, and while on probation was again, caught with possession of firearms. Although this was a clear violation of his parole he was, curiously, released. At another point he escaped from Soledad Prison and immediately organized the SLA. It seems like nothing could stop this guy, neither law enforcement nor the prison system. DeFreeze had been suspected of undercover work with the FBI in previous operations. The New York Times ran some articles pertaining to his association with the FBI. These articles came out around the time of the violent end of the SLA and they received little attention from the public. Years later (1993) Hoffman and Headley wrote a book entitled "Vegas P.I." which presented a strong argument that Donald DeFreeze had been a police informant and provocateur. To activists and revolutionaries in the Bay Area the whole operation was a media frenzy to discredit Communist ideology and to stop the growing unity between the population and the Communist activists. I think that the only people who could have cheered this government operation, if in fact it was a government operation, would be a few impatient and angry people who had a grievance against the system. There were plenty of these people through-out the country, just as there are today. The truth is, the SLA was nothing more than a terrorist group that appealed to a romantic/individualist idea of revolution. There also were a lot of right wing, free market ideologues that portrayed them as a glaring example of why we don't want a Marxist revolution. It was a real publicity attack on the growing social movement. Most people who have had no knowledge or experience of the underhanded and dishonest methods of the FBI may view my negative view of them as nothing more than paranoia. But I stand behind my criticism of them historically playing a negative, subversive role against the struggle for political, social and economic justice. I feel that there is some objective evidence and history to support my view. Regardless of who orchestrated or influenced the SLA they certainly had nothing to do with revolution or Socialism. Further, all the biased attention they received in the media, at the time, had some effect on discrediting true revolutionary struggle. To me the whole event will be remembered as a politically motivated dog and pony show, the likes of which we haven't seen the last.

Many readers can remember the FBI's negative direct influence during the turmoil of the 60s, 70s and part of the 80s, but for those of you too young I just wanted to emphasize the extent to which the ruling class will go to spread misinformation, propaganda, lies and even covert activities such as the SLA and other activities more sophisticated and less detectable. I am sure that the FBI still gets involved in domestic unrest issues with all of their covert actions and that they understand that Socialism is the long term threat to Capitalism and its benefactors, whom they represent. Today, other government groups such as the National Security Agency have moved into the spotlight under the patriot act and the NDAA, (National Defense Authorization Act). The NDAA allows the NSA the flexibility to label any political activity as *potentially terrorist* in nature and hold people in *indefinite detention* without the right to legal representation and without the ability to even contact their friends or family. The NSA has already used the NDAA against certain individuals in the "Occupy" movement. I went to a march by "Occupy Los Angeles" that was around this very issue (the main chant was that "we are not terrorists"). So the draconian society written about in Orwell's book <u>1984</u> which was supposed to represent Communism taking over society and removing all civil liberties is coming true. The only catch is that it's a Capitalist Society, not a Communist Society, that's behind "big brother" attacking civil liberties, putting cameras and monitoring devices everywhere. They read our E-mails, monitor our phone calls and Facebook accounts, and use their huge propaganda machine to spread lies and confusion on some of the most serious issues facing us today. So don't put it past our government to get involved in violent forms of action, such as the SLA to spread misinformation. When brave Americans like Edward Snowden expose these attacks upon our privacy by exercising his 1st amendment rights, he is branded as a "traitor." Tell me, who are the real traitors? Edward Snowden, or the corporate controlled U. S. government? But these threats and intimidation tactics by the government will not stop people from speaking out and fighting for justice, it will only expose their propaganda, solidify distrust and strengthen and focus the resolve to continue the struggle.

The political activity today is starting to remind me of the activity in the Bay Area and around the country during the 1960s, 1970s and early 80s. The Occupy Wall Street movement appears to have been the dress rehearsal for the continuing level of marches and demonstrations we see today. The issue that "Occupy" raised about the disparity in the distribution of income has now become a national issue, even among politicians. But the issue of classes, the 1% versus the 99%, was the main reason the federal government orchestrated the shutting down of their encampments around the country. The encampments served as 24/7 free speech areas and their message of class struggle was not tolerated. The key issues during the 60s and 70s were many of the same issues as today: black poverty and police brutality, a growing weariness among the people for the endless involvement in foreign wars, the loss of American jobs, and lack of healthcare for far too many Americans. Homelessness and racial hatred have gotten much worse since the 60s and 70s, as well as the upward shift of wealth. On the positive side, in the 60s the "gay rights movement" was struggling. Today the LGBT movement has made great strides forward. There are two noticeable differences. Today the intensity of the problems has reached much deeper into the working class and now is including the disappearing middle class. Many white people are now feeling the economic hardships that minorities have always experienced. The "rich get richer and the poor get poorer" has progressed in the United States to where we now have the biggest disparity between the rich and the poor of any country in the world. Another noticeable difference is that in the 60s and 70s people didn't see the class nature of society as they do today. The "Occupy Movement" started right out from the beginning emphasizing the 99% versus the 1%, which was readily accepted by the general public in their support of "Occupy." As the leftist, progressive, and revolutionary trend of direct action grows, the neo-conservative right wing will become smaller but much louder. The reactionaries will have to be dragged kicking and screaming into the new world of the 21st Century. This is a 21st Century where objective economic conditions grow worse and the political unrest grows. It will become much more difficult to walk a grey line and people will have to decide which side they are on.

The division of working people along national lines has been the most effective way of weakening the past struggle for political, economic and social justice, and it still is. We are divided: Asians against blacks, blacks against whites, whites against all minorities and many Americans of all nationalities against immigrants. So let's turn for a moment to the subject of dividing people by nationality and color, and what better place to start than with the "Bakke decision?"

CHAPTER SEVEN

The Bakke Decision
The impermanence of reforms and
racism as a class divider

In 1863 President Lincoln issued "the Emancipation Proclamation" by executive order. It was to free the slaves in all of the states that had withdrawn from the union. In 1865 the 13th Amendment outlawed slavery. In 1870 the 15th Amendment gave voting rights to black men. In 1920 the 19th Amendment gave all women the right to vote (women's suffrage). In 1965 the Voting Rights Act final gave some enforcement to the 15th Amendment of 1870. But for nearly 100 years, from 1870 to the 1964 Civil Rights Act and the 1965 Voting Rights Act, black people were on their own to struggle for full citizenship. In fact, the 100 year period was filled with "Jim Crow" laws in the south to insure that black Americans were treated as second class citizens. Laws like pole taxes and literacy tests. The Civil War and the subsequent Constitutional Amendments certainly did not end discrimination. It took the civil rights *movement* to force the issue. After the Civil Rights Act, there was various legislation to implement the "Act." Affirmative action and quotas were a part of these laws. In 1978, *only 14 years* after the Civil Rights Act was passed, the Supreme Court of the United States ruled on what has been referred to as the Bakke case. The conservative leaning Court's ruling outlawed "quotas" and opened the door for attacks on all affirmative action programs for minorities. It's the unfortunate history of the Capitalist system responding to the demands for justice until injustice raises its ugly head and the system takes back previously won concessions. In the 21st century, there are ongoing attempts to water down the 1965 Voting Rights Act. The voter I.D. laws in several states, based on the idea of voter fraud, is a current example. These laws will prohibit many poor and minority communities from voting. Reforms are only temporary.

Alan Bakke was a young white male from an affluent family. He had graduated from college with an engineering degree and as the story goes, worked for a while in engineering, but found it to be an ungratifying profession. He did some introspection and decided what he really wanted was to be a medical doctor. He had applied to several colleges for acceptance into their medical programs but had been turned down based on his qualifications in comparison to other applicants. One of the last colleges where he applied was U.C. Davis in Northern California. He was once again turned down based on his standings with other candidates. He then discovered through a sympathetic (perhaps racially biased) counselor, that the college had set aside (16) medical program slots for minority candidates.

The 16 reserved slots (or quotas) were a part of the affirmative action programs in follow up to the Civil Rights Act. These slots were quotas to insure that some minorities would be admitted into the medical program. The quota system was based on statistics that minority applicants were at a disadvantage when it came to entrance tests, which were skewed in favor of white culture. Also, white students receive a better basic education in the lower grades because of the better schools available to white children. So the quotas, recognized past discrimination within the system, and were intended to give minority students access to medical school based on the minority percentages in their communities. When the percentages of doctors more reflected the ethnicity of minority communities, similar to white communities, the quotas would end. The goal was never met anywhere in the United States, even to this day. Alan Bakke got together with this sympathetic counselor at U.C. Davis and they came up with the idea to challenge the quota program as *"reverse discrimination"* against him, as a white applicant. If you are a person that doesn't believe that racial discrimination against minorities still exists, then these quotas for minority students might appear as skewed against whites. But if you understand that racial discrimination is still a part of society and that minorities are still struggling for equality then the idea of "reverse discrimination" is illogical. How can you have reverse discrimination if the problem of discrimination against minorities has not yet been rectified? In my view the term "reverse discrimination" is a racist term. (See chapter 17 for other code names and "Orwellian doublespeak.") Alan Bakke was apparently serious about becoming a doctor because he did actually become a doctor. But the 16 minority students who lost their chances of becoming doctors were also serious about becoming doctors. Alan Bakke's selfish individualism left no sympathy for the dreams of the 16 other people he had to step on to get into the medical program. The chances are that some of those 16 minority students were more qualified than Bakke without the quota system. But the idea of reverse discrimination took hold and passed the *questionable objective scrutiny* of the Supreme Court. The Supreme Court ordered the University's medical school to accept Alan Bakke and further eliminated all 16 minority quota slots. This systemic cycle of give and take away will repeat itself again and again until we make big systemic changes to eliminate the private property interests that benefit from keeping working people divided.

There were many demonstrations of minorities and whites opposing the Bakke case before the Supreme Court decision came down. I personally spoke to black churches in Oakland, California to inform the congregations of the significance of the Bakke case. Political Activists, including Marxists and Socialists, in the 70s recognized the Bakke case as a major turning point to set back the Civil Rights Act.

Viewed from the perspective of minority people the notion of reverse discrimination reinforces their belief that white people don't understand their discrimination and how they struggle in their everyday lives. The sad truth is that too many white people *don't* understand racial discrimination and some don't care. And just as the Bakke case turns whites against blacks, Hispanics and Asians, the concept of reverse discrimination turns these minorities against whites. That is the underlining effect, some would say intention, of a system run in the interest of a ruling and wealthy class: to keep us divided, weaken the class struggle, and preserve the status quo.

Everyone today, all nationalities including whites, are suffering under the economic attacks on our incomes, living standards and decreased social mobility. But because of racial discrimination, past and present, these attacks are far worse for minorities. Whether it is unemployment, home foreclosures, mass incarceration, educational opportunities, or police killings the dreadful statistics are worse for minorities. This is a *class struggle,* not a struggle of whites against blacks and browns as the Neo-Nazi ideology would have us believe. The Nazi mentality looks to a future of genocidal civil war rather than revolutionary class struggle. The proponents of Nazi/KKK philosophy are out there pushing the message of hate both overtly and more subtly. The white uneducated segment of the working class who listen to talk radio show hosts, with all of their conspiracy theories, are hammered directly with racist ideology. The rest of us are subjected to more subtle racism by politicians who target immigrants, undocumented workers and appeal to religious and cultural differences. Both methods use fear and are driven by hatred and/or political motivation. The intentions of these demagogues may be unclear to some people but the message is clearly to portray all non-whites as the problem, to further divide us, and draw attention away from the real enemy: the ruling class or the 1%.

The fact is we the people are divided, and race or nationality is the single most effective method of dividing us. But, as divided as we are, 99% of us are still part of the same social/economic class: the working class. If some of you don't believe that the benefactors of private property - the 1% or owning class - are encouraging the racial divide with all of their influence and in some instances orchestrating it, then you are being deceived by a "divide and conquer" technique that may be appealing to your own deep rooted racial biases (and with this statement I am speaking to both whites and minorities). We are all oppressed by the forces of Capitalism, but minorities are doubly oppressed. They are additionally oppressed because of the color of their skin and their race or national origin. Minority women are triply oppressed because they are oppressed as all working people are, plus discriminated against because of the color of their skin, plus discriminated against because of the fact they are women, as all women are.

So among the multinational working class who should be initiating the action to reach out to people other than their own race? Who needs to reach out and start this "national dialogue" to bring us together and start the healing from the wrongful thinking that the powers of capital have imposed on us for so long? Well the bottom line is that it is the responsibility of all nationalities to open up their minds and hearts and extend kindness to each other. It is the responsibility of all nationalities to realize that although there is a difference in the type or degree of oppression, we are all suffering. Although there are cultural differences between us, the overwhelming similarity we all have in common is that we are all of the same _class_ and we have a common enemy. We are all human beings with the same hopes, heartaches, and needs that vary only in degree. We are not each other's enemy and our common enemy is Capitalism. We are involved in class struggle, not the civil warfare that some politicians like Donald Trump are encouraging.

That being said, it is _primarily_ the task of "white" people to reach out and support minorities in their special struggles, to prove to them that we are sympathetic to their special situations, and to recognize that they are still subject to racial discrimination. Why is it the task of white people to reach out more than blacks and other minorities? Clearly it is because the white establishment started the whole disgusting and immoral situation. We uprooted African Americans from their homes on another continent, separated them from their families, threw them into the hulls of ships, brought them to America and enslaved them. We beat them, hung them, raped them and worked them until they dropped. Our whole abusive history of non-white nationalities goes further than just African Americans. Our internment of the Japanese Americans and the genocidal attacks on Native Americans represent the same hate and fear. When I hear the expression _"white pride"_ I sometimes think to myself, what is it that we as white Americans have, as a culture, to be proud about? Certainly not the history of our treatment of other nationalities. After the Civil War with Jim Crow laws discrimination in the south continued. Even in the northern industrial states blacks and other minorities were given the worst jobs with the lowest pay, while the better jobs were reserved for white workers. This discrimination in the work-places continues to this day all around the Country. It took the civil rights movement before we would even let black people sit at the same lunch counter, pick their seat on a bus or live where they wanted to live. My grandpa, who was a Lincoln Republican picketed, a small drug store in Southern California because they wouldn't serve black people at the lunch counter. This was in the 1940s. My, how the Republican Party has changed. Much of the same still goes on today and in some ways it has gotten worse. Many, black people es-pecially, have an ingrained distrust for white people be-cause of the history of the abusive, hateful and inhuman way we have treated them. In my opinion, much of this distrust is justified. So it's up to us as whites, in every-thing we do, to prove to minorities that at least _this_ white person understands our past history of racism, that we are sorry for the immoral actions of the past and present, and that we are striving to change our-selves and other whites away from our flawed way of thinking. We need to extend this outreach to Hispanics, Asians, Muslims and all other minorities as well as black Americans.

The whole terrible history in the treatment of black Americans was made possible by the private property rights of slavery and continues with the private proper-ty rights of Capitalism. It's the whole idea of individual ownership: the "mine" mentality we see in young chil-dren instead of the idea of sharing. Individualism is a driving force in the idea of private property and it starts at an early age. Capitalism pits us against each other even within the same economic class. Capitalism under private property has a built-in divisive nature to it, and racism is a natural ally to this divisive nature.

In the 70s the Bakke Decision was a landmark turning point to take away the gains of the civil rights movement. My generation of politically active "boomers" saw this trend coming and fought hard to stop it. You can't win them all, and we lost that one. Since then, and with the continuing conservative politics of Reaganism, Bushism, Trumpism and Republicanism the attacks on civil rights are growing and are reflected in court decisions and actions by individual state legislators. These attacks, along with the physical attacks by police on black communities are bringing people out into the streets. White protestors are joining hands with the "Black Lives Matter" movement. Class struggles, with strong racist overtones against police brutality, voting right restrictions, deportations, housing discrimination, and unemployment are again representing the special struggles that Blacks, Latinos, Asians, and Muslims face. At the same time, the continuing economic crisis is reaching into the more affluent level of the working class (the so called middle class) which is disappearing with lower wages and the sky rocketing costs of higher education. Home ownership is also becoming an unrealistic goal for everyone. If we could only learn to stick together and fight for each other's interests as well as our own, we could accomplish so much more. My trade union experience has convinced me that minorities are open to uniting with white people in struggling towards a common goal. I can see future decades of civil unrest and direct action including civil disobedience in store for the U.S. A part of this may be Union organizing drives, which created the middle class in the first place. The equal pay concept in Unions also helps level the playing field by taking away the pay disparities suffered by minorities and women in non-organized workplaces. Currently it is the community organizing which is addressing police murders, the homelessness and the deteriorating conditions in the inner cities that has more than reached a boiling point. Much more direct action, civil disobedience, and reforms are necessary regarding the out of control police departments. The government has continuously kicked that can down the road. The courts and politicians both have failed to bring any justice in response to the killings of innocent black and Latino people by the police. They have left the people no other alternative other than direct action in the streets.

The bright side of the racial division situation (in politically active circles referred to as the "National Question") is the changing mindset of the millennial generation. The political and judicial establishment may not be helping the situation, but the cultural, social acceptance of rightful "color blindness" in society is becoming obvious. It is wonderful, as well as ethically, morally and politically correct. As the older generation, my generation passes away, many of the holdouts of racial discrimination among us will also pass away. Then with these new generations coming into power who are more socially tolerant and have been "color blind" all their lives, then the racial class division will hopefully disappear and we will be more compassionate with each other and stronger in the class struggle against Capitalism. A united working class can overcome any obstacle. The more we all unite and come together the less vulnerable we will be to the rhetoric aimed at dividing us. Social and political change is a slow, gradual process. The growing inability of Capitalism to provide for society is also a protracted process. But eventually, the two changing phenomena will come together and the demands will no longer be for just reforms within the system, but rather for political/economical systemic change: a second revolution in America.

CHAPTER EIGHT

"Dump the Shah"
And the Iranian Question

The history of turmoil in the Mideast has always been about oil. The world has become dependent on fossil fuels as the main energy source for approximately a century. The oil industry and their drive for profits is responsible for this dependency. The U.S. government's view on who is an alley or an enemy, in the Mideast, has evolved around the ready availability of oil. The human cost to these political/economic policies, and the resulting violations of ethics and morality mean nothing to Corporate America or to our government. Instead, they use misinformation, denial, secrecy, patriotic propaganda and demonizing against whatever country or leader suits their purpose at the time. In the end it all comes down to profits! The human misery, global warming, and terrorism are all related consequences to these relentless imperialist policies for oil. Iran, Iraq and Saudi Arabia have been central to the conflict over oil for a long time. So, is Iran really the axis of evil that the western world has portrayed them? There is always two sides to every issue and the Iranian question is no exception.

Direct action in the form of political protest has been an essential form of free speech on many different issues. The purpose of all direct action is to effect change. Both domestic and international issues have resulted in political protest and criticism of government and corporate policies. International issues regularly include the U.S. government's involvement in other countries. Most of these government policies abroad are corporate driven. The education of the American

120

public on any particular issue is an important aspect of calling for change. Our government, in cooperation with corporate interests, would prefer that the American public not know about many of its involvements in other countries. Today, with the global internet, this is becoming much more difficult for them to hide. All world governments represent the interests of the influential status quo far more than the interests of the people. The U.S. government is no exception. My unity is with the people of the world and I have no illusions about the lack of moral and ethical standards of any government, including my own. The support of the Iranian people's struggle against the Shah of Iran and against the American government's relentless backing of the Shah was an example of supporting the international working class. Today Iran remains a controversial player in the Mideast and the target of right wing propaganda worldwide.

In the 1970s the struggle to depose the "Shah of Iran" was an international struggle where the Iranian people reached out to the people of the United States for support. Today, with all the turmoil in the Middle East, Iran is again in the spotlight. There are a lot of ill feelings toward Iran from the American public. Some of these negative feelings arose out of past actions, such as the hostage taking and arrests of Americans in Iran. But many of our ill feelings have grown out of the constant barrage of propaganda that only portrays one side of the picture. All we hear today is that the Iranian government cannot be trusted. This may or may not be true, but it disregards our past role in Iran which our government would just as soon we forget. The truth is that Iran has ample reason to distrust America. The American installation of the Shah in Iran is where a lot of the problems with Iran started. Most of the American public are unaware of the facts of how the Shah came to power, and the humanitarian atrocities he committed while in power.

The Shah (Mohammad Reza Pahlavi) of Iran ruled from 1953 to1979 and he was a brutal dictator who represented American oil interests. He was installed in power in 1953 with a U.S. backed coup by the CIA that overthrew the democratically elected Prime Minister Mohammad Mosaddeq, who had briefly nationalized the Iranian oil industry. This was the CIA's first successful overthrow of a foreign government. This coup which installed the Shah in power was motivated by the western oil cartels and their leverage on the United States government. The action by Iran's Prime Minister to nationalize the oil industry was unacceptable. The CIA action was a blatant example of American imperialism. This overthrow of power and replacement with "our man on the ground," the Shah, has since been replicated throughout the world. South Viet Nam and the overthrow of Ngo Dinh Diem government in 1963 comes to mind, which immediately preceded American troop involvement in Viet Nam. Although you no longer hear Iran chastising America for this despicable act of overthrowing their democratically elected government nearly 60 years ago, you know they have never forgotten it, just as America will never forget 9/11. The Iranian people had to live under the regime of the Shah for over 25 years. They shouldn't forget it and I am sure that Iranian distrust of America's moral authority started with the installation of the Shah and the many years of suffering by the Iranian people, that followed.

I first heard about the Shah of Iran in an international relations class in college in the late 60s. There were foreign exchange students in the class from Iran, Iraq and other countries. It was the Iranian student that was explaining the atrocities committed by the Shah on any Iranian who spoke out against the Shah or U.S. foreign policy in Iran. Later, in the 70s, there were Iranian activists on a speaking tour across the entire United States with lectures aimed at obtaining American support against this terrible dictator who had the full backing of the U.S. Government. By the 1970s, the struggle in Iran against the Shah had reached a full scale open revolutionary struggle where tortures, murders and imprisonment conducted by the Shah were daily occurrences. It was estimated by the Iranian speakers on tour that one in four Iranian families had suffered from the chopping off of feet, hands, legs and arms in an effort to intimidate and terrorize the movement to depose the Shah. The American Government and the oil cartels were well aware that the Shah was committing these atrocities. They had been able to suppress any widespread knowledge of the Shah's action from the American people. But the speaking tours of the Iranian students in the U.S. were beginning to educate Americans, especially American activists. American activists in the 70s embraced the Iranian people and, with the students, organized demonstrations and speaking forums around the country to expose this terrible U.S. backed dictator. "Dump the Shah" and "Down, Down, Down with the Shah" were the chants, along with a call on the American government to end their support for this terrorist regime. I was politically active in the Bay Area at the time, both on the job and in the community, and helped spread the word in a united effort with the Iranian people. I helped organize and participated in several demonstrations to "Dump the Shah," and there were other demonstrations all around the United States. This was not *just* a righteous struggle in support of oppressed and brutalized people in another country, which in itself was enough reason to support it. This was a terrible situation that had been created by the private property interests of the U. S. oil companies and promoted and implemented with the full backing of the U.S. government. It was all about controlling the world's oil supply with complete disregard for Iran's national sovereignty and void of any moral considerations. This was a dreadful example of American imperialism that was brought to the attention of Americans by the efforts of Iranian students who had reached out in class unity directly to the American working class.

You see, there is always another side to the story of official government press releases and sound bites about how Iran cannot be trusted, their support of terrorism, and the nuclear threat. But the Iranian government has just as much or more reason to distrust the United States than we have to distrust them. *Our distrust of Iran is based on speculation on what they might do. Their mistrust of the United States is based on what we have already done.* They suffered for over 25 years from the oppression of an American puppet (the Shah). The American involvement in Iran did not end with the Shah. The United States continued their violence against Iran by supporting Saddam Hussein in the Iraq/Iran war from 1980-1988. The U.S. government was attacking Iran through their proxy, and ally of the moment, Saddam Hussein. It's no wonder Iran is so distrustful of American foreign policy. We have interfered in their internal affairs for decades with horrific covert actions and military action. We have demonstrated throughout the world that we will side with any dictator who represents American economic interests of the moment. On the one hand we support Saddam Hussein in the Iraq/Iran war and then, on the other hand, falsely accuse him of the 9/11 terrorist attack and launch an ill-advised all-out war against Iraq to remove him from power. The Iraq invasion alone added to the distrust of American foreign policy by Iran and much of our western allies.

It would at first appear that there is no method to the madness with which the U.S. vacillates between support and demonizing of different countries and their leaders. But the common denominator in changing sides on international issues is always economic profits. When Iran was supplying us with their oil they were our trading partners. When they resisted and nationalized the oil industry, they became our enemy and had to be forced to comply (enter the Shah). Once the Shah was overthrown, then they became our mortal enemy again and we backed Iraq, siding with Saddam Hussein in a war against them. When Saddam Hussein invaded Kuwait, in Desert Storm and jeopardized our oil interests there, he again became our enemy. With Saddam Hussein now our enemy he became an easy target to blame for 9/11. The invasion of Iraq was also an attempt to regain control of oil in the Mideast; a control we had lost with the departure of the Shah of Iran. All of this political posturing was driven by the corporate interests on American foreign policy. It's a part of the imperialist game of musical chairs driven by the private property interests of world Capitalism. The invasion of Iraq after 9/11 was, in my opinion, the biggest mistake (supported by lies) in the history of U.S. foreign policy. The repercussions of the Iraq invasion will haunt the world for decades. World-wide terrorism began with the invasion of Iraq, and not with the terrorist attack of 9/11.

Whenever I hear the reactionary cry to "bomb Iran" I reflect on the craziness of the remark. It is motivated by ignorance and sometimes racial and religious prejudices of right wing Americans. This is encouraged by the news media, just like they encouraged the invasion of Iraq after 9/11. I remember T.V. anchor person Katie Couric with her gravelly voice saying "right on" to the Iraq invasion. The only thing an attack on Iran would accomplish would be to set off World War III. I will give the Obama administration credit for pursuing the nuclear arms agreement with Iran because without it the right wing would have had more of an excuse to start World War III. The Republicans attacked the nuclear arms agreement with Iran because some of them actually want war with Iran. With other Republicans, and a few Democrats, the opposition to the agreement was purely a political opportunity to grandstand their military posturing and secure votes from conservative voters.

The 70s demonstrations to dump the Shah didn't force the U.S. Government to change course in Iran. The U.S. government stubbornly held fast and supported the Shah up to the bitter end. The demonstrations, along with the Iranian student speaking tours, did however, educate many Americans on the skullduggery of our government in that part of the world. It also created an alliance between hardworking Americans and hardworking Iranians. It let Iranians know that the actions of the U.S. government does not necessarily represent the views of the American people, at least not all of the American people. The poor and the working people of the world in all countries, including the United States, always have more in common with each other than with the ruling classes that dominate their respective governments. It's the international working class that Marx referred to and the reason for celebrating "International Workers Day" (May 1st). The struggle to dump the Shah is another struggle I am proud to have been a part of.

In the final analysis, it's up to the people in each country to take matters into their own hands and that is what the Iranian people did in 1979. The revolutionary struggle against the Shah was finally successful and it culminated with the Islamic revolution and with the Ayatollah Ruhollah Khomeini replacing the Shah. Today it is a parliamentary government with right and left factions and a strong religious influence by the current Ayatollah. I feel that completely secular governments are preferable to theocracies because I support our constitution that upholds the separation of church and state. Unfortunately we don't have the separation of private property interests from the state. But in 1979, Iran did achieve their independence from U. S. influence. The different cultures will determine the form of government that the people choose to support, and that is their right.

There are Americans who criticize the influence of the Ayatollah and religion on the political system in Iran, and I agree with much of the criticism. Yet some of those same critics are Christian fundamentalists who press for more religious influence upon the politicians in the United States; politicians like Ted Cruz. Do I sense hypocrisy? These religious influences on governments and differences between secular democracy and theocracies are secondary to Capitalism's private property influence on governments and politics. Most Marxists/Socialists believe that countries have to rid themselves of political and economic influence from outside imperialism or colonialism, prior to the revolutionary struggle for internal democracy and Socialism. Like the Russian Revolution which deposed the Tsar, the Chinese Revolution which help defeat the Japanese occupation, and the Cuban Revolution that overthrew the U.S. backed Batista regime, the rise to power of the

Ayatollah Khomeini in Iran which overthrew the Shah and rid the country of imperialist control, was a progressive step forward for the Iranian people. It represented national independence from the U. S. backed dictator. The process of Socialist revolution is not always a one step process. In countries dominated by outside influence national independence may be a necessary precursor before the economic system of private property within the country can be addressed. In the United States we have already had our *first* revolution against outside tyranny. Marxists refer to this as the American *Bourgeois* revolution. Our struggle against Capitalism and private property continues and a second, Socialist revolution, will most likely be necessary. "Down, Down, Down with the Shah."

CHAPTER NINE

Dialectical Materialism
The Philosophy of Class Struggle

My story is about my experiences, my observations, my insights and opinions regarding the cause of injustices in the United States and the world as a whole. I hesitated on whether or not to include the "philosophy" supporting Marx and his critique of Capitalism. Philosophy is by nature abstract and subtle. But the application of philosophical concepts are what is behind so much of our human beliefs and the societies we create. It is not necessary to understand the philosophy of "dialectical materialism" to appreciate Marxism. I personally am not intellectual enough to fully articulate the philosophy to anyone. But I will do my best to explain my understanding of dialectical materialism in as popular and down to earth a way as possible. It is far more important that you remember and internalize the *definition of Capitalism* in the introduction. I just want readers to know that Marx and Engels' views of Capitalism and the need for Socialism have a rational and scientific philosophical side to them that is well grounded in the real world. It is more than just a common sense observation of the rich get richer and the poor get poorer.

Meaning of Dialectics

"*Dialectics*" in the Marxist sense is the progression of change through the interaction of conflicting ideas and interests. Dialectics is the tension or struggle of opposites. It is the new rising from the old in a continuous movement upward to new and better things. It is the method of an inevitably changing world. It results in the emergence of something new (Socialism) accompanied by the decline or disappearance of the old (Capitalism). The change can be incremental (quantitative), but at times the struggle involves big changes (qualitative) which result in major leaps forward in the struggle. The progress of the dialectical process is sometimes inconsistent and non-linear, and often gets side tracked as the dying old fights back against its inevitable demise. There are many steps backwards and sideways in the protracted forward progress.

Dialectics is a way of viewing life. Its close relationship to change ties it to the facts of real life and the Universe where change is inevitable. Life is never constant. Life is constantly changing and impermanent. The dialectic process can be applied to human relationships such as marriages or parent/child relationships. In marriage, it can be the differences of opinions between married couples where struggle takes place. With parents and their children, it can be the struggle between adolescents struggling for independence which is in conflict with the parents' concern for protecting their children and exercising parental authority. Dialectics is a philosophical overview of the changing world as it evolves through the tension of opposites. Dialectics *drives* change. In "evolution," dialectics would be the struggle for survival between different species with older species dying and new species arising. It is the essence of "natural selection" responsible for the human race. In cosmology, it could be the struggle between dark energy and dark matter for the continued expansion or the eventual collapse of the universe. The principles of dialectics reach beyond Marx's political application of class struggle. It is a philosophical view of the entire universe that never remains the same. In the political and social arena it is the direct conflict between a ruling "owning" class and a "non-owning" working class.

Within the subject of political economy, Marxism embraces dialectics as the method of social/economic change. Socialists view the opposing interests of the classes as the opposites essential to dialectic struggle. It's the private ownership of workplace versus the public nature of the workforce. A very small owning class benefits at the expense of the huge working class, and they are locked in struggle for a new order. The new order would be Socialism, stressing the public's interest in community, and the need for sharing the wealth. The old dying order will be Capitalism, stressing individual interests and selfishness. Private property creates the opposites of this dialectical struggle. The end game of this struggle is to build an economic system based on public property where society takes control of their own destiny in the collective interest of everyone rather than a handful of billionaires. Now let's examine the meaning of materialism.

Materialism

The *philosophical* meaning of materialism is *not* the same as the more common use of the word materialism. The common use describes the "materialistic" consumer society under Capitalism, where people mold their personalities, and establish their self-worth and status in society based on the accumulation of material objects.

In philosophy, "materialism" is one of the two major schools of philosophy. The other school is "idealism." Materialists believe that everything in the world comes from matter. That matter is nothing more than what we perceive it to be. That our perception is accurate and objective and no blanks need to be filled in by human concepts or metaphysical idealism. What you see is what it is. There is no need for the mind to create its own reality. Humans are capable of seeing the truth and essence of the extended world of objects, humans, society and everything external to our own minds. Scientists are, for the most part, materialists. They view thought and consciousness exclusively as a product of the material brain. Scientists have confidence in human perception and the observation of the natural world. This trust in observation is at the heart of the scientific method. Idealism, on the other hand, is meta-physical, spiritual, and it questions the exclusiveness of the material world. Religion and spiritualism are idealism. The old question "if a tree falls in the forest and nobody is around does it make a noise" is an example of idealism. It views the essence of the external world as existing only in the mind's eye. Idealists view human perception as incapable of understanding what we see because of our limited senses and knowledge. Idealism further posits that we modify what we see with the ideas, concepts, experiences and superstitious beliefs ingrained in our minds. As the philosopher Kant implied, we may be incapable of understanding *"the thing in itself"* or the real nature of what we perceive with our senses. This statement reflects idealism. The opposing views of religion (idealistic) and science (materialistic) sometimes come into conflict with each other. The current opposing beliefs between "creationism" and "evolution" are in themselves an example of a "dialectic" struggle which may never be resolved, because the concept of religious *faith* cannot be proven or disproven.

In political economy, Marxism embraces *materialism* as opposed to idealism. Marxism looks at society as what it seems to be, not what we would like it to be. Society consists of people living, working, paying bills, buying food, struggling, loving, playing and suffering.

Marxists view nearly all of the social, political and economic injustices of society as a product of the relationships of people to the means of production: the material world, the real world of struggling for survival. Your position in the workplace is the materialist approach to reality and determines the relative material conditions of life. It is the basis of Marxists and Socialists defining Capitalism. The common grounds between science and Marxists, both being a materialist discipline, lends further credibility to the view that the Marxist critique of Capitalism is a scientific approach. What goes on in the workplace, what it gives us and what it doesn't give us defines our lives and the nature of society.

On the other hand the *Idealist* approach to defining Capitalism is what the Capitalist economists since Adam Smith put forward. It is a very superficial view of Capitalism that avoids any discussion related to the workplace. They don't talk about who owns what and who works for whom. To them, Capitalism is all about the free market, consumption, consumerism, supply and demand, healthy competition and mass production benefiting everyone. They go on about how the free market satisfies the needs of people in the consumption process. This is an idealistic approach based on abstract notions, hopes, and desires, and void of any observation of the real material world and the way private property creates classes and suffering on a widespread basis. It is short sighted, and sees only what it wants to see instead of what it actually is to most of the society. It is idealistic rather than materialistic.

Well that's my best shot at explaining the "dialectical materialism" philosophy of Marxism. *Dialectics* is the unavoidable struggle and *materialism* focuses on the aspect of Capitalism (ownership of the means of production) most important in the lives of working people.

Together they define the unavoidable class struggle of Capitalism and the need for Socialism. The other aspect of the Marxist philosophy is "historical materialism" which studies the history of private property prior to Capitalism. I will not go into historical materialism although I do touch on the history of private property in the following chapter.

A Closing Comment

When it comes to politics, sociology or economic justice *"materialist"* philosophy is certainly the most appropriate and practical way to consider issues and devise solutions to the problems. That is because our society has been conceptualized by humans to accept the existence of matter. So when we move about in the world that we have created in an effort to make changes, whether of an economic or political nature, we need to stay within the materialist perimeters of the accepted mindset we have chosen. If we instead approach political change from an idealistic philosophy then we will not even be able to recognize the nature of the problem. Likewise, our methods of solution will be unrealistic and ineffective.

That is not to say that idealism doesn't have its place in an effort to view the universe in general. There certainly could be truth to Immanuel Kant's view that we are not capable of understanding "the thing in itself": that our limited perception does not see what is actually in front of us. Modern atomic and sub-atomic science tells us that there *is* no matter or solid anything. That the universe is all energy and that matter is a temporary form of energy. The equation $E=MC^2$ reflects this relationship between matter and energy. Quantum physics has further confused the view of the material world and scientists have been struggling with the implications of quantum physics for nearly 100 years now. Maybe someday our whole view of the universe will be turned upside down. But for now our accepted science and our concept of the world is materialistic. Our whole society that we seek to change is built around this materialist philosophy. So for a political/economic philosophy to be relevant today it must adhere to the current material world view and accept the scientific method of observation we have created. Marxism is based on viewing the economic/political world from this materialistic perspective. That means acknowledging the dehumanizing effects of Capitalism on people, rather than the idealistic concept of a consumer society of commodity distribution, prices, and free market competition. That is why Marxist *dialectic materialism* centers on the *ownership* of the means of production which is at the heart of the material conditions of life.

CHAPTER TEN

The Molders and Foundry
Workers Union
Local 164

As discussed previously in Chapter One, there has never been a Communist state, only attempts at Social-ism, with some more successful than others, such as Cu-ba. The closest experience that I have witnessed, in an organizational form, that reflected Socialist ideals, fol-lowed truly democratic practices, and set itself above the legal restraints of American Capitalism was the Molders Union in the mid-1970s. If all unions in the country were like the Molders, we would be a lot closer to accomplishing workers' political, economic and social justice than we are today.

The Molders was founded in 1859, just before the Civil War, and was one of the first, if not the first, union in the United States. Its founder, William H. Sylvis, (1828 to 1869) was a Marxist and in the Socialist camp of the "International Workingmen's Association." Karl Marx (1818 to 1883) himself, had drafted up the provi-sions for the IWA. There were many followers of the IWA in the United States and around the world. One of their basic beliefs was that the "wage" system of labor reimbursement was designed by the owners of the means of production to confiscate the value created by labor in the form of "profits," leaving the working class with barely enough to survive on. This of course was in keeping with the Marxist analysis of "surplus value" and the term "wage slavery." The Molders Union had a proud history of Communists and working people struggling together against "capital." Over a hundred years after the death of the union's founder, I was privileged to have continued that history of struggle in the Molder's during the 1970s.

The Molders Union represented the foundry industry workers. A foundry is where scrap metals are melted down and recycled into new products. The metal is melted down in a furnace and transported to the pouring deck by an overhead crane where workers, mostly Hispanic and black, hand pour the metal into the sand castings for the new products. The pouring deck is an extremely dangerous place to work, for obvious reasons. The racist excuse for having mostly dark-skinned minorities assigned to this job was that they could take the heat better because of their darker skins. Just before I got a job with the biggest employer in the local union, in Berkeley, California, the union had come through a "wild cat strike" that received national recognition. A wild cat strike is when the local union defies the international union's reluctance and decision not to strike and the local rank and file vote to go out on strike anyway. Wild cat strikes have been viewed as illegal by the courts. It takes a lot of determination, a lot of organizing and courageous local leadership to do this. There was always a lot of talk amongst rank and file workers of other unions to defy their international leadership and wild cat, but it is seldom done. Well, the Molders had a local president by the name of Joe Navaro. Joe was a young, early twenties, Chicano who had his head in the right place and the leadership abilities to match. My experience in working with Joe was that he was a Marxist, although he never publically declared himself as a Communist or a Socialist. But he spoke proudly of the Socialist/Communist background of the union's founder William Sylvis and his unquestionable dedication to working people. So whether Joe considered himself a Marxist or Socialist, he clearly saw the down-side of American Capitalism in the lives of working people. His union meetings were a refreshing example of democracy in practice. You could speak and express yourself and propose anything you wanted to without restriction or getting ruled out of order. This was in stark contrast to the Teamster Warehousemen's Union meetings talked about earlier. Joe was not a union bureaucrat who left the workplace and became part of the union hierarchy. Joe worked on the pouring deck for Pacific State Steel in Berkeley, CA. the same company where I worked as a maintenance mechanic. Joe had led the local out on a wild cat strike that received national attention. After the strike ended the local was placed into trusteeship by the union's international leadership who attended all the meetings. But the president still had complete control of the meetings and procedures. It was broadly assumed that the FBI were present at all the meetings after the strike. In the United States, the international leaderships of most unions discreetly work with the companies to prevent strikes. When any union defies the international leadership and "wild cats," the corporations around the country and their representatives in the U.S. Government become concerned. That's when the FBI gets involved to try and divert the movement. Anything that threatens the status quo of Capitalism becomes a "national security issue" and the FBI gets involved. Today, the NSA would probably be involved as well. There were several very active union representatives who all worked in the foundry shops around the union and there were also a lot of Socialists/Communists like myself. Many if not most unions, during this period, had leftist/Socialist members as well. I feel that this is still true today, and always has been, as Marxists have always played a leading role in all unions. The difference being that the Molders had defied union protocol with the wild cat strike. The leftist members who were aware of the systemic nature of Capitalist oppression were an encouragement to FBI involvement and the center of their attention. But these activists, like myself, were not outsiders. You had to be working on a job in the local union in order to obtain union membership and some of these activists had been on the job for many years. I personally was hired by Pacific State Steel after the strike but there was still plenty of activity in the local union to try to pursue issues that had received momentum during the strike.

Let me explain a little more about the foundries. The ethnic makeup of foundry workers in the Bay Area was 90% Hispanic and Portuguese. There were a few black workers. There were also a few white workers, mostly all in the skilled trades. All of the Portuguese and most of the Hispanics did not speak English. Joe Navaro, the president, was bilingual in Spanish but not Portuguese. All of the better jobs, the skilled maintenance jobs, were reserved for white workers. I was hired as a maintenance mechanic. Although I had several years' experience in industrial employment as a mechanic, there were plenty of Hispanic workers who were as qualified (or more) in the trades than I was. Some had worked in the trades in Mexico and South America before entering the U.S... But because of discriminatory practices, they had no chance at the better jobs. It's the old *keep the working class divided* and pitted against each other tactic of the system, along with blatant racial prejudice. The situation in local 164 was different with the Molders and we were not as divided as would normally be the case. Joe Navaro had led the local in a manner that clearly represented the interests of its members and had stood up against any moves to undermine the special interests of the ethnic minorities who were the bulk of the rank and file membership. The politically aware activists, like myself, were helping to educate the rank and file on the nature of Capitalism in the course of the struggle for improved working conditions. The struggles that resulted in the wildcat strike were the issues of discrimination, low pay and job security. There also were specific issues, like improper layoffs that violated seniority rights in the union/management *contract*. These illegal layoffs mostly affected Portuguese and Hispanic workers who couldn't speak English and the contract was in English only. It reminds me of today where the mortgage agreements were only in English and Latino home borrowers, who couldn't read English, were being taking advantage of during the recent foreclosure process.

In addition to its dangerous, life threatening aspects, the foundry was a very unhealthy place to work. The molds for the products were made of silicon sand which filled the air throughout the working day. If anyone was unfortunate enough to work anywhere in a foundry for very long they would eventually get silicosis and die early of a lung disease. Anywhere in the foundry was an unhealthy, nasty job even for the maintenance people. I won't go into all of the terrible assignments I got as a mechanic once the company figured out I was an activist. They were trying to get me to quit. I wouldn't and eventually they gave up and fired me.

In a discussion one time with a white friend he told me that if some of these hard jobs, like working in the fields, the slaughter houses and chicken factories, jobs performed mostly by minority and immigrant workers paid more, then white workers would gladly accept them. I know there are exceptions but in general this is not true. If it's just the low pay that keeps most white workers from taking these jobs then why do white Americans flock to Walmart, and all the fast food jobs? They're low paying. I'm not making any stereotypical judgments about *all* white Americans. I just think that as Americans, and especially white Americans, we have been spoiled. We have unemployment benefits, food stamps and other government benefits that immigrants and illegals don't have. Furthermore, white people still have an edge on all minority workers for a variety of different jobs simply because they are white. So white Americans have more options. There is an old saying in the UFW that if it were up to white Americans to harvest the agriculture then the crops would rot in the fields. I personally worked in the fields with a friend of mine alongside immigrant Mexicans (for about 2 days) and I absolutely could not keep up with the migrant workers. We were topping and boxing carrots and the immigrant Mexicans left the two of us behind in the dust. An aerial shot of the field would have shown a strip of green where two white boys were failing to keep up with the Mexicans. They work harder and faster because they have to and it's expected of them.

In keeping with my own beliefs that white people have to take up the special struggles of minorities, and work to tear down the divisions between us, I volunteered to head up a committee within the Molders Union to get the contract translated into Spanish and Portuguese. The very mention of it on the Union floor sent the international representative into a tizzy. One of the white business agents who was uninterested in the basic rights of the minority workers chimed in with his opposition. Remember now, 90% of the workforce in the Bay Area Local, which included various companies, were minority workers who, for the most part, could not speak English. The English only contract was of no benefit to this 90%. The international representative and the business agent knew that if the contact was translated into Portuguese and Spanish that workers would discover that there was a grievance procedure, and seniority rights and that they were being cut back and laid off out of seniority and in violation of the contract. Seniority rights are the main advantage of union-ized workplaces over non-unionized workplaces. With-out seniority rights, when it comes to layoffs, the com-panies are allowed to pick and choose (practice favorit-ism) who they keep and who gets fired. Seniority helps prevent employer discrimination on the job. It protects older workers from being replaced by younger workers and provides better job security based on how long you have worked for the company. The bottom line was that if the contracts were translated, then these sell out union leaders, who vetoed a sanctioned strike over these same issues and forced a wild cat strike, now would have their hands full challenging the companies whom they had allowed to violate the contract. Since the strike, many of the minority workers were coming to the union meetings in follow up to the issues they went out on strike for in the first place. The union meetings were packed to standing room only with a flood of rank and file participation. Even with the oppo-sition of the international representative and one of the business agents, Joe, the union president, was able to get the measure to translate the contracts to the floor and it passed overwhelmingly. It was my role to see that the translation happened. Even though I had not worked in the local during the wild cat strike, I was now able to help complete one of the demands of the strike. That was to get the contracts translated. The challenge was that the motion had to be voted on (ratified) in all outlying locals like Lodi and Exeter nearly 100 miles from the Bay Area. These locals consisted almost entirely of white rural rank and file members. The international representative and the business agent were confident that this would never happen because these white workers, in their opinion, had no interest in translating the contract, and they set about to make sure it didn't happen. At night after work, a couple of "contract translation committee members" and myself traveled to these rural locals to speak to these white workers for support to get the motion passed. The business agent went to these union meetings as well, talking down the motion and at times openly "red baiting" me as a Communist. But it didn't work. The last local to ratify the motion for translation was in Exeter. It is a small local in the Sierra Nevada foothills. The membership of the Exeter local was all white men of rural background. There were about 20 to 30 rank and file members at the union meeting and the small hall was nearly filled. The business agent did his thing of talking down the motion and implying that I was part of a radical group. The rank and file membership were unimpressed with his derogatory remarks. They had come to the meeting to hear about the translation issue and were sincerely interested in the recent strike of local 164 in the Bay Area. The 20 to 30 men who attended this union meeting represented a large turnout. I sensed that they were having their own problems trying to get the union to take up their issues in Exeter. I tried to convince them of how different it was in the city with the minority makeup of the rank file of Local 164 who couldn't read or speak English. I emphasized that the translation of the contract would make the union much stronger in the city and when you make any part of the union stronger it benefits the union rank and file everywhere, including in their small community of Exeter. The motion passed unanimously. The contracts were going to be translated. I had helped finish what the wild cat strike had started. None of this would have been possible without the unique leadership of President Joe Navaro who brought the "translation" motion to the floor for discussion and a vote. Joe had organized the local to go out on strike and had tremendous respect from rank and file workers, both white and minorities. Likewise, none of this would have been possible without the majority of white workers setting aside their perceived differences with the Mexicans and Portuguese or without the minority members trusting in their white brothers to do the right thing. The Molders contract was the first contract in the United States of America to be translated into three different languages. The cost of the translation and printing it was around 3 or 4 thousand dollars.

The whole struggle just shows what working people can do if they stick together and don't allow the system of Capitalism to divide people along ethnic lines. It also shows how a real union with honest leadership can approach the economic and social needs of working people better than any organizational form in the workplace. I hope that this story will help open the eyes of some of the readers who have negative attitudes towards unions and to the positive role that Communists have played in the struggle for rank and file control of their unions.

The unions were the primary mover for the creation of the middle class in America and with the decline of unions from 35% to 7% of the workforce so too goes the middle class in a downward spiral. Lastly, I sincerely hope that you can see that Communists / Socialists / Marxists are definitely on the side of working people in their struggle against American Capitalism. What happened in the Molders Union is possible in any local union given the honest, devoted leadership and the determination of the workforce membership. The determination of workers can be manifested outside the union structure but it is more difficult. If the union organizational form already exists then workers have a ready-made structure to challenge management's opposition to their needs. The Molders Union in the 1970s was well known and respected by activists and other unions in the Bay Area. It was Joe Navaro's leadership that led the union and brought it the respect during an intense period of class struggle in the U.S. This is an intensity that is again surfacing in the United States. As for my role I look back with a sense of accomplishment in getting the contract translated. I made many Latino friends in the Molders' struggle and showed them that white people are perfectly capable of acknowledging and fighting for the special oppression of minorities. One of the Mexican green card union representatives voiced this respect for me; the fact that I was fighting for something that would not benefit me personally. I treasure that acknowledgement.

One other aspect to keep in mind about the above struggle: this whole successful struggle got going with an "illegal" wild cat strike. The system is set up so that government, corporate and sometimes union bureaucracies can control when workers can strike. But the Molders disregarded the legal restraints imposed upon the working class. The laws and courts of private property interests are slanted against the interests of working people. Many times it takes civil disobedience and infractions of the law, as long as they are non-violent. We don't always yield the streets when ordered to by the police. We don't always disperse when ordered to disperse. And when the entire system is legally trying to prevent a strike we sometimes strike anyway.

CHAPTER ELEVEN

Private Property: the Creator of Class Societies

In 2013 I went on an adventure trip to the eastern extremities of Mexico: the State of Chiapas. It is adjacent to Central America and right across the Usumacinta River from Guatemala. Chiapas is one of the poorest states in Mexico, but it is also beautiful with jungles, mountains, and Mayan ruins. I was traveling with a friend and we were traveling on the cheap. We stayed in huts in the jungle and low priced hotel accommodations in the cities. We were about as close to a backpacking trip as you can get and we met back packers staying in some of the same accommodations. Not only did this save money but, more importantly, it kept us close to the working people whom we both relate to. We really got down to the "no hot water" basics and stayed very close to the mainstream poor and working class both in the country and cities. I speak a little Spanish and my friend was bi-lingual, having spent a good portion of his life south of the border.

In the rolling hills and flats of the jungles there are scattered numerous clearings for corn fields, which is the mainstay diet for the populations of the city and rural communities. There is currently a big political movement in Mexico against the U.S. world conglomerate *Monsanto,* who is controlling the seed supply (in this case corn) and is claiming ownership of genetically developed crops through the international patent rights, made possible under laws of *private property*. It's complicated, but they are making it illegal for the rural farmers to use and even possess their own natural corn seeds. This natural agricultural process is at the heart

147

of their culture and their ancient nature based religion (the anti-Monsanto movement is happening in other countries too, such as India). Chiapas' rural areas are truly beautiful. There are also beautiful cities like San Cristobel with a multi-ethnic population from all around the world, especially from Europe. San Cristobel is one of the cleanest large cities I have ever seen and a favorite for tourists. There are also many artists and culturally minded individuals who have moved there from different areas of the world. I was in a half a dozen other cities and nowhere did I see the degree of blatant poverty and the homelessness you find in the cities of the United States. The United States has the biggest disparity between the wealthy and the poor of any country in the world. Mexico does have better safety nets with government created jobs, although they are low paying. I am sure there is plenty of poverty in the cities of Chiapas, but it just isn't as "in your face" with people sleeping in the streets as in the U.S.

There is a real revolutionary movement and atmosphere throughout Mexico, both in the cities and in rural areas. San Cristobel has a revolutionary cultural to it as well. I spent an evening in a restaurant with live revolutionary music and posters of Che Guevara the Argentine Marxist and hero of the Cuban Revolution. Mexico is far more than drug wars and murders, more common in the border towns, that the U.S. media would have you believe. There is still an armed revolutionary presence in rural areas (jungles). The Zapatistas (ESLN), an armed revolutionary group led by "Marcos" are currently hiding in the jungle as a guerilla movement. They have surfaced from time to time with sporadic attacks against federal troops in some of the cities which, include San Cristobel. The Zapatistas have strong support among the rural population and their support is voiced everywhere. These rural communities is where the direst of poverty exists. The poor people living in these rural, jungle, settings are second class citizens with much closer cultural ties to their Mayan heritage than the urban Mexicans have. The entire rural area of Chiapas is under federal troops' occupation with barracks and road blocks and search stops every 10 to 15 miles. They are mostly concerned with arms supply to the Zapatistas coming through Guatemala, but also in searching the peasants for any contraband associated with the ESLN.

The main revolutionary struggle and struggle for reforms, however, is mostly in the more sophisticated populations of the main cities, which is separate from, and skeptical of, the armed struggle of the Zapatistas. They have the same enemy: the Mexican government and big private interests. The level of poverty in the cities does not approach the impoverished rural people. The more organized urban movement is mostly peaceful civil disobedience and direct action, while the Zapatistas have turned to armed resistance, and only occasionally in the last few years. The unions are strong, the teachers are a powerful force to be reckoned with as well as the students. They are fighting against the privatization of the public school system, as many are in the United States. There are Communist groups right in there with the other activists, struggling together just the same as in the United States. There are demonstrations and rallies throughout Mexico. Strikes, mass blockage of highways with demands for economic, political and social justice similar to the U.S. are common, but just a lot more widespread and intense.

The American born "Occupy" movement and tactics are well recognized and revered in Mexico, as it is throughout the rest of the world. Even in the area of the Zapatistas some of the pro-Zapatista signs have been

modified to include "Occupado."   The Occupy movement, which originated in the United States, has had a
galvanizing and influential effect on political struggles
worldwide. The occupation tactic, which in the 60s and
70s were referred to as sit-ins, now display the little
domed pup tents made popular by the occupy movement.   Many occupy slogans, such as the "We are the
99%," have also been adopted worldwide.

One evening in the small city of Comitan we were in
the public square talking to activists who were protesting in front of the local government offices. They were
picketing and chanting for the release of some student
political prisoners who had been incarcerated for several weeks. I was having a discussion with a bilingual
Communist who was one of the leaders of the protest.
As we talked a small circle of protesters, many of them
young, gathered around us, listening intently to our
conversation which was in English, out of necessity, because of my lack of fluent Mexican. A few were bilingual
but the Communist I was talking with, kept interpreting
what we were saying for the benefit of the others who
didn't understand English. We talked about the class
struggles in Mexico and in the United States. The struggle in Mexico is far larger and more conspicuous than in
the United States. He was aware that the struggle in the
U.S. was very small in comparison. He also felt that the
situation in Mexico was about to explode. Because we
both were Marxists, supporting the reform struggles
wasn't all we were interested in. We both believed that
Capitalism was the problem and were both interested in
raising the consciousness of non-Communists to understand this. I told him that the hardest thing in my experience was to convince people that private property was
at the root of the problem. I further said, that when you
approach people in the United States with the proposi-

tion that private property was the driving force of Capitalism and would have to eventually end and be replaced with public ownership, a common response would be *"you mean you want to take my house?"* He smiled and said that has been his experience as well, except in Mexico, being far poorer, people say *"you mean you want to take my shirt?"* The problem of moving people beyond the favorable view of private property is not easy. There is more propaganda out there selling the idea of private property than any other bourgeois message. That is because the ruling class behind the propaganda, the benefactors of Capitalism, know full well that the idea of *public ownership* strikes at the heart of their way of life and if they lose public support for the concept of *private property* then their days are numbered.

The term private property has been so revered by the working class in America, because of the phenomenon of home ownership. The fact is that home ownership in America is truly an illusion, even for most home owners. Unless you have your mortgage paid off all you really have is a 30 to 40 year lease. All you have to do is refinance it once or twice along the way and it will never be paid off. It's just like your automobile, which is registered in your name, but the legal owner is the Bank. The real owners of the homes are the banks and Wall Street investors. But if you really think you own your home any more than a person who rents or leases an apartment or house then just miss a payment and you'll find out real quick who really owns the home you call yours. This is a reality that millions of Americans found out during the recent great recession of 2008 that was triggered by the mortgage crises. It wasn't only those sub-prime loans that were foreclosed on. Many people who had been in their homes for years lost their jobs and incomes and subsequently their homes. Under Capitalism, financial disaster for working people always lurks just around the corner. In past generations, many more people did actually get their homes paid off, but not in today's world. People have had to constantly pull equity from their homes just to get by with day to day expenses because of shrinking incomes. In many cases, their mortgage balances grow larger instead of smaller and the hopes of ever getting the mortgage paid off is secondary to just keeping the mortgage payments current. Many of the younger generations don't even seriously plan on buying a home. A lot of the younger generation don't even have automobiles.

Actually, you don't need to *own* a home to have a roof over your head, and under Socialism with public property most people would be better off with government organized housing for everyone and the elimination of the "homeless" in the bargain. Most all of the real property (land and houses) is and always has been vested in the hands of the upper wealthy owning class. Almost all of the foreclosed homes of the 2008 crisis are being purchased by large investment groups and private investors, and turned into rentals. This is in keeping with the changing realization on the part of the public that owning a home is becoming economically impractical. Still and all, the dream of home ownership, as rare and increasingly impractical as it is, remains one of the only potential advantages that private property offers to working people. But the home buyers' market has become a financial racket that mostly serves the Wall Street mortgage and investment companies. All the other benefits of private property are in the exclusive interests of the wealthy class and work to the disadvantage of the rest of us. But this hope of owning your home is why people defend the private property concept, sometimes adamantly. Almost everyone believes that the security of having their own home, with exclusive living rights, can only be obtained through owning and private property. Well, there are many ways that a Socialist society could assure people their own guaranteed residence for them and for their families without private property. A government guarantee to residency rights at an *affordable* payment to a government that represents and works in the interest of everyone is an alternative to the way it is done today. The money paid to the government could then be used for social needs, including housing, instead of profits to wealthy stockholders. I, for one, would feel a lot more secure with this type of arrangement than with the free market Capitalists, holding my mortgage and just waiting for the opportunity to foreclose and resell the property. The banks and mortgage companies make a bundle off of refinancing of homes, foreclosures, reselling the homes over and over again while raking in the loan interest in an endless cycle of broken lives and shattered families. They couldn't care less about all of the personal failures and family bankruptcies left in the shadows from this revolving door practice of selling, repossessing, re-selling and refinancing in the big business controlled housing market. The Capitalists are callous to the heart breaking effects on the people who have lost their homes and their dreams. This callousness was made clear during the recent mortgage crisis and the endless string of repossessions, many of them illegal, and most of them filled with deceitful and misleading tactics.

The reason I discussed home ownership first in regards to the subject of private property is because in the minds of Americans the term private property brings to mind owning your own home. This is true even if people haven't purchased a home yet. Unfortunately, it is another aspect of the disappearing American dream. Most Americans, 86% of the population, have only Social Security when they get too old to work. You can't make mortgage or rent payments and cover your food costs with just Social Security. The fact is that in a "Capitalist society" to have a house "paid off" when you get old and can't work is the traditional way most Americans will be able to stay in their life long familiar surroundings. I knew an old couple that *rented* the same house for decades at an affordable rent from a sympathetic owner. When the owner died his heirs sold the house and the old couple had to leave. No telling where they wound up, they were very old and had been in the neighborhood for many years. But getting your home paid off just doesn't work out for most Americans. So the laws of private property pertaining to home ownership is not a bad idea in the Capitalist world, it's just unrealistic for most people. Under Capitalism, getting your home paid off is the only way to survive in later years for the vast majority who will have only Social Security to survive on. In my experience, I have run across many older people who turned to a reverse mortgage in order to live out their life in their homes. There seems to be more people going this route of the reverse mortgage than actually getting the house paid off. Under a reverse mortgage, the payments on your existing mortgage are eliminated but when you die the bank usually gets the house, not your heirs. Reverse mortgages are structured so that the lenders, in the long run, make huge super profits above the profits made on traditional mortgages and eventually wind up owning more and more of the real estate in the country.

That being said all of the other effects of private property are clearly in the interest of the ruling elite and work to the disadvantage of working and middle class people. Private property under Capitalism drives profits and is the cause of climate change, low wages, unemployment, unavailable health care, wars, crime and unbelievable levels of incarceration. The private ownership of the *means of production* is the template for the control and exploitation of labor in the workplace which filters down through all aspects of society. We are all dependent on the workplace for our livelihoods. Private property serves special interests and under-mines and controls the democratic process to the point where the power of the rich and the corporate world has become more powerful than the governments of the world. It is the economic system represented by "the corporate state," that runs our lives and the political system has come to serve their interests. Without pri-vate property, there would be no corporate state.

According to the *historical materialism* of Marx and Engels, Capitalism is not the first political system that instituted private property but it will hopefully be the last. The ancient Greeks had a slave society. What more terrible use of private property than to own other hu-man beings for their entire lives? The history of slavery in the U.S. is a shameful abuse of private property in modern times, the effects of which still linger in Ameri-can society. Slavery still exists in America through "human trafficking" for profit. In a feudal society, the feudal lords owned all the land and all but owned the serfs who were subservient to their lords in every way. Both of these societies were class societies as well be-cause "social *classes*" and "*private property*" go hand in hand. Social classes are created by private property. The private property laws in relation to Capitalism are no exception.

Under Capitalism private property has attained its

highest pinnacle of development. The workers and the owners of the means of production meet head on at the point of production. A class of oppressed workers develops, and a class of wealthy owners develops. The accumulation of capital, of wealth, cannot happen without private property laws. That's what Capitalism is: the accumulation of capital. But the accumulation of capital only occurs for the owning class. The working class who owns nothing but their labor power supply the profits for this capital accumulation. Capitalism brings together the combined labor power of hundreds and thousands of workers, which creates profits on a scale unheard of in the history of class societies. Eventually, it sucks the life out of society and the wealth that the owners of private property accumulates gives them the unlimited power over all of society including the political system. That is why the final struggle will be this struggle against the private property of Capitalism. But the struggle against Capitalism in itself is not enough. The struggle has to be a conscious struggle for Socialism, as well. You have to have a plan that makes sense. To dump one economic system without a conscious understanding of what to replace it with could result in anarchy. This being said, the next logical social change is to Socialism and that's what "historical materialism" through the struggle of "dialectical materialism" is about.

Look for a moment at ancient Greece: the ancient city states had the owner class (the aristocracy), they had the warrior class of soldiers, and the slave class. There was no room for movement between the classes. If you were a slave you stayed a slave until you died. If you were a soldier you were raised to be a soldier and that's how you served your life. If you were from the wealthy aristocracy, who grew out of land ownership,

your role was to get educated in philosophy and government and participate in the city state forums of political debates and to rule the community. Of course this
ruling elite ruled in their own interests. You can believe
what you want about the so called golden age of ancient
Greece with their invention of democracy, but the bottom line is that it was a slave society. The wealth of the
ruling aristocracy was mostly land based wealth and
trade, both predicated on private property. In addition
much of the wealth was created by the free labor of the
slaves. You also didn't question your class status and
there were no aspirations of the lower classes to move
upward.

Under feudalism, the ruling class were the monarchy of kings and the individual lords and barons with
their castles and private armies (the soldier class). The
lower classes of serfs and peasants tilled the soil and
served their lords while residing in villages near the
castles on lands owned by the war lords. Feudalism
was also a mostly land ownership society which was
made possible by laws of *private property*. Again, very
little upward social mobility to speak of and a pretty
much fixed division of labor with fixed classes just like
under slavery.

But private property under Capitalism is different.
It is the same as in other class societies, in that it is
based on private ownership and creates and perpetu-
ates social classes. But it is different from previous
class societies where upward mobility was difficult or
impossible. Class mobility under Capitalism is encouraged and offers hope for anyone to *attempt* to climb the
social ladder and accumulate more wealth. In most instances, this upward mobility is false hope. Currently,
social mobility in the United States lags behind almost
all other western countries. In earlier American Capital-

ism it was possible for more people to move up into the middle class or on rare occasion become wealthy and move above the middle class. But these opportunities, although more available in the past, never were feasible for the vast majorities of Americans. Under "monopoly Capitalism," upward mobility is even worse and disappearing for more and more people. But the illusion is kept alive, through government and corporate propaganda, contrary to the reality of the situation. This concerted attempt to keep the dream alive serves the wealthy class. It creates aggressive and selfish individualism and divides the working class into a dog eat dog atmosphere. It creates the frustration of not being able to get ahead and adds to the stress and mental illness of society. The main exception to the lack of social mobility was the development of the middle class due to the efforts of Unions. This period of a growing middle class was short lived however and too illusive and temporary to become a permanent class of any sizable scale. Through the government rhetoric of politicians the idea and hope of middle class life styles is kept alive. President Obama has been particularly adamant about raising middle class hopes while ignoring the needs of the poorer working class. His affordable health care program was a positive exception to his obsession about the middle class and the American dream. But like many politicians before him, he has been far too chummy with Wall Street and corporate America. I guess that is a characteristic of all politicians: they believe we can tweak Capitalism to provide political, social and economic justice.

Borrowed money has become the way to subsidize unlivable wages. People are offered easy credit and home credit lines to subsidize their working class incomes. This gives them a taste of middle class living standards and creates a false sense of class mobility. But borrowed money to maintain life styles eventually collapses. Advertisers and movie makers play their role by scripting all sort of sales pitches and drama scenes around middle class situations of families and individuals. This form of subliminal propaganda, in the entertainment media, creates the belief in the working class that most of society is affluently middle class. This puts social pressure on people to role play middle class living standards at all cost, including borrowing. This eventually leads to financial bankruptcy for many who would have been better off just living within their own limited means. The real mobility trend today is downward. The ruling class becomes smaller in numbers and richer in concentrated wealth. The middle class disappears and is pushed down into the working class. The working class itself grows in numbers and many times becomes homeless and poorer and dependent on public assistance. The working class is gradually becoming the unemployed working class. Right along with this process in the United States is the world-wide phenomenon of the disparity in the distribution of wealth between the very rich and the very poor with less and less middle ground.

I just read an article in the local newspaper where "Oxfam" now calculates the 85 *richest billionaires* in the world including Carlos Slim, Bill Gates and Mark Zuckerberg hold the same amount of wealth as the bottom 50% of the world's population combined, and that disparity is growing. The article concluded that we can no longer separate this issue from the issue of "class warfare." Let us pursue this a little further. Take a hypothetical situation where all the wealth of the world or, if you prefer, all the wealth in the United States, was somehow commandeered and redistributed equally to every individual or family unit including the formerly rich and the formerly poor. But after this confiscation and redistribution the "*law* of private property" was left intact. How long would this redistribution last? What, five years? A decade? Who knows how long, but rest assured that eventually we would be right back to where we started. The masses of poor and working people would be no match for the greedy, the driven, the con-artists, and all of the people who feel they should have more and live above what the planet offers to the average human being. So if the law of private property was left intact, after this hypothetical redistribution of wealth, we would sooner or later see the money moving back upward into the hands of a few. No, the redistribution of wealth will have to be accompanied by the elimination of private property as well. Without private property laws, Capitalism would have no *legal format* to exist. There is only so much wealth created in the world and every time someone takes more than their share someone else gets less than their share (the reality of this statement couldn't be proven more accurately than by the Oxfam study cited above). For every person who makes a million dollars in a year, thousands are forced below the national poverty line. To redistribute the wealth and leave the law of private property intact, most people would just not be equipped to play the Capitalist game. Most people don't have the financial educational level, the ability to communicate and organize and invest their money. Many would squander it away. Others would be subject to and particularly vulnerable to the greed and selfishness of the players.

Actually, most of the honest poor and working people are limited in the dog eat dog atmosphere of Capitalism by their working class moral ethics. There are exceptions, but my experience in life has convinced me that working class moral and ethical views are more honest, admirable and caring for other human beings when compared to the moral and ethical views of the wealthy and the more affluent. I can even see the difference between Democrats and Republicans on the question of ethics and values. But many, not all, of the social climbers and middle class people adopt this bourgeois ideology and subsequently their ethics and values, to one extent or another, degrade as well. When it comes to the super rich their lifestyles and ethics become down right decadent. That's why I have always felt more of a closeness with the down to earth working people and poor people than with middle or upper middle class people. Again, there are plenty of exceptions. I am not attacking all rich or more affluent people either, including the few philanthropic wealthy people like, for example, Bill Gates. But rather than relying on a relative few philanthropic billionaires to give back to society, which is actually a drop in the bucket as to what is needed, wouldn't it be better to have a philanthropic government that would stop this shifting upwards of the wealth in the first place? Well the only government, in my mind, that could possibly do this would be one that instituted public or collective ownership instead of private ownership. This would be a government that followed the Marxist principle "*to each according to their needs and from each according to their ability*."

CHAPTER TWELVE

Public Property and the "Socialist Dream"

Capitalism developed side by side with the Industrial Revolution. With the development and growth of Capitalism, the factories initiated the mass production of commodities and began to eliminate the handcrafted products of the skilled artisans and their collective guilds. With the growth of the new means of production came the demand for a large concentrated labor force. Farmers, tradesmen and the unskilled and impoverished populations gravitated to the factories and the wage system became the means of survival for the vast majority of society. The private property wealth was shifting from the owners of the land to the owners of the commodity means of production. The ruling aristocracy was being replaced by the new Capitalist class. All of the working people developed into one class, the working class. The Capitalist class began accumulating unheard of wealth compared to past class societies. The conflicting interests between the owners of the means of production and the non-owning workforce is what created these fundamentally different social classes. The working class interests centered on providing for the necessities of life. The Capitalist class was driven to make more and more profits, avoid physical labor and have lavish, sometimes decadent living standards far above the barely subsistence levels imposed on the working class. It gradually became one small non-productive ruling class living off the productive efforts of the entire society. Capitalism was the new format for class exploitation resulting from the *"profit driven"* development of science and industrialization.

The scheme devised to exploit the workforce under Capitalism is the *"wage system."* The wage system pays employees just enough to provide food and maintain the energy necessary for labor to continue the production process. It amounts to nothing more than wage slavery. Workers are paid for only a tiny bit of the value they create while the rest of the value is confiscated by the owners. This wealth, or value, taken from the workforce is traditionally referred to as "profits" by the Capitalists but, simply put, it is unpaid wages. Marx refers to the profits as the *surplus value* that working people create but never see. Yet the arrogant millionaires and billionaires claim they *made* the profits. In reality these profits are no more than legally stealing from working people most of the wealth they have created. For the first time, under Capitalist production and the wage system, the people as a class were able to see the exploitation of their labor by the factory owners. It became clear how their impoverished life styles differed from the life styles of the factory owners. They began to see themselves as a class sharing the same interests and having the same position in society. But not until Marx and Engels critiqued and articulated the private property nature of Capitalism were the working class able to see the necessity of a Socialist society based on public ownership. Humanity is worthy of a better system than Capitalism.

Once the Communist Manifesto and Marx's "Capital" were available and in world circulation, the followers of Marx used the theory to educate the workforce on the necessity of a political/economic revolution. Thus the class struggle was being guided by a scientific theory which continues into modern times. The working class has struggled for over two hundred years and has won many victories such as unions, abolishing child labor, workplace safety, economic benefits from employers and many others. But with the inevitable progression of Capitalism into monopoly Capitalism, the hammer of cutbacks has again been lowered against working people. Many of the victories for working people have been reversed. This is the history of the struggle to reform Capitalism. The reforms and gains become harder to achieve and existing benefits come under attack. This is also reflected in the growing disappearance of the middle class and the extreme shifting of wealth upward.

According to the Marxist theory of "historical materialism," Capitalism will be the final stage in the progression of societies based on private property. Socialism will be next! What else is there? It's been private property throughout all class societies. Public property is the obvious alternative, and that is what Socialism is: public ownership, or collective ownership, of property. If one form of ownership of property doesn't work for centuries through three different economic systems; Slavery, Feudalism, and Capitalism, it is time to consider its alternative. Unfortunately, the system of Capitalism was necessary to intensify the oppression, to create the largest class in history and usher in the next economic system. By creating the working class, Capitalism was guaranteeing an eventual revolution and literally digging its own grave. As monopoly Capitalism (Imperialism) progresses in society, the intensity of the oppression will continue to grow. It's a natural social/economic evolution, but human consciousness, awareness, and a targeted future goal will be necessary to bring this social/economic change to fruition. *Capitalism may destroy itself and collapse on its own but the Socialist revolution will have to be built.* The building of Socialism starts with a dream. Currently the dream is in the minds of a relatively small percentage of society, but as the conditions of Capitalism continue to deteriorate, the dream will grow along with the revolutionary movement.

So what would a new society based on a government dedicated to the public interest without private property be like? It may be considered premature to start drawing a picture of a Socialist society when the vast majority of Americans aren't even convinced that Capitalism and private property are a problem. Besides, by the time Americans come to the conclusion of giving a completely different economic system a chance, many of the concrete conditions of today will be intensified and new problems will exist as well. So the priorities for a new society will change. The oppression will be more severe and may include forms of injustices that we can't even imagine today. The exact details and priorities for the building of Socialism and the working model for implementation will be finalized by the people and their leadership of the revolution in the closing hours of Capitalism. But the dialogue on what it could and should be, has already started with a small percentage of the population. Revolutionary change is more than likely a long way off so we have time to expand the discussion to more people. There is no fixed blueprint for the leaders of a new Socialist government to follow in the transition to public property. The transition will differ as the conditions of monopoly Capitalism progresses and will also be different from country to country. The leaders will need to sum up the mistakes made in past attempts at Socialism and consider the concerns of the working class at the time. But no one knows when Capitalism might implode with another crisis beyond the capacity of a government bailout. So we must create a working model based on the current failures and conditions of our private property driven economy.

If we get caught short without a consensus on a new economy, an irretrievable collapse of Capitalism could result in anarchy and the end of America as a nation state. It's not enough to simply say "replace private property with public property." Building a working model of the future requires that we visualize concrete examples of what a public property driven economy might look like. So the struggle to educate people of the necessity to dispose of Capitalism includes encouraging all working people to participate in visualizing a future system that addresses the real problems that Capitalism cannot resolve. Capitalism was created in the interests of rich opportunists and was imposed on society from the top down. Socialism must be grass roots originated from the bottom up. The ideas and dreams of a new society are not just the responsibility of a few political activists. Real democracy requires the participation of society, with people reflecting and contributing. The way Capitalism and politicians have failed us has discouraged many people from participating in the political process of voting. Our voices, when restricted solely to the ballot box, far too often go unheard. But the hopes and dreams of a completely new society, with no limits to what we can do, should encourage people to participate in the planning for Socialism. We will need to work together and plan the future together. Revolution begins with an awareness of the causes of injustices but also must include a dream to cure the problems. Try to be open minded. Be creative and use your own imagination and visualize the change with hope instead of fear. So much anti-Socialist and anti-Communist propaganda has been flooded over the minds of Americans for decades. Visualize what _you_ would want to see in a new society. Cast aside the characterizations by the establishment that Socialism has been tried and proven wrong and threatens the American beliefs of democracy and the beloved free market. This is the propaganda crap that serves the interests of the Capitalist class and leaves the country hopeless with no alternative to the current system. Try to keep in mind just how bad things are getting today under Capitalism, and how the growing problems of working people are just not being addressed. This will help you to see the need for major change. Many of the major changes you can visualize are probably impossible under Capitalism, but without private property interests to throw up road blocks, anything is possible. As you imagine a better society and reflect on the impracticality of these new ideas under Capitalism it will also help you to see the necessity of replacing Capitalism with Socialism. Just try to embrace the dream. The sooner people do so the sooner we will reach a majority of people demanding revolutionary change. All Socialism does is change the ground rule from private to public property. A simple idea with huge implications that can reap historically unique rewards for humanity.

The following are just a few ideas that I have to address the unfulfilled needs and obvious problems existing today under Capitalism. But what do you think? How would you change my views and create new ideas of your own? A Socialist revolution must be a democratic forum from inception to implementation and beyond. So participate in this democratic process, by visualizing a new society, and help to create the new American dream.

In building Socialism there would be short term, tactical things that would have to be changed more immediately, and long term strategic goals that would require a more gradual approach. The short term tactical policies would be overwhelmingly directed at the very

rich and the very poor. Following are some of the priorities, as I see them:

- The private ownership of the workplaces would be transferred over to the
  public sector. This could be done by nationalizing large industry under the
  new government. It could be accomplished in smaller businesses through
  workers taking over and running the
  job sites themselves in co-op fashion.
  In some cases, especially very small
  workplaces, the private ownership
  might be allowed to exist for a while but
  under regulated, livable wages and
  benefits. As in any process of change
  there would have to be flexibility. But
  regarding the workplace, which is the
  focal point of Capitalist exploitation and
  oppression, the needed changes would
  have the highest priority and require
  action to begin immediately.
- Most of the assets of the billionaires
  would need to be commandeered at
  once. Most of their money in their bank
  accounts would be confiscated and used
  to finance the necessary changes. The
  redistribution of wealth would have to
  begin immediately. In order to secure
  the cooperation of some of the 1%, they
  may be allowed exceptions like not taking all of their assets at once. Other super rich Capitalists who adamantly resist the changes mandated by the revo-

lution would have everything confiscated and in some cases even be jailed. What a novelty that would be: rich people going to jail. Or maybe they would be ordered to rehabilitation centers and struggled with. But rich families like the Waltons, would not be allowed to have more than one or two estates and the rest would be used to house the homeless, or used as medical facilities, drug rehab or child care centers, community art centers, academic education facilities, or public vacation spots.

- The banks holding the mortgages on homes and multi-unit landlords would take a hit as well and the properties would be taken over by the government. Mortgage debt would be cancelled. The payments of renters and people with the previous mortgages would have their payments reduced and paid to the new government to be used for public projects. People would still be able to remain in their existing housing but now their financial contract would be with the government instead of the mortgage lenders and their lives would be more affordable and secure.

- In all of these issues, and other issues, there would be a concentrated effort to not disrupt the lives of the working classes any more than absolutely necessary. The kind of treatment you would expect from a caring government that looks out for the interest of the everyday people rather than representing the wealthy under the old system of private property and a corporate state run government.

- Instead of soup kitchens, every area would have publicly owned restaurants where good wholesome food would be prepared daily for anyone who wanted it and it would be available at a cost (if any) that people could afford. Fast food chains would become collectively owned and converted to only healthy foods, or closed down. Think of just the health benefit alone. This is my dream. Think of all the jobs that would be created with the expansion of the public sector to accommodate the needs of society that were neglected under Capitalism.

- In all cases, the Communist principle of "to each according to their need" and "from each according to their ability" would be a guideline in the appropriation of income and what labor would be expected from each individual in the growing labor force. No one would go without, even if they couldn't work and everyone would work according to their ability to do so. Once the public interest and needs become the driving force of the new economy, instead of profits, there will be plenty of work to do, no surplus labor force, and no layoffs or unemployment.

- The healthcare system would be transitioned rapidly from the private market force to a public run healthcare system similar to Western Europe and Canada. It would be better than the current government subsidized, market run healthcare systems because there would be absolutely no private interests to undermine or interfere with the new system. Private owned hospitals would gradually be taken over by the government and run similar to the Veterans healthcare model except with adequate financing. The health insurance companies would be unnecessary and eliminated. A more urgent change would be to open the doors of medical facilities and hospitals to everyone. Eventually there would be no private doctors. Only government employed doctors similar to Britain and our own Veterans healthcare system.
- The manufacturing of goods would be determined by what the people of the country need and not based on what might sell for a profit. Goods would also be manufactured which could be traded internationally for needed goods that couldn't be produced in America for whatever reasons. The manufacturing process would be planned and the booms and busts of Capitalism eliminated. Millions of jobs would be created and job security would become a reality. Many more jobs would be created

to fulfill needed public services and re-furbish the decaying infrastructure. The whole profit driven economy would eventually be transformed to the actual needs of the people and the country. Commodity production would be based on what is needed for the country and for trade and never again would manufacturing workers be una-ble to enjoy the products that they pro-duce.

- Public education will be free and avail-able to everyone, which was originally the goal of Capitalism. Except that un-der Socialism, free public education would include higher education. Teachers would have smaller class-rooms and assistants in every class-room. There would be no private sec-tor or education for profit (charter schools) to attack or undermine public education, which would prosper and excel in quality because of the elimina-tion of cutbacks to the public sector ex-perienced under the previous Capitalist regime.

- All religious and non-religious beliefs would be respected with no govern-ment interference, and any hateful con-frontations between different religious dogmas would be dealt with severely by the government. On the other hand, re-ligion will be kept completely out of the political sector and the democratic pro-cess as was originally intended under the concept of "separation of church and state." No religious lobbying interests or religious platforms of candidates for office. The separation of church and state will be just that. Religion will become a personal and private matter and will not be allowed to influence political decisions.

The money to pay for the new society will come from the increased productivity and creation of wealth beyond what was created by Capitalism because everyone who can work will be working and creating wealth. The wealth, through wages and benefits, would be distributed equally, but would also take into consideration any special needs. There will not be a privileged class siphoning off the wealth for their own selfish interests with cash sitting around in off shore bank accounts. So there will be more wealth to finance the new society than ever before. The cash flow and the monetary management of society will need to be reorganized just as the political system will need to be changed. The democratic political system would really be democratic, based solely on the popular vote and no undermining electoral college to manipulate close election outcomes. No political candidates will be allowed to advocate a return to private property interests. A new Constitution would be created that would clearly outlaw private ownership of any institutions or organizations. The new Constitution would include the good aspects of the old Constitution such as freedom of speech, civil liberties and civil rights but would eliminate all the bureaucratic election procedures and restrictions on grass roots politics. The states' rights would be limited so as not to interfere with the overall planning for the country as a whole, and to avoid inequalities among U.S. citizens depending on which state you live in. All the institutions of Capitalism such as the Federal Reserve, private banks, and stock exchanges would be eliminated, along with Wall Street investment firms and brokerage houses. They would no longer be needed. Other institutions would be created in the interests of all citizens instead of the interest of capital. There probably would not even be a need for taxes. The new government might be similar in function to a super escrow company administering the cash flow of wages, payments, manufacturing, housing, healthcare and public services and projects. Wages would probably be lower because much of the needed commodities and services would be handled directly through public owned and run entities. But the standard of living for the average American would be higher. The wages and benefits of elected officials would be based on their individual needs as well with no special perks or private sector lobbyists influencing them. All campaigns would be publicly financed equally among candidates. There would be no more millionaires or billionaires running for office, because there wouldn't be any millionaires or billionaires. All candidates would be on equal financial footing, and dedicated to *sharing and community* instead of individualism and selfishness and promoting private interests. We would in essence, all be government employees, except the government would be us working for ourselves and each other. Don't worry about all the details now. Organizational experts will be part of the new government. Just use your imagination and believe in the future without private interest obstructionism. The transition from private ownership to public ownership could take years to organize and implement. But in no case would there be any form of private ownership left intact that could in anyway favor anyone getting a bigger slice of the national wealth.

What would _not_ happen under the transition from private property would be the confiscation of your shirt or your home. Personal items that are dear to your individual life wouldn't even enter into the picture when it comes to eliminating private property. Most of these items don't even require ownership agreements under Capitalism and have nothing to do with my indictment of private property. The question of home ownership has already been discussed in the previous chapter and hopefully the stigma of that aspect of private property has been somewhat lessened. It's really not a problem as long as you have a guarantee of your own family or personal living quarters, a housing guarantee that no one enjoys currently under Capitalism. The concept of home ownership has served the 1% far more than the mortgage borrower. My concerns deal specifically with the ownership rights responsible for the movement of wealth upward in the concentrated hands of a few, the workplace role of wage slavery and a commodity production based on profits rather than actual needs. I only mention these ideas to remove some of the fears of Socialism that have become a part of American culture. These fears have been spread throughout American society through misinformation, propaganda and incorrect political / economic philosophy. Ever since the idea of Socialism was conceived, the Capitalists have attacked it. The only people who should fear Socialism are the ruling wealthy class. They know that their privileged lives depend on the concept of private property. The idea of Socialism or Communist philosophy will constantly reappear until finally it remains at the center of attention. It's the only permanent solution to the ever failing model of Capitalism and the benefactors of the status quo know it. The use of fear has been a common tool used by government and the status quo for a long time on many social, political and economic issues. It's how they remain in power. There is the fear of terrorism, the fear of not having enough insurance (until you become insurance poor), the fear of the unknown and the fear of change, and the fear of Socialism. If you let your life be controlled by fear you become depressed and devoid of hope. But if you can see that not only is the transition to a new society not threatening, but that it would be positive, then it could become the new American dream. To myself and others, the hope of a Socialist society has already become the new American dream. A dream that you don't have to be asleep to visualize. In fact you had better be awake, focused, informed and engaged in the discussion of Capitalism vs. Socialism so that you and your grandchildren will be equipped and able to participate in the struggle for a new and better future America. The struggle for Socialism started over a hundred years ago. It may be another hundred years before change occurs as it won't happen in a day. So I, and others, will struggle to keep the dream alive and wait patiently for others to join the dream. As the conditions of Capitalism grow worse others will surely join in.

Above I referred to the *planners* of a new society. Planning would be the key requirement of a Socialist system of government and a main difference from the existing Capitalist system. Capitalism has no planning to speak of and when there are attempts to plan by local, state and federal governments they are confronted head on by private interests. Marxists/Socialists have often referred to the Capitalist mode of production as the "anarchy of production." That is truly an appropriate definition of the way Capitalism works. Companies do not plan their product production rate to provide

steady long term employment for workers. They produce as fast as they can with overtime and pressure
(speed ups) of workers to produce more in a given period of time. It's a rush to layoffs for private interests.
When you hear that the productivity rate in the country
is up that is not a good thing for American workers. It's
only good for profits and the owner class. To the 99%,
it generally means there are fewer people working and
working much harder and often with lower wages. This
eventually builds up inventories and is the cause for
layoffs. It is the method responsible for the regular
booms and busts peculiar to a Capitalist economy. This
method of producing everything as fast as you can instead of spreading out the production over the months
and years is driven by profits, quarterly income reports
and stock share price considerations. It creates havoc
in the lives of working people living under the constant
threat of layoffs. The instability it causes in the lives of
American's makes it nearly impossible to plan family
budgets and retirement plans. The stress bought down
on society is responsible for much of the mental and
physical problems of Americans that have contributed
to America's unparalleled drug addictions. Every company is in its own little world with fierce competition
with other companies in the same industry. With the
exception of some behind the scenes *price fixing* there is
no industry level planning either. The rate of production and booms and busts is only part of the story involving the "anarchy of production." Even the products
produced are subject to the free market anarchy of production. What people actually need plays second fiddle
to what entrepreneurs want to sell us. Our garages become filled with broken down junk from yesterday's
marketing strategies. We buy cheap Walmart crap that
is poorly constructed or soon to become outdated by

technology. Chinese imports and "*planned product ob-solescence*" on behalf of American Companies insures this. Society requires a large degree of overall central-ized planning which can only occur with publically owned factories and a government dedicated to serving the people's needs and uninhibited by private property interests. Just like monopoly Capitalism is not an op-tion, the *anarchy of production* is not an option. They are hard wired into Capitalism and a private property based economy, and are inevitable. Socialists see the need for economic planning so that the workforce can be steady, so that society actually produces what it needs, to conserve the natural resources and provide the essentials of life. Yet all we hear from the "*right*" is let the free market prevail! Well, it has prevailed, and here we are today.

The above views for a better society built on public rather than private ownership are based on a lifetime of observation, seen through a critical eye enhanced by my understanding of Marxism and Capitalism. My views on building a future society based on public property are admittedly very general, but are based on a realistic dream for a better world. The specifics of the changes to society under a truly democratic government based on public property will be up to the future generations of the most class conscious, educated and experienced leaders. The planners will undoubtedly include, but not be limited to, educated Marxists, model building ex-perts, and financial and currency experts, all with the knowledge of previous attempts at Socialism and the mistakes made. But all of society will need to play a role. The inputs of everyone must be solicited and be-come a part of the planning dialogue. As the conditions of Capitalism continue to deteriorate, the priorities and the model for change after the fall of Capitalism will change as well. Simply getting food and shelter to people could be the immediate agenda for a new government. So the whole process of developing a Socialist society will be in a much different atmosphere than in the past and the present. However, the time to understand the causes of society's problems and began developing the foundation of a new society is now!

In the future, the Capitalist world will have been tried and tested, propped up and failed again and again, and the conditions for everyone will be far worse than today. The struggling people of the United States and the world will be demanding drastic systemic change. In the past, Socialism may have been ahead of its time, but in the future its time will come. The writing is on the wall and the predictions of Marxist theory are progressing on schedule. The time to come together and start planning is now. John Lennon's words, from his song "Imagine" ring in my ears; *"you may say I'm a dreamer but I'm not the only one"* - *"I hope someday you'll join us and the world will be as one."*

CHAPTER THIRTEEN

Military Life Will Change You Forever

Willie Nelson wrote a song about "don't let your babies grow up to be cowboys." He should have written another entitled "don't let your babies grow up to be soldiers." You can be a modern day cowboy, you can be a scientist, a political activist, a recluse in the mountains, a doctor, a teacher, a plumber, a waitress, a mail carrier, a taxi cab driver etc. You can at least try to do anything you want, even be a "politician," <u>but if you decide to be a soldier and experience live combat, the one thing you will never be is "the same."</u> I was in the U.S. Navy for 4 years from 1959 to 1963. One of the few peace time windows between a never ending series of wars during the 20th century which are continuing into the 21st century. I was honorably discharged just before the Viet Nam War really got going. I thank my lucky stars I never saw live combat. Many of my friends, a few years younger than me, were not so fortunate. No one that I have ever known or heard of is ever the same once they have killed another human being. Even if they never killed another person, and have just been around the carnage, or shot at constantly, or suffered the loss of a friend in combat, they're never the same. It's not something that you get over or can ever get out of your mind. Some veterans are able to go on with their lives and raise families, have careers and seem to function normally, but inside they are never the same. They have dreams and wake up in the middle of the night sweating or have vivid flashbacks. A few come home and turn their violence on society. If wars don't physically dismember you or put you in a wheel chair the rest of your life, the mental damage done is usually irreparable.

The PTSD talked about today is not something new, it's been around forever. It's just since Viet Nam that it has been talked about and finally, today, recognized as the mental destroyer of our servicemen that goes beyond the terrible physical injuries. Military veterans don't like to talk about their war experiences and other veterans know not to ask questions. But if you get to know someone more closely they will open up to you on occasion. Usually it's their wives and parents that have to relive their experiences, or just parts of their experiences. But a lot of combat veterans can't open up to anyone and so the people close to them just have to painfully experience the effects of their trauma. Some of the trauma is driven by anger, some by fear, some by the ongoing shock and some by guilt for what they had to do. In the last 15 years, since Afghanistan and Iraq, it has become a national disaster to society. The Veteran's Administration cannot really handle the amount of PTSD veterans flooding the system. The veteran's hospital in Loma Linda California, where I go for my veterans' health care is expanding its building facilities to handle primarily the mental disorders of veterans. These veterans are the ones who have come in and asked for help. The worst of the lot are those who have turned to alcohol, drugs and are out there on the streets. Veterans make up one of the largest elements if not the largest group of homeless people. The terrible human effects of wars are one of the most glaring problems in society and should be of the utmost concern. But the way our government has turned its back on the problem and only given it a cosmetic consideration is a national disgrace. I am not going to go off too much on the politics of this situation and its causes. By now you can tell what I feel about war's relationship to Capitalism. My concern is with the young men and women who are considering military service. My appeal is to the parents who are encouraging their sons and daughters to even consider the military option. In fact, as a parent if you don't struggle adamantly against your child's desire to sign up then you are not performing your responsibility as a parent.

The human brain, specifically the frontal lobe, is not complete until around the age of 21 or 22 years. Until then, the two sides of your brain have not grown together to where it can function as a full brain. So young teenagers of 17, 18, 19 and sometimes even 20 or older cannot think clearly and don't know what they are doing, especially on such serious adult matters as going off to fight in other countries against people they don't even know. But these young, hardly out of their adolescence, individuals are exactly what the military wants. They don't think and maybe physically can't think outside of the box and they are also in a top physical stage of their lives and can perform physical feats that in just a few more years they won't be able to do. Just go to a skate board rink and watch them if you don't believe me. Basic training in the military is not about getting young men into good physical condition so they can fight. It's about brain washing them and teaching them to take orders, stripping them of their individual personalities, of developing a hive mentality so that when the leaders say <u>kill</u> they kill without question.

I was a wild teenager who couldn't wait to grow up. I left home for the summer once when I was 15 and lived and supported myself working in the orchards and packing houses and saved a little money for school clothes in the coming fall. I joined the Navy at 17 to get out on my own and be an adult and for the adventure of seeing the world. Well I didn't have to get any further than boot camp, or basic training, to see the world and for the first time experience the evil in it. The company I was assigned to in boot camp was uniquely harsh and I would say brutal compared to the other companies. All of the other outfits were mostly involved in brain washing tactics such as sleep deprivation and marching everywhere you went and never allowed to be alone. But my outfit was far worse. There was physical abuse and beatings, with recruits being called into dark rooms in the middle of the night to receive this physical abuse. I had difficulty peeing for weeks after one of those beatings. The leaders in my outfit were sick, perverted alcoholics who took the goal of *brain wash* to the extreme. They were demanding complete mental submission if they had to beat it out of us. My company turned out to be the sharpest trained in the whole division of companies. We were a 4.0 meatball company as represented by the scores we received in the classrooms and the perfection with which we marched together. But the word somehow got out as to what was going on. I heard one of the recruits, who had gotten his head bashed into a wall, had somehow gotten the word out to his father who knew a U.S. congressman. There was a congressional inquiry and a resulting court martial into the misuse of authority and physical abuse that went on in our ranks. Several people including the company commander received other than an honorable discharges.

The basic approach in military training is to break down the individual aspect of a person. I don't mean individualism talked about earlier in the sense of being opposed to community and as a selfish attitude. I mean all the things your mother and father and the community instilled in you in the past before you joined the service. To be what you are: a unique human being. The individual aspect of your personality, your sense of humor and your ability to think for yourself and hold the values to do the right thing. The military tries to strip you of these qualities so that you think in terms of a fighting unit, a group as opposed to a separate person so that when any commissioned officer, no matter how young or naïve, gives you an order which may be sending you to your death, when they send you into a situation where you either kill or be killed or kill and get killed anyway, you will not question this order or you will be subject to disgrace, a firing squad, dishonorable discharge or indefinite detention if you refuse. There is no justice in the military justice system. So this is what all basic training and subsequent military training is about, but in my situation, in my 4.0 company, it was far worse. In my company, the general goal of tearing down your resolve to be an individual was driven by people who had real issues within themselves and abused their positions. Well I was one of the recruits who overtly refused to be broken in spirit and stubbornly would not conform to the extremes demanded in the program and was subsequently beaten. We all came out of boot camp several weeks later than other recruits as our company was held over for all the court martial proceedings. During the proceedings I kept my mouth shut partly out of fear but partly because I had been raised not to be a tattle tale. Some of the abused recruits were given discharges and some of them were glad to get out. But I just kept it all to myself because I still wanted to see the world and be an adult, which in this case included all the scars I had picked up in basic training. So I went into the Navy with all the adventurous ideas of being on my own and I came out of basic training hating the Navy. This was a feeling that only grew the more I learned about military life.

My experiences don't come anywhere close to the experiences that combat veterans go through. A lot of combat veterans still embrace patriotic views about their horrific experiences. I don't know for sure, but I expect there are many injured veterans who no longer have that patriotic zeal but instead are bitter at the country's government responsible for their condition. There are certainly thousands of combat veterans who are angry in the way the government has not taken care of them after their injuries incurred in combat. I know this for a fact because I have talked with many of them. We never hear much about these bitter or outspoken veteran critics against the government and the military in general. There are veterans against the war groups scattered around the country but they sure don't get much notoriety. During the Viet Nam war, there was the "winter soldiers group" who came back and burned their medals and joined the anti-war movement that was in full swing. The current Secretary of State, John Kerry was one of those who spoke out against the Viet Nam War and burned his metals. Kerry actually per-formed heroic feats in Viet Nam, but when he ran for president he was attacked by the right wing as a liberal blah, blah, blah and was defeated. But the news media is so controlled now a days that there is no voice for these dissident veterans of Afghanistan and Iraq. It's mostly about the injured and heroic soldiers who still cling to their misguided patriotism. But I know they are out there, because even though they don't want to dis-cuss their particular combat experiences (which is un-derstandable) I have talked with many veterans who see the political sham of Afghanistan, Iraq and Viet Nam.

I marched in a Veterans Day parade last year in a contingent of veterans against wars. I carried a sign that read "*I am against the next war wherever it is*." My sign was well received by civilian by-standers and a group of old soldiers, undoubtable WWII veterans sitting in a group among the by standers. One woman called me over and yelled to me that she loved my sign and others cheered her remarks. So don't tell me that there aren't plenty of wounded veterans and civilians who feel differently than those who speak only of patriotism and defending the American way of life. These bystanders were honoring veterans for their sacrifices but that didn't mean that they agreed with the nature of the wars the veterans were sent to. There are also many veterans that don't see the hypocrisy and futility of wars and still hold to the patriotism that drove them to enlist in the first place. I don't agree with their politics but I feel for them just as I do all veterans and relate to their suffering and the terrible ways their lives have been changed or destroyed.

The phenomenon of post-traumatic stress disorder has been around as long as wars have existed. This was true even in World War II. I worked for a WWII veteran a while back who had been in a fox holes somewhere in Europe. He lived out in the country, was in his 80's and had run off his wife and his daughter who just couldn't tolerate his mental sickness that had stayed with him since the war. They had eventually given up on him although his daughter would still check on him from time to time. He was really impossible to be around, because he was so mentally damaged from whatever he had experienced in combat. Years earlier, he had dug a huge fox hole out in the front yard of his rural home. The fox hole had a bed down in there and a refrigerator and steps cut in the dirt to get down to it. He still related to it more than to the house he lived in and wanted me to clean it up for him, which I did. I could tell he had spent some time down in there recently because of the scattered garbage. He was real mean and not clear thinking at all. He would obsess on things of the slightest signifi- cance. No one was really able to handle him. But to him that fox hole represented the type of foxhole he proba- bly wished he had in Europe, with a bed and a refrigera- tor, etc. He was destroyed from the war and just unable to break free from it. It had destroyed his life and his family. There were plenty of others in WWII, many of whom wished they had never gone to war. The flight crew who dropped the atomic bombs on Japan, once they had seen what they had done, were stricken with guilt and wound up in psychiatric care and one or two of them committed suicide. I was in Japan about 15 years after Hiroshima and you could still witness the birth defects in the subsequent generations. The super sad thing was that the bomb wasn't even necessary, the war had already been won. Yet today we spread fear mongering on what our political adversaries might do if they get nuclear weapons, yet we are the only nation on earth that has ever used nuclear weapons against hu- manity.

Once I got out of boot camp and out into the regular Navy, I started seeing more of what the military was about. The military is a perfect example of a _class socie- ty_. In a recent discussion with a woman in regard to the class differences between enlisted men and commis- sioned officers, she viewed the military as an outright "caste system." I didn't even know what a class society was until years later. What I did know was that officers were in a world of their own. They lived in houses if they were married and luxurious quarters if they were single. The enlisted men lived in barracks all stacked on top of each other in keeping with the "hive mentality." Officers were paid much better and didn't get their hands dirty. They were fed much better, even aboard ship. The ate roasts and steaks and drank wine while the enlisted men ate powered eggs and recombined milk with chipped beef and gravy on toast for a treat. Compared to the enlisted men, the cannon fodder, the officers lived like royalty. You damned well better treat them as royalty. To be candid, there were a few officers who came up through the enlisted ranks. They were called "Mustangs" and some of them were actually down to earth and had some empathy for the common folk. But these officers were few and far between and limited on how far in the officer ranks they could progress.

So my growing contempt for military life was rendered more profound as I lived and observed the double standards of a class society, very similar to today's world of Capitalism but more overtly so and officially sanctioned. But of course to see it, and not question it, is not one of the personality traits that boot camp tried to take away from me. So I fought it, many times to my detriment and almost to the point of my complete demise. I am sure the way I was abused in boot camp added to my aggressiveness. At one point I zeroed in on a particular officer who had been building his entire military career on the discipline of enlisted men. I would resist his methods and at times defy him and in keeping with the organizational part of my personality would encourage others to defy him as well. Anyway, this poor excuse for a human being who obviously had issues of his own, exemplified by his arrogance and contempt towards enlisted men, almost took me down. He came very close to getting me sent to a retraining command where the military can hold you indefinitely and the time spent there does not come off of your agreed enlistment time. They keep you there for years, if necessary, until they break you of the bad habits of being an honest free thinking individual that basic training, at least in my case, was unable to do. I was saved by a more senior mustang officer who liked me and could see that I was a good person. He was the commander of the base and one whom I had gotten to know. Probably the only officer that I ever befriended, at least as much a friendship as was possible considering the "class restrictions." So I guess that my first exposure to a class society and also my first attempt as a political activist was in the military and certainly in a very dangerous, intimidating and threatening atmosphere. But then I guess I didn't realize the danger of the situation because my brain hadn't grown together yet, I was only 19 years old at the time.

A very good friend of mine who went through the above episode with me once asked me, if the Navy told me to grab a gun and go and fight in Viet Nam, would I go? This question was in the context of the Viet Nam war heating up and the military was beginning to hold over some of the enlisted men from their normal discharge dates. In other words keeping you in when you were supposed to get discharged. I really didn't know much about Viet Nam as most people didn't because the build up for the oncoming war was just in the preparatory stages and the government hadn't gone public with their plans as yet. Anyway I thought for a moment and then answered "Yes, I guess I would." A few years later you couldn't have forced me to serve in Viet Nam. I just wasn't politically conscious at that stage of my life and I was involved in a little war of my own against the injustices of a class based society and abuse of authority. I hadn't yet questioned my conformity to the popularized view of patriotism as an *exclusively militarized patriotism.* This was a patriotism based on "American Exceptionalism:" that we are better than other cultures and know what is best for them. This typical form of patriotism is no more than arrogance, based on ignorance and many times with strong ethnic racial overtones.

Well somehow I got through the military with an honorable discharge, no good conduct medal, but an honorable discharge nonetheless. Oh, there were a few notations in my service record about "showing slight contempt towards military authority" which are entirely true. One of those notations was the result of defying an NCIS officer (the NCIS is the Navy CIA) who wanted me to hold my boat crew past the scheduled departure time, while he was conducting an investigation. I had just been lectured on keeping the boat runs on schedule by my immediate boss. I also got busted in rank once in keeping with my drive to see the world and have a good time. The situation was having a good time with several senior officer's daughters my own age. I organized a party in a beautiful outdoor garden patio of a huge bachelor officer's quarters that had only one or two temporary officers there in transit. Hey! The enlisted men didn't have any facilities like this and it wasn't even being used. But I earned the rank back and before I got discharged moved up one more rank to an E-4. No one ever called me stupid. I was just unable to remain silent in the face of injustice, the same as I am to this very day. I was also extremely lucky. But during my entire four year enlistment I never once considered staying in the Navy.

So anyway returning to the yet to be released song "don't let your babies grow up to be soldiers." I wish there was some way to cut through all the current enlistment propaganda that entices young people to enlist. I wish there was some way instead to enlist the parents to struggle with their children when their children present these thoughts about joining the military or at least not encourage it. I wish that some of these young adults would read this book, be more open minded, do a little firsthand research and talk to some wounded veterans, anything other than just jumping off the bridge, sort of like I did. Certainly not all of the people who join the service wind up in combat. I am proof of that. I just don't think that young people realize what they are getting into and in the worst case scenario the huge risk they take in risking their lives and limbs and minds. There are worse things than dying for your country. You can live out your life as **a** quadriplegic or with incurable brain damage. One of the things different today which is causing such a huge amount of PTSD over years past is that soldiers are going back for 2, 3, and more tours and the stress of combat exposure is intensified and cumulative. The primary reason for this is that we just aren't getting enough bodies through the volunteer army to satisfy all the military occupations that the system continues to initiate.

You know with all the fear mongering about who's coming to get you, be it the Communists, the terrorists or little green men, the United States has not had its shores invaded since the War of 1812. I know some of you are thinking what about 9/11? This was a single act that the Bush Administration might have avoided. They were told by the FBI that there was going to be a terrorist attack and it might take the form of terrorists commandeering commercial airlines. There were many other red flags as well and the Bush administration turned a deaf ear to the warnings and then we lashed out at IRAQ who had nothing to do with 9/11. The administration knew they didn't and lied about the facts to the American people and Congress. But as terrible as 9/11 was, it was one terrorist act with no chances of a military invasion or occupation on American soil. If we continue with these deceitful military adventures, if we turn to violence as a first resort instead of a last resort and sacrifice the lives of our children in the process, we are probably going to have to go back to the draft or military conscription to match the pace of these economically driven, foreign occupations. I don't think that young people of today would stand still for a mandatory draft any more than they did during the "resist the draft movement" in the Viet Nam war that ended conscription. As a percentage, there probably aren't that many young people tempted towards enlisting in military service any more. I think that some today, as well as in the past, feel they don't have a lot of economic options in a shrinking economy. Minorities and poor whites from the south do seem to be filling a higher than average percent of enlistees. So I think I am again back to square one. It's Capitalism, stupid! The cannon fodder are the working class and within the class are the economically deprived and within the economically deprived working class are the minorities that always suffer more than the rest of us no matter what the issue.

But all of society suffers the guilt of what we do to our children. We throw their lives away as if they were nothing and then celebrate their death or ruined lives in the form of heroic pronouncements. Whether you believe that it is Capitalism or simply politicians that perpetuate the senseless carnage, the fact is that we as a people are all responsible for our acts as a nation. We can applaud our violent actions against our own children as acts of patriotism or just shake our heads in passive complacency. Either way, we the people, the parents, the politicians, the Wall Street barons, rich and poor bear the responsibility for allowing it to happen. Until we rise up and take our destiny in our own hands this atrocity against our children will degrade our humanity and move our smug self-righteousness into the depths of social and moral decay. It makes a mockery of the love that is a part of humanity and casts a shadow of hypocrisy on our religious beliefs. War is not the answer. It only makes matters worse.

CHAPTER FOURTEEN

Violence in America and the Question of Terrorism

Violence and terrorism are inseparable. Terrorism is violence that elicits terror, and is directed at innocent people. The following is my best effort in defining the multiple aspects of terrorism.

A definition of terrorism: Terrorism is the violent attacks targeted against innocent people or when innocent people are treated with disregard and caught up in the violence against terrorism. Terrorism is also living under the fear of violence. The motivation for terrorist acts can be religious, political, racial hatred, disrespect for women, revenge, economic instability and the mental disorders exacerbated by the growing stressful world conditions. It is sometimes the depraved acts of individuals and groups who welcome their own death. Regardless of the motivation terrorism is never justified. It is an outrageous form of violence in the world that speaks to the deterioration of moral values and callous disregard for human life. It is directly proportionate to the increasing failure of international Capitalism to provide for the basic needs of a growing percentage of the world population. This in turn fosters lack of hope, mental disorders and growing despair. Terrorism is an extreme manifestation of a decadent society. The phenomenon of terrorism is not limited to the violence itself but includes the fear and anticipation of the violence. It can cause the fear to travel, to venture into public places, or to hear the sound of police sirens or helicopters overhead in our cities. Terror causes women and children to lock themselves behind closed doors in defense against raging husbands. In some countries the anticipation of drone attacks can cause great fear among civilian populations. Terrorism is not limited to radical movements within the Islamic world and its only relation to Muslim religion is in the deranged minds of religious fanatics bent on violence.

Terrorist acts pre-date 9-11, Al-Qaeda, the Taliban and ISIS. They include the bombing of the Federal Building in Oklahoma, disgruntled employees in the workplace who go postal and start killing innocent workers, the massacre at Columbine High School in Littleton Colorado, The attacks on Planned Parenthood in Colorado Springs Colorado, the Sandy Hook Elementary School tragedy in Connecticut and the killing of 9 people in a black church in Charleston S.C. by a lone white racist gunman. They also include hate crimes directed at the LGBT community. The 2016 lone gunman attack that killed nearly 50 people in Orlando Florida represented one the worst mass killing in American history. Terrorist acts have been around for a long time. The December 29, 1890 "Wounded Knee Massacre" of between 150 and 300 men, women and children of the Lakota Indian Tribe by the U.S. Cavalry was certainly an act of terrorism and a disgraceful part of American History. Probably the oldest and most common form of violence that evokes terror occurs in the home where women live in fear of recurring violence. Home violence is as much a form of terrorism as all the rest and often spreads out into the streets where it then becomes recognized for what it is: terrorism. None of the above forms of terrorism had much, if anything, to do with the Islamic world or Muslim religion. Yet recently, when San Bernardino, California, was subjected to an attack which killed 14 and wounded 21 people, both the government and the news media waited several days before calling it a terrorist attack until they could determine if it was orchestrated or inspired by ISIS, Al-Qaeda or another Muslim group. The position of the U.S. establishment is to reserve the term terrorism exclusively to violent activity influenced by, or directly orchestrated by, the terrorist groups within the Islamic world. When terrorism is referred to as "radical Islam," it is an attack on the religion of peace loving Muslims at home and abroad and encourages racial hatred and religious divides. This exclusive definition of terrorism has also been used by Republican politicians to support their anti-immigrant position, to stir up racial prejudices and secure votes from the far right during election campaigns.

In the United States violence has too often become an accepted way of settling individual differences within the general population. But in my opinion the violence in our society starts at the top. It *"trickles down"* by example from our government on a national level through the sanctioned use of force. Whether in the communities of America through the militarization of the police forces or in the never ending military involvements around the world, violence spreads from the establishment to the people. Violence is contagious. The frequency of wars and military occupations reached historic levels during the 20th Century. The early 21st Century has seen increased levels of violence by our own government involved in overt acts of assassination, torture and indefinite detention of suspected war criminals without trials. The casual use of military drones targeting terrorists with little regard for innocent civilians is a form of violence that is seen by much of the world as an example of state terrorism. All of these actions on behalf of our nation are examples of violence and many violate good moral principles with respect for human life and civil liberties.

When the establishment engages in sanctioned legal violence it is described as patriotism or enforcing law and order. When individual citizens commit violence and people die it is seen as murder. When state

sanctioned capital punishment takes lives it's called justice. These examples illustrate the hypocrisy and double standards of our society on moral issues involving
life and death. The world leaders rightfully decree that
world terrorism is unacceptable, but they have been
perpetuating the same violence for decades with weapons of mass destruction. The people of the world
watched with amazement and horror the bombing of
Hiroshima, Viet Nam and Iraq which annihilated tens of
thousands of innocent people and they listened to the
justification offered for these actions with raised eyebrows. But over the decades many of us have become
immune to the violence and gradually consider the human casualties and suffering of this legal use of violence
as somehow justified. Then, in too many instances, we
handle our own disagreements with the same violence.
On the home front we are one of the most violent,
weapon accessible, nations in the world. We also have
the largest, most powerful military presence in the
world. It's monkey see, monkey do. Our society is
tainted by the government's embrace of violence.

The world in general and the United States of America in particular, have an abundance of violence these
days: murders, mass homicides, gang killings, family
domestic violence and individual acts of terrorism. If
there is a clear "red flag" to signal a potential terrorist
act ahead of time, it would be instances of man on
women domestic violence, regardless of whether it involves weapons. It is a strong indicator that, many
times, leads to community acts of terrorism, on down
the road. We must no longer turn a blind eye to the
abuse of women and children in the home, if only because it often evolves into violent men *"taking their
guns to town."*

The United States has the highest proliferation of

guns per capita, by far, than any country in the world! I am a supporter of the Constitutional right to bear arms. Unlike many other supporters, who see the National Rifle Association primarily as an advocate for the 2nd Amendment, I see the NRA as the main lobbying group for the gun manufacturers. The armament industry in America profits from the proliferation of weapons worldwide. With the relatively unrestricted gun sale laws in the United States many of these guns wind up in the hands of international black market weapon dealers. They are ultimately destined for international terrorists, armed resistance groups and drug lords around the world. Some go directly to criminals and wind up on the streets of America. The proliferation of weapons around the world by American weapons manufacturers helps perpetuate world conflicts and many times these same weapons wind up being used against American troops. The ready availability of weapons in America also adds to the problem of domestic terrorism.

As a supporter of the 2nd Amendment, I have no problem with legislation for reasonable gun control reform such as background checks to scrutinize people with histories of family violence, hate crimes, and threatening remarks on the internet. I agree with restrictions of certain military style weapons as well as the monitoring and tracking of large quantity gun or ammunition sales regardless of the *stated* destination. I am, however, wary of background checks aimed primarily at people who seek psychological counseling or use mind healing medication. I think the bigger threat are people who need psychological counseling but haven't asked for help or have no access to mental counseling. These people would not show up on screening anyway. We don't want to turn the process of gun control into a witch hunt for everyone who takes anti-depressant medication. I also don't see reasonable improvements to gun control laws as a precursor to outlawing individual gun ownership. The 2nd Amendment, regardless of the NRA propaganda and views of some avid gun owners, is not under attack by any reasonable opinion. Many gun owners see every attempt at gun control as a step towards collecting all guns. This view is encouraged by the propaganda of the NRA, talk radio and conservative politicians, all of whom, objectively represent the interests of gun manufacturers to maintain and grow their unrestricted domestic sales. Every time there is a domestic act of terrorism, people line up at the gun stores and stock up as if it was Black Friday shopping at Walmart or J.C. Penny's. Sounds to me like the 2nd Amendment is alive and well. I also oppose the _unlimited_ right of just any citizen to carry a concealed weapon and view these laws as a recipe for disaster that can often turn an argument among strangers into a homicide. These "right to carry" laws in some states also encourage a vigilante approach to law enforcement and are a prescription for more social violence. Even though the majority of Americans favor some form of gun control reforms, the propaganda based around the fear of eliminating gun ownership has strong backing from Republican politicians who use this fear as an appeal to single issue voters. This solidified, politically motivated position within the Republican Party is the main roadblock to reasonable changes in gun control laws.

So the growing gun violence in America is a result of both the violent nature of society, which begins with the government model of violence at home and abroad, and the unrestricted proliferation of domestic gun sales. Both of these phenomena are directly caused by a decadent Capitalist society based on the bottom line of profits. Capitalist economics also creates stress on all working people, with a growing number of people going over the top and engaging in terrible acts of violence which they see in every direction they look. So now let's take a closer look at violence on steroids: the acts of *international* terrorism.

The use of military drones is becoming another ugly side of American military policy abroad. If you disregard the hundreds of innocent lives lost, disregard the new ethics of open assassination directed by the White House and overlook the fear and apprehension in countries like Pakistan, where a widespread use of drone attacks occur, then initially the official position of saving American troops lives on the ground sounds convincing. The casualties of the innocent people in the countries caught up in these attacks on terrorists has become an international issue even in the United States. It was one of the first criticisms by the liberals and progressives in the Democratic Party of the Obama Administration. I agree with the Obama position of using military force only as a last resort and turning to diplomatic solutions. But the extensive use of so called targeted assassinations with drones is not using military force as a last resort. It is simply using another form of military force other than manned troops on the ground. It is far more frequent and more casually used than sending in troops or calling for manned air attacks. The cavalier process of using drone attacks and the seemingly disregard for a growing number of innocent people being killed in these attacks raises issues of morality and ethics. Its effectiveness in fighting terrorism is also questionable. One terrorist leader is killed along with innocent bystanders and 2 more move up to take his place. With every innocent man, woman or child that dies alongside the targeted terrorist the world wide political opposition to drone attacks by the United States grows.

Drone assassinations have become a form of "state terrorism." My definition of terrorism is when innocent people are targeted or else are treated with disregard in the war on terrorism. When the violence affecting innocents comes at the hand of world governments, such as drone attacks by the United States, then the action qualifies as state terrorism. It is not only the killing of innocents but also the fear that innocent people have of becoming victims of drone attacks, the sleepless nights of anticipation. Whether it is war planes overheard in their communities, armed helicopters or missiles coming out of the skies from silent drones, it simply creates an atmosphere of anxiety and terror. Drone attacks hit populated streets, public events, festivities such as weddings and homes where terrorists *might* be. The use of U. S. drone attacks meets the criteria of state terrorism on both accounts. Drones both kill innocent people and create a climate of fear in anticipation of more attacks. Looking at the case against the United States drone policy as a form of state terrorism keep this in mind. It doesn't matter what the intentions are of those performing the drone attacks if it includes killing innocents. If you are ISIS or Al-Qaeda your intentions are clearly bad. If you are the United States your intentions could be to combat evil, which is good. But *disregard* for innocents killed in the process is in itself evil. To the innocent victims the terror created in their lives is the same whether it comes from the terrorists or the U.S. military. That's what terrorism is, violence or fear of violence against innocent people regardless of the source.

A sad fact about all wars is all of the civilian casualties which have come to be viewed as a necessary side effect. In Viet Nam there were 50,000 American troops killed but several million civilian casualties. During the bombings of Europe in World War II the civilians suffered the brunt of casualties. During the Iraq War, the so called "strategic bombings" caused the maiming and loss of life of innocent men, women and children in the pursuit of one man, Saddam Hussein. Although he was a terrible dictator he had nothing to do with 9/11. The continuous bombing by the U.S. military was a human tragedy and the main reason behind the demands by the Iraqi people for American troops to leave the country. All of these examples are a form of state terrorism, regardless of which country does it and regardless of whether or not civilians are the intended target. The missile attacks of Iraq were particularly disgusting because they went on for many weeks even after it became apparent that they were killing and maiming little children. That is very close to the intentional killing of innocents. At the very least it represented open disregard for innocent lives.

Today we hear the cry against drone strikes by the Pakistani people for the same reasons. In the age of technological warfare, coupled with the unquestioned tactic of overt military assassinations, the drone activities and its effects on the innocent are rapidly becoming the source of the modern day sentiment "ugly American go home." The American Flag has come to represent a symbol of fear in some parts of the world. I don't mean fear experienced by the terrorists but rather the righteous fear of the civilian populations. This fear or concern has time and again proven to be justified because wherever the U. S. military gets involved there is a huge escalation in violence and innocent deaths. In Pakistan, one of the main countries being targeting for drone strikes, the civilian losses have reached such a level that communities are organizing against U.S. drone attacks.

These are communities who have no allegiance to the Taliban and only fear them. But they have come to see the drone attacks against the Taliban as nearly as devastating to their communities as the fear and tactics of the Taliban itself.

What makes the U. S. drone policy even worse, and completely unethical, is that the U. S. drone attacks have been used against the people that speak out against the drone attacks, as well as the terrorists. A recent report on "60 Minutes" covered the use of drone attacks in targeting community activists who speak out against the attacks. There was a 15 year old Pakistani school boy, a soccer player, who was involved in the community meetings being organized in protest to the drone attacks. This young adult was returning home by automobile from a soccer game and was targeted and assassinated by U.S. drones on a country road. I don't know where "60 Minutes" got the video footage but it actually showed the hairline sighting mechanism of the drone operator (probably a young military man, with a patriotic video game mentality) in a bunker somewhere in Nevada, bringing the Pakistani boy's automobile into the sights and launching the drone missile with a direct hit. This is after a 10 minute scenario by "60 Minutes" covering the young Pakistani protestor's growing interest and involvement in the struggle to stop the drone attacks within his community. This young Pakistani was not someone in the wrong place at the wrong time. He was a part of a protest movement against U.S. drone attacks. So what has our government come to in this relentless war against terrorism? Here in the United States, the Patriot Act is used to label the free speech of the Occupy movement as potential terrorism and an excuse for making arrests. In Pakistan, we assassinate protestors against drone attacks as if they were terror-

ists themselves. This is state terrorism and is no different than the terrorists' practice of targeting the innocents. The only difference is that ISIS is up front about
their terrible deeds and we try and cover it up, justify,
or deny it. The similarity is that both the U.S. and ISIS
have become blinded with self-righteousness and arrogance over their individual acts.

Our government, in the name of fighting terrorism,
is attacking free speech, and especially free speech
against government policies. If we don't struggle
against these attacks on free speech before they become
more engrained in our society and political system it
could develop, along with the growing police state, into
Fascism which can evolve from Capitalism in trouble. I
say damn the Patriot Act. The dark days of the Patriot
Act didn't end with the *temporary* end to torture. The
Patriot Act, and the 2012 changes to the NDAA (National Defense Authorization Act) have become an excuse
for an attack on the civil liberties of American citizens.
We talk about countries like North Korea and Iran as
terrorist states. But we don't have to look to other
countries for examples of state terrorism. How long will
it be before drone attacks are used against American
protestors or people suspected of some form of immediate threat to the interests of the corporate or government status quo? We should no longer tolerate these
oppressive domestic and foreign policies and stop supporting politicians waving the flag with pronouncements of America's role in leading the fight against terrorism while trampling on the civil liberties of Americans and innocent people around the world. These are
hollow, hypocritical pronouncements which are in
sharp contrast to our Constitution and what we are
supposed to stand for.

Al Jazeera News interviewed a woman in one of the

ISIS strongholds in the Iraq/Syrian area who was weeping and reaching out to the world for help because of what the terrorists were doing in her community. She was calling for help against the ISIS terrorists because she didn't want to live under their regime. But she also knew that the drone attacks would also kill the innocents in her community including herself. She knew that she too was going to die as a result of the drone attacks and she was resolved to this fate. She was pleading for someone to "bring it." If that was the only way someone could see fit to help us, by killing us all in the process, then "bring it." She didn't want to live anymore.

The efforts of the United States corporations to achieve international hegemony in the marketing of its commodities worldwide is the driving force behind our foreign policies. The American military assaults are extensions of economic policies. Marxists view imperialism as the export of capital in pursuit of these economic policies and imperialist wars a result of failed economic policies. But the aggressiveness in pursuit of these policies is what sets the United States up as the *"go it alone"* modern day Capitalist country. Just as our domestic policies at home are laissez-fair right wing with a nearly unrestricted form of Capitalism, so too is our foreign policy a go it alone right wing policy. We do what we do with or without the support of our western allies. We sometimes defy the United Nations and raise our own nationalist/economic interests above the democratic intentions of the United Nations. We have the biggest economy in the world and the largest military budget (four times that of China). Our enormous military budget is needed to support our private corporate investments. National Security has become the *code word* for the economic security of our privately owned companies abroad.   The aggressive nature of American companies is reflected in the aggressive nature of our military. There are a lot of American retailers using Pakistani sweat shops for cotton goods. They have to keep these shops churning out products for shipment to the U.S. We can't let some Pakistani protestor against our drone attacks interfere with exporting American jobs to Pakistan.   Someday we'll want to put sweat shops in Iraq and Syria. After all, we can't let a poor, oppressed and *hysterical* woman hell bent on dying stop the drones. We can't have free market expansion in an atmosphere of terrorism. I talked to an ex-marine who was in Iraq during the height of the Iraqi terrorist insurgency.   He and several hundred marines were assigned to protect a large American oil company headquarters in the middle of nowhere. It made him stop and think a little bit on what our role in Iraq was about. Upon discharge he later became involved in the "Occupy" movement.

The United States, along with many western countries has a formal policy of not negotiating with terrorists or paying ransom. Many countries with this policy have engaged in negotiations and in some cases have paid ransom to terrorists privately. The United States has negotiated prisoner swaps and may have paid ransom unofficially behind the scenes regardless of the official policy. In 2014, the U.S. refused to pay ransom for an American free-lance photographer named Luke Somers who was kidnapped by terrorists in Yemen. Instead, we initiated a failed rescue attempt during which the American hostage was murdered by the terrorists. The U.S. has officially been refusing to negotiate in any way with terrorists and has turned a blind eye to several beheadings of Americans. The difference with this failed attempt is that a South African hostage, Pierre

Korkie, was also murdered by the terrorists during the failed raid. The South African government had been negotiating with the terrorists for the release of Korkie and he was due to be released in two more days. Immediately after the failed rescue attempt and the murder of the two men, criticism came down on the Obama Administration for causing the death of the South African hostage who was to be released within hours. The Administration press secretary denied any knowledge of the South African negotiations. Immediately, the South African government responded to the U.S. press secretary's denial, stating that the U.S. knew full well of their negotiations and that some level of U.S. representation was even present for the ongoing negotiations between them and terrorist group. If the United States had participated in full partnership with the South Africans and negotiated for Luke Somers' life as well, it is possible that both Korkie and Somers would be alive today. It is certainly reasonable to question the stubborn policy of the U.S. to never negotiate with terrorists especially when innocent human lives are immediately in danger. But when this policy is so adamant that it undermines the right of other governments to negotiate for the lives of their citizens, do we have that right? Then when we get caught in the lie of denying any knowledge of the negotiations doesn't that indicate that we knew what we did was wrong? What does that say about the honesty, morality and transparency of our government in the "war on terror?" The South African government was clearly irritated by the rescue attempt which undermined their agreement and cost the lives of two innocent human beings. When the U.S. denied any knowledge of the ongoing negotiations they were enraged enough to publicly expose the U.S. denial as a lie. President Reagan first exposed the government's right to lie to the world by referring to it as _misinformation,_ which he justified as deceiving our enemies under the umbrella of national security interests. Nowadays the veil of secrecy using "national security" reasons goes far beyond the implied safety of American citizens and has come to include embarrassments to state officials, the economic interests of private American corporations and virtually anything that the government just doesn't want Americans to know and much of what we should know. The case of Edward Snowden comes to mind... I think the reader can fill in the blanks and I'll let it go at that.

So where does this international terrorism, inappropriately referred to by the right wing as "radical Islam," come from? Where does this hatred manifested in terrorists' tactics towards America originate? What drives other human beings to kill their own when they can't get to us to kill us? Without a doubt, they are religious fanatics who could just as well qualify as criminal serial killers or suicide candidates who want to take others out with them. But they grow out of an environment in their individual countries that is dominated by international Capitalism, especially American corporations and military occupations. The history of international Capitalism, or Imperialism, helps create terrorism. The private property foundations of Capitalism's economics creates classes, inequalities and poverty. Poverty feeds extremism and terrorism is a form of violent extremism.

When American corporations go into these third world countries be it for resources, cheap labor or markets for their products the countries are not allowed to develop their own balanced economies. U. S. corporate interests in these countries are heavy handed and bent on serving the exclusive interests of the companies involved. This can result in undiversified economies and sustained poverty. It's a banana republic approach serving the exclusive interests of the foreign investors. These policies of Imperialist economics have always created resistance against America and the dictators that serve American corporations. With the American economic involvement in these countries also comes American lifestyles and American values, such as separation of church and state, developing a consumer society, women's rights and free speech which are many times in conflict with the theocratic political systems and social mores of Islamic countries. There is a resistance against the secular/democratic form of American politics even among the peaceful Muslims who are daily worshipers and look to their religion for guidance in their everyday social lifestyles and political decisions. Many if not most Muslims want to maintain their religious influence over cultural mores and in political decisions and don't embrace the American cultural model of secularization, especially when it is imposed through aggressive outside nation building.   So the resentment towards America comes from decades of our corporate involvement and political arrogance towards Islamic countries and the emphatic belief that our way of life is best for everyone. Again, "American Exceptionalism."

I agree with our secular government, separation of church and state, and equality for women. There are some Americans who want to de-secularize American politics and establish the church over the state. These are the fundamentalist Christians, the single issue voters, who politicize religious dogma and are "over the top" of mainstream Christianity. Knowingly or not these Christians are advocating theocracy over democracy. The Islamic countries are still more theocratic even where voting is allowed. The problem is that you

can't force social and political change on another society. It has to evolve naturally and slowly on its own and
not through outside forcefulness. That is exactly what
corporate high handed intrusion, economic imperialism,
combined with our political opinionated message for
secular democracy does. We have no right to impose
our values on other societies. When it comes to wom-
en's oppression there are many Muslim women around
the world who are activists for women's rights. But
there are also many Muslim women, through intimidation from the male dominated society or who still hold
to the old cultural beliefs of a woman's role. They are
not as anxious to become more in step with the western
world's increasing advancement for women's equality.
For instance, in Saudi Arabia the monarchy recently
took the first step in allowing women a limited right to
vote. This is in a society where women are not even allowed to drive automobiles. The step was positive and
some women embraced the change, but others did not.
The point is that positive political and social change
must come naturally and doesn't happen overnight.
The women's rights movement in the United States was
a protracted struggle going back over a hundred years
and it still continues.

Our pushy, profit driven world economic agenda
coupled with a self-righteous political view, colored as it
is by racial prejudice, has caused resistance, resentment, and in the case of the terrorist movement outright
hatred. This does not excuse the fanatical violence of
the terrorists like Al-Qaeda and ISIS (and our hatred
towards terrorism doesn't excuse the drone attacks that
also kill innocents). It only explains where the hatred
towards America, expressed by the terrorists, comes
from. The vast majority of the Islamic world would
never think of turning to terrorist acts even though

many may be resentful of American corporate and political dominance in their countries. Likewise in America the stress in society created in part by the failure of the economic system to respond to the needs of the majority doesn't turn everyone to acts of violence. In America it's only a small percentage that turn to violence, just as it is a small minority amongst Muslims that turn to terrorism. But terrorism both in America and in the world is directly related to the failure of international Capitalism to provide for the needs of far too many people. The world is dominated by Capitalist economics, the free market and private property. There is no Socialism anywhere. Even the so called Communist countries are well immersed in the world free market. After 9/11 our invasion of Iraq made matters far worse and added to the growth of Terrorism.

The international war against terrorism is not our responsibility to solve militarily. We can try to use our influence and diplomacy but the main responsibility is clearly in the hands of the Islamic nations. It's in their back yard and it is an immediate threat to the existence of their governments. Countries such as Turkey, Syria, Saudi Arabia, Iran and Iraq are slow to step up to the plate. They have so many differences among themselves, and the United States involvement makes matters even more confusing. All we can do, rather than diplomacy, is stay out of their internal affairs. The problem is that this is not just a political decision to be made on behalf of our government. It's an aggressive economic decision that is being dictated to our politicians, and politicians of the western world, by international corporate interests. The Marxist view is that international Capitalism does not have a choice. It must continue to expand in order to survive.

The U.S. invasion of Iraq upset the whole balance of

power in the area. We pretty much destroyed the civilization of Iraq. We destroyed their military, their infrastructure, and changed the religious orientation of their government from Sunni to Shia. We elevated Iran to the most powerful country in the area. Didn't anybody see that coming? Those that did were not listened to. Terrorism flourished after the Iraq invasion, and Iraq and Syria became the target for ISIS. We now know that there was at least some truth in Bashar al-Assad's early claims that terrorism was threatening his country. It wasn't solely a dictator waging war on the righteous resistance of Syrians against his regime. But western influence saw this as an opportunity to overthrow *another* dictator and began backing and building militias to overthrow Assad. The whole ground war in the area is very confusing as to who is fighting whom, a complicated mess of political and religious differences. But clearly the United States was lagging behind by not recognizing ISIS and the terrorist threat in Syria at the time. In Iraq, the right wing philosophy of Bush and Chaney saw only what they wanted to see. The cry to overthrow the Assad regime in Syria was the position of the U.S. State department under Secretary of State Hillary Clinton, until we learned more about the terrorist threat that Assad referred to. I remember going to an anti-war demonstration in Los Angeles at the time against a pending Syrian invasion by the U.S. There were many people there from the Syrian community in Los Angeles who weren't particularly fond of Assad but did not want a U.S. invasion to overthrow him. I guess in part, they and their relatives in Syria had witnessed the outcome of the U.S. invasion of Iraq to overthrow Saddam Hussein and the terrible consequences that resulted for the whole area. There is not an easy solution and the countries in the area are going to have to work it out and it may take many years. It also may not turn out exactly the way we want it to. But one thing is clear. The United States started the whole mess with the Iraq invasion and can only make it worse with our own lack of understanding of the situation and the push for our own political and economic agendas.

The United States made a similar mistake in taking out another dictator, Muammar Gaddafi of Libya, which is now a failed state with a growing terrorist presence. We just absolutely don't know what we are doing in that part of the world. We are still blindsided by our tunnel vision to promote democracy. We should be more concerned on how democracy is failing at home with the control of the corporate state over our own domestic political policies. We can't even get our own house in order, yet we are out there telling the rest of the world what they should do. At the same time the corporate world needs to expand its presence in this part of the world which make purely political decisions regarding American foreign policy even more difficult, if not impossible. The United States needs to back off. More military involvement will make things worse. Will we ever learn from our mistakes? History says no we *don't* learn. Marxist Socialists such as myself understand that Capitalism *can't* learn, it digs its own grave. Americans need to understand that our involvement so far has been negative and that there is no instant gratification in the solution to international politics. The drone strikes and other militarily efforts can be controlled somewhat by our political system and the office of the President. But the corporate interests have a mind and agenda of their own, with a huge influence over our government. So I am not too hopeful of our government's ability to back off. Imperialism / Colonialism is not a policy even for the corporations. It's a necessity.

But maybe, hopefully, with all the turmoil in the area, American Corporate interests can be drawn somewhere else long enough to give peace a chance in the Mideast area. The downside to this "backing off" means that someone else, another country or continent will be on the U.S. military short list. I am against the next war no matter where it is. Ultimately only the end to private property can lead to world peace.

The continued terrorist attacks around the world are something we may have to live with for a long, long time. As frightening as this situation may be it is preferable to an all-out 3rd world war, driven by Capitalist economies to re-divide the world. That would involve winners and losers and the shifting of power. The world is smaller now with computers and weapon technology, and the next big war will not be limited to the suffering of only European citizens. American citizens will also suffer the bloodshed and tragedies of a world war amongst nation states. In previous wars, only the American troops suffered. In future wars American citizens will be victims of weapons of mass destruction right along with the rest of the world.

The answer to defeating terrorism is not a matter of giving up civil liberties and privacy laws as guaranteed by the Constitution. This is however the mantra of the FBI, the NSA, Homeland Security and too many of our leaders in their quest to obtain unlimited surveillance rights. In a recent terrorist attack in San Bernardino California the FBI attempted to intimidate Apple to co-operate in writing a code that would leave all customers without any privacy rights in their conversations, e-mails and message texting. The CEO of Apple refused a court order to help break the encrypted code of the terrorist owned iPhone. Apples refusal was supported by Google and Facebook who agreed that this would set a

far reaching and unnecessary precedent upon the privacy rights of millions of Americans. These companies
were also driven to this position out of concern for the
continued sale of hardware and software of their respective companies. The FBI then initiated a lawsuit
against Apple which was destined to go to the U.S. Supreme Court. I had seen an earlier interview on Public
Television of a national security expert who said that
the FBI was perfectly capable of breaking the encryp-
tion on the iPhone and was only suing Apple to establish a precedent over the corporate world to cater to
National Security interests. This would have been a
precedent with complete disregard for the privacy
rights of American Citizens. Then an unpredictable
event happened. Supreme Court Justice Anthony Scalia
died unexpectedly. Scalia had been influential in the
recent conservative leaning of the Court. Scalia's suc-
cessor to the court would probably be either a moderate
or liberal and the new Supreme Court would more than
likely not favor the FBI's hopes for far reaching national
security interests over privacy issues. Well upon Scalia's death the FBI dropped the law suit and stated that
they had come up with a 3rd party who could break the
encrypted iPhone for them. If you believe that sudden
change of heart as authentic, then I have a bridge in
London I'd like to sell you. My distrust and many times
contempt for the FBI hasn't changed and neither have
they changed. Their role of deceit, blackmail, misinformation and covert activities against the working class
has not changed since the days of J. Edger Hoover.
American citizens should have at least as much fear of
the FBI and the NSA as they do of terrorism itself. Fascism can be, at least, as scary as terrorism. Americans
need to get control of their fear when it comes to the
ISIS/Al-Qaeda terrorism. It is this runaway fear among

the American people that supports the government and its security agencies, such as the FBI, NSA and Homeland Security, to push for more surveillance, police action and suspension of civil liberties. In FDR's first inaugural address he said *"the only thing we have to fear is fear itself."* All of these actions are aspects of growing Fascism which, if it occurs, will be far more of a blow to America's way of life than the random senseless bombings by terrorists, which in most cases, are nearly impossible to guard against anyway. It is the misguided reaction to emotions such as fear, revenge and anger that always comes back to haunt us and raises the recurring question "will we ever learn?"

The importance of world terrorism has been elevated to a disproportionate level of priority. This is in part because of the love for violent sensationalism on behalf of the American news media and the uncontrolled spread of fear by the media, and rightwing politicians. You can't blame the media completely for their coverage of violent sensationalism. Everywhere you look in the country and the world there is violence, and not just from terrorism. The chances of any individual American becoming a victim of terrorism is very small, but the anticipated fear of it happening, no matter how slight, is what drives the effectiveness of terrorism. Even if ISIS, and all other international terror groups were to be destroyed, we will still have instances of terrorism in America as long as we are driven by violence, hatred, ignorance, and stress created in part by the grim economic prospects in a world in the stage of monopoly Capitalism. You may not agree with me that international Capitalism is the main cause of terrorism, but many of you would agree that our reaction to terrorism has rendered it more profound: just causing it to spread everywhere throughout the world.

A far more threatening and urgent issue for humanity that we should be concerned about is climate change, which is imminently threatening the life of the entire planet. So let's turn now to the most pressing issue that has been shoved into the background by the attention given to endless world violence.

CHAPTER FIFTEEN

**Climate Change
A struggle all but lost**

If you are one of the few people on earth that still thinks climate change isn't happening, or that human beings haven't caused it, then you are probably un-reachable. You are either in a stubborn state of denial, prompted by your conservative political leanings, or you just cannot bring yourself to believe that humans are responsible for such a threat to humanity and all life. It wasn't too many years ago that the question was a political one with the Republicans firmly holding the view that the phenomenon didn't exist or that it was part of a natural, long term cycle. The problem of global warming is now more obvious and widely accepted. The Republican politicians are still adamantly against regulations or mandates to limit the spewing of fossil fuels into the atmosphere. Although both parties have commitments to, and reliance on corporate America, the Republican Party, has always been more deeply dedi-cated to corporate interests, no matter what the issue. From 2000 to 2008 the Bush administration spent con-siderable effort to promote the false science that climate change wasn't real.   The effects of those eight years, with all the brainwash and lies, still lingers in the minds of many Americans today. The American public lags no-ticeably behind the rest of the world, whose populations have been demanding action against climate change for a long time.   President Obama finally accepted the overwhelming scientific evidence, and has officially rec-ognized the growing threat of climate change. Obama's administration included many Wall Street executives which was, in part, responsible for his delay in address-ing the problem. The ongoing contradictions between the profit driven Capitalist class and the concerns of the people couldn't be more obvious than it is with climate change. It lays bare the class struggle of opposites for all to see.

The progressive people of my generation tried in earnest to approach many environmental concerns. There were a lot of successful victories such as ending the use of fluorocarbons which cause long term damage to the ozone layer, the Clean Air Act, many chemical clean ups and attempts to step back from the potential disasters of atomic energy. There were also many ad-vances made toward renewable energy such as solar and wind power, which are continuing today. But when it came to eliminating the burning of fossil fuels, the in-fluence of the oil, gas and coal industries were just too powerful. Although today there is a growing awareness of global warming and the fossil fuel emissions causing it, the powerful corporations of big oil continue to spread doubts, and resist any meaningful restrictions and regulations to stop or slow down the release of fos-sil fuels into the atmosphere.

The world scientific community has been telling us for several years now that the increases in global tem-peratures have noticeably risen since the beginning of the Industrial Revolution. The scientific community understands that human activity is responsible for the jump in world temperatures and climate change. Natu-ral cyclic changes in the climate are slow gradual changes that are barely noticeable at any given point in time, and are not clearly observable for many genera-tions. On the other hand just within the last half centu-ry global warming has produced the frightening effects of icebergs melting rapidly, the loss of species and many

more threatened, rising sea levels affecting human populations around the world, and unbelievable weather
patterns. Just in the last ten years the United States has
seen droughts, fires, flooding, tornadoes and hurricanes
reaching historical levels in frequency and intensity. On
a world basis the amount of high magnitude earth-
quakes is also increasing. All of these patterns have surfaced almost overnight. So it doesn't matter if there are
20% or 30% holdouts who are still in denial. You can
never get 90% or 100% of Americans to agree on anything. The majority of us know what is happening and
what is causing it, and it is our responsibility to speak
out and force change.

The fossil fuels industry has been doing everything
in its power for over 100 years to keep our citizens dependent on fossil fuels. In the Bay Area, around the
time I was born, the old Oakland Bay Bridge which con-
nects Oakland to San Francisco had rail tracks on it. It
was an early form of mass transit. The oil industry and
automobile industry successfully lobbied the local and
state governments to tear out the tracks and install all
roads on the bridge for the exploding automobile industry which was the oil industry's biggest emerging customer. They have been lobbying against mass transit
ever since and promoting the one or two or three cars
per family scenario. These are the same cars that have
brought our intercity freeways to a standstill in frustration and smog. I remember when Los Angeles and outlying communities were all equipped with electric
street cars, most of which were eliminated to make way
for the gas guzzling automobiles. (Today, in our cities,
there is a trend to bring back some of these electric
powered forms of public transportation.) Even as early
as 50 years ago, electric automobiles tried to make a
debut but were suspiciously collected, put out of circu-

lation in storage yards or destroyed and the production was stopped dead in its tracks. All these acts were done in the interest of the fossil fuel and automotive industries to keep society dependent on fossil fuel powered cars. That corporate influence is still with us today with continued lobbying attempts to preserve the energy industry profits and even roll back many of the environmental gains of the past. The fossil fuel industry has no social conscience on this question. Their only interest is to continue their profits and keep the world dependent on their product. They do this through denials, lies and through their overwhelming power over the political system. It's part of the "corporate state" I have referred to. They desire to exploit every last drop of oil and lump of coal from the earth before embracing the clean air technology we already have.

When the scientific evidence shows that the exploding changes in the world's climate have happened since the "Industrial Revolution," does that mean that the Industrial Revolution was responsible? Well, yes and no. Certainly the development of the internal combustion engine was a major technological blunder for scientific research with its resulting environmental impact on the planet. That is part of the imperfection in human beings and our science: we don't discover until later that we went in the wrong direction. The Manhattan project, the splitting of the atom, the atomic bomb and the so called non-polluting atomic energy is a classic example of acting first and figuring out the consequences later. But what if the Industrial Revolution had been directed in the interest of the public under Socialism rather than the exclusive profit driven interests of Capitalism? Would that have made a difference? Once we saw the changing air quality and early effects on human health, we might have been able to change directions away from fossil fuels. The Industrial Revolution, guided by Capitalist interests, did not consider these factors at all, even after the negative effects began to surface. But working from the premise that humans have caused global warming and climate change, what can we do about it?

Not only is climate change the single most serious social/political issue, it also stands far above all the other problems of society in *urgency.* Because this pending environmental disaster is now immediate it takes precedence over all the other political, social and economic problems, including terrorism. All the other issues are protracted struggles that, although serious, are not as pressing as climate change because of the potential consequences it presents to the world. So if we don't approach climate change immediately, with *our own direct action,* none of the other issues will matter. We need to take direct action on our own. We can no longer wait for the traditional political process which may never get there in time. At this point we may not be able to stop global warming from running its ultimate course, but we must do all that we can now, or resign ourselves to the possibility of eventual extinction.

We have to change our living habits and life styles now! The planet has made it very clear that it cannot handle our polluting way of life. Regardless of whether you believe that climate change was caused by the free market of Capitalism it doesn't matter. It also doesn't matter whether you believe that Capitalism eventually has to go and it doesn't matter if you are convinced of the need for Socialism. This is not just a political ideological struggle about the Capitalist economic system. This is a struggle to save the planet. We must stop the fossil fuel industry, or at least slow it down from spewing its products into the atmosphere. The struggle must

involve the actions of everyone who is currently convinced that the phenomenon of climate change is urgent
and is the result of burnt fossil fuels entering the atmosphere. Decreasing the *demand* for coal and petroleum products is the best way to counter the global
warming phenomenon. By eliminating or significantly
slowing down carbon emissions, we will leave the door
open to the developing market for clean energy technology, which is now positioned to gear up and become
the new energy industry once the end of fossil fuels becomes apparent. The problem has always been, for decades, the fossil fuel industry dragging their feet and undermining all of the efforts to switch to cleaner energy.
If left unchallenged the oil companies will keep the
world dependent on fossil fuels for generations to come.
Big oil corporations don't care what another 50 or 100
years of continued pollution to the atmosphere will do.
They can see no further than their balance sheets or the
next quarterly report. But the scientific community and
the people of the world know that we have to pull in
their reins now. The method of action I am talking
about is a determined *boycott* of all petroleum products,
including clothing, plastic items, and energy derived
from fossil fuels. We need to become more politically
and socially conscious shoppers, and much more conservative in the way we use all the energy sources that
come mostly from the burning of fossil fuels. Before I
offer some specific approaches to boycotting petroleum
based products, let's just take a brief look at the current
state of climate change and the scientific forecast.

    We have already set in motion the pattern that will
result in major changes to weather patterns, not yet experienced by civilization. These changes will be in the
nature of violent storms, increases in the sea level
which will make human dwelling in certain coastal re-

gions and island populations impossible. This will cause mass migrations and chaos. We are currently seeing droughts, flooding, fires and storms that are more frequent and severe than in past decades. These will only continue to increase in frequency and intensity. Although we cannot foresee all of the specifics of this revolt of Mother Nature, the effects will be severe enough to cause famines, social unrest with possible insurrections, and major economic problems. Although the poorest people of the world will suffer the most initially, in the long run your money won't be able to shield you from the changes that are in store for us. The troublesome world of the near future will not distinguish between the haves and the have not's, it will be "class" blind and for the first time the old saying "we are all in this together" will have some real meaning. These predictions by the scientific community are not forecasts that will start happening off in the future "by the end of the century" as was earlier predicted. It is happening now, much faster than what was thought only a few years ago. It is set in motion and rapidly progressing within a shorter time frame. The changes we are experiencing in the weather patterns might trigger some unforeseen and immediate event such as a permanent or prolonged power blackout in the energy grid or a violent mega storm over large portions of the planet. The only hope or potential bright spot still held by the environmental, scientific community, is that if we were to stop, or cut in half, the pumping of fossil fuels into the atmosphere right now then maybe we can slow down the pace of climate change and buy a little time. So there it is good people, the factual situation as it stands today. What if we fail? From a religious viewpoint, it will ironically be the greatest sin ever committed by the human species and quite likely the last one. It will also be the parting farewell from the otherwise laughing, arrogant and condescending free market Capitalists responsible for the situation. The lives of all species and all social classes are threatened, along with the beautiful little green emerald delicately afloat in space.

I am, at the same time, driven by anger against the system I believe caused this crisis, and also full of sadness over the situation which didn't have to be. But no matter how slim the prospects are for stopping this human created Armageddon there is always hope. That hope will have to be followed up by determination, sacrifice and direct action of all the clear thinking people to an extent that has never before been required by human beings. The biggest polluters in the world, the U.S., India and China, have finally recognized the reality of the problem and pledged to reduce fossil emissions. This is after decades of dragging their feet and lagging behind the curve of climate change awareness. But governments act too slowly and it will clearly have to be the people leading the effort. Direct action aimed at our government, to enact extreme environmental regulations cannot hurt, but the primary target for all direct action must be directed at the fossil fuel industry.

The three major fossil fuel vehicles of pollution are the smoke stack petroleum based industries of textiles and plastics, the fossil fuel powered electric generating plants, and the automobile. So, for instance, when we cut back on the use of our automobiles we are at the same time immediately reducing the emissions into the air and also the profits of the oil companies, both of which we want to do. The reason we want to cut back on oil company profits is we want to hurt them where it counts, in their bank accounts and balance sheets. This could force major changes in their attitudes and bring them to compromise. The major companies like Exxon,

Chevron, BP and Arco are stubbornly resistant to social concerns. Instead they consume a lot of time and money spreading lies and doubts of the seriousness of climate change and stifling all efforts at regulation. But the truth eventually comes to light. As Abraham Lincoln said, "you can't fool all of the people all of the time." Recently (2016) a group of students from the Columbia University Graduate School of Journalism broke the story that Exxon had done their own climate change study that confirmed that the burning of fossil fuels is causing global warming. Yet, with full knowledge of the truth, they continued to publicly question the science. This is reminiscent of the Tobacco industry knowing that smoking is addictive and causes cancer but openly challenging these facts for decades. At this date, the powerful Exxon Company is attempting to silence the study from Columbia University which exposes their willful deception. What more proof can any continuing doubters of the human causation of climate change need than the breaking story of Exxon's deceitful tactics? When armed with this truth people have an ethical basis to despise the oil industry and should have no reservations in pressuring them through boycotts and determined demonstrations. The major news stations are doing their typical role in not covering this Exxon story which has only been pursued somewhat by public radio. It's much more in the interest of the American news media to sensationalize terrorism than to offend their corporate advertisers and owners like General Electric who is a major shareholder of NBC. All large corporations have similar lack of ethical and social consciousness. There is a lot of truth to the Marxist view of Capitalism digging its own grave; right down to the last stubborn shovel in the ground.

Of course when we hurt any industry there will be a

loss of jobs. Well the loss of jobs has been an argument used against environmental reform for decades, so now we have to get past the consideration of job loss and force this industry to a more conciliatory and humble position. Clean energy technology is already creating new jobs and stands ready to go full bore on job creation. Besides, if we let climate change take its own course, according to the scientific and political think tanks on climate change, there will be even more widespread industrial and economic collapse, which I presume will cost jobs. The American people should have no sympathy for the conscious lies and smug arrogance of the Oil Industry. Let's get more specific now about the life style changes and the boycott.

The use of our automobiles should only be for the most absolute necessities, like getting to work. If you can car pool, take public transportation or ride a bicycle do it. It may be inconvenient and take more time and effort but just do it. When you get home from your job park that car and leave it in the driveway. If you are able to walk, then walk to the store, have your children bicycle to school and sporting events, or organize carpools for them. End the phenomenon of the single family soccer mom trips in the gas guzzling SUVs. In an effort to reduce the use of your car except as a last resort, we will all need to shrink our communities to 2 or 3 miles for all necessary services, not the 25 miles expanded by the use of the automobile. People did it for hundreds of years before the automobile. Buy your produce from local farmers markets. You will get better produce and eliminate the fossil fuel pollution from ocean steamers bringing produce to supermarkets from all over the world and adding heavily to atmospheric pollution. No you will not be able to get all the fruits and vegetables year round, so change you eating habits to correspond to locally grown products. Try to eat foods that are in season in your area. You will find that the food is better than imported food and you will learn to appreciate those fall apples and summer strawberries more. Didn't Al Gore say something about the _inconvenient_ truth? By the way, as you and your family will be spending more time at home, think seriously about cultivating a backyard or front yard garden which will supply you with the very best unmodified produce possible. The produce in the supermarkets are tasteless and lower in nutritional value compared to home grown. Many adults and most city children have never tasted anything but supermarket produce. No wonder encouraging kids to eat their vegetables is so difficult.

Are we talking sacrifice or just major lifestyle changes? Probably more lifestyle changes and less of a sacrifice. By walking, shopping locally, working in the garden and parking your car you will save lots of money and you will live longer and become healthier. That doesn't sound like much of a sacrifice. It sounds more like getting physically active and adopting smarter lifestyles which are healthier and can fight climate change at the same time. Some people, based on their individual situations, will have better luck with parking their car in the driveway than others, but everyone needs to do it as much as their situation will allow. A few people will be able to get rid of their cars. Whatever you do to reduce driving, let your friends know what and why you are doing it and solicit their support. Use social media to express your concerns and the actions you're implementing. You will be doing your role as an advocate or activist and probably make more friends and contacts for car-pooling; opening up more options when you need to venture outside of your community radius of 2 or 3 miles. Grocery cooperatives in your immediate neighborhoods are a good way to avoid trips to the supermarket and provide better tasting more nutritious fruits and vegetables. These grocery, or food, cooperatives purchase foods from local farmers markets and fill orders delivered to individual households. They have a long history in inner city communities. It involves individual households taking turns on filling orders and delivering the produce. It takes less time than cultivating your own garden, less use of individual automobiles and provides healthier produce. Food cooperatives can start with two or three families taking turns on going to the farmers markets and bakeries. They can grow to include whole neighborhoods. So just start changing your own family buying habits. The more individuals and family units change their life styles away from petroleum products the more effective the boycott will be. Many young single people are already living without an automobile and many poor people have never owned a car. I have met poor people who don't know how to ride a bicycle because they never owned a bike as a kid. In a worst case scenario, if the power grid goes down indefinitely, the people less dependent on fossil fuels for their cars, electricity etc. will be more seasoned to adjust to such a disaster than those who indulge in *fossil fuel technology* right up to the last moment. Your decision to adopt a more austere life style in advance will in essence make you a leader against climate change. You will have set an example for your friends and neighbors ahead of time so when a tough situation is imposed on everyone, people can look to you with hope because you will have demonstrated that life goes beyond the conveniences we have all taken for granted and think we can't live without. It will be those who have already lived without abundant energy availability, by necessity or choice that will have a calming effect on others and help prevent social anarchy out of despair and fear when the worst effects of climate change happen.

All products of the free market have a product life. The automobile is no exception. In the major cities cars are rapidly becoming an inefficient mode of transportation. The crowded freeways and traffic jams are now driving mass transit development. Where in the past the "powers that be" undermined the development of mass transportation today there are just too many cars for the metropolitan areas to accommodate. This fact, coupled with the environmental effects are bringing the product life of the automobile gradually to an end. Rural areas aren't faced with the same congestion problem and also have less access to public transportation. But the writing is on the wall. There is an effort to sell more hybrids and electric cars, but they too have no extended future. They congest the highways and city streets just as much, and even though they do not put out as much pollution in the air where they are driven, there is a ton of pollution pumped into the atmosphere where the fossil fuel generation plants created that electricity to charge them. So when you drive that electric car in Los Angeles don't be overly satisfied with your environmental contribution because you're still adding to the climate change problem in the atmosphere somewhere in Texas, or maybe West Virginia, every time you plug it in for a recharge. Although the end to the era of the automobile is becoming visible at the end of the tunnel, the urgency of global warming can't wait another 50 years.

This brings us to the other aspect of fossil fuel pollution. The use of electricity is equally or more destructive than the automobile. Most of the electricity is generated around the country by the burning of *oil, coal and natural gas*, by the smoke stack turbo electric generating plants. It takes a lot of automobile tail pipes to match the amount of carbon pumped into the air by these monster smoke stacks. The smoke stack industries around the world are also what is creating petroleum products like iPhones and cheap polyester clothing.

So you park your car in the drive way for the weekend pledging not to use it except for an emergency, and then we go into our homes and engage in a 72 hour assault on the environment. Television's blaring in every room, computers sucking up energy for hours, air conditioners running all night and video games, yes those beloved video games. Lights on in vacant rooms and all of this goes on into the wee hours of the night and early morning. It's an onslaught of electronic entertainment indulgence that has replaced physical activity with the couch potato syndrome of overweight Americans. It's not just costing you money in huge electric bills, that's the least concern of all home electric use. It's contributing to the smoke stack pollution of oil, natural gas and coal burning electric generation plants which is driving global warming. Electronic digital entertainment, with its lack of physical activity, is a main contributor to the growing health problems of children and young adults. So step back from all of those video games. Sure they are a great escape. But one of the things you are escaping from is facing up to climate change that is being aggravated by addiction to the digital screens and virtual reality, all of which is promoted by commercial interests and repetitive advertising. If you get away from all the digital screens you won't be subjected to as much advertising. I remember an instance when I was working in a local *Occupy* planned event and a group of young activists didn't show up for their role in the event because they got hung up in a group session of video games and literally could not tear themselves away from the game. I would say that is an unhealthy addiction. Many of the video games are also violent combat games that train and encourage some young people to continue the internet violence in the military bunkers directing drones to kill people they don't even know. Don't be so naïve to think that there isn't a conscious effort, with the corporations who design these violent video games, to start preparing children to fight wars that support their economic expansion abroad. Setting war aside, don't we have enough violence right here at home without further encouraging it? So the game continues. Really, come on, unplug those polluting electronic devices that are directly or indirectly burning fossil fuels; grab a basketball and head for the courts or play catch in the back yard. Take a step back from the unhealthy aspect of the digital world and experiment with the real physical outdoor world. Bicycle to the park and get out into nature and live a physical life instead of an exclusive sedentary one. Who knows maybe you can prevent a heart attack at 30 or diabetes at 15. Anything but sitting around mesmerized to a digital screen growing fat and physically impaired while at the same time bringing the planet to an early end! Come on parents, take charge, and get the kids out of the house while there is still air to breath. Discipline them to step back from their computer screens and have real contacts and relationships with their peers. This separation from the environment and the physical world is part of the blind side to climate change and shows a lack of human understanding of our dependence on the environment we are destroying. What's that, you say that you did the same thing when you were their age and in fact you still are playing video games or other forms of digital addiction? Well there you go, I rest my case. Our energy consuming habits and their effect on the environment and our minds and bodies have been a long time in the making. My mother use to call the television set an "idiot box" because if you watch it long enough you will become an idiot. She was no dummy. I think smart phones have the same effect today, they are certainly a lot smarter than the bulk of people who are addicted to them. Seriously though, there is too much digital activity in our lives. We carry them with us wherever we go and can't turn them off even when we are driving, sleeping, eating or having a live personal conversation; talk about a dangerous and rude addiction! So like anything else in our lives whether its video games or ice cream, the answer is "moderation" as opposed to hedonism or unchecked self-indulgence.

So here is the austere target plan for changing your life style in the home full of electrical goodies. You really do need a refrigerator and hot water heater, at least as long as there still is a power grid to support them. But turn them both down to the point where the food won't spoil and you can at least have a lukewarm shower. When it gets dark, go to bed, and don't get into your car and start driving around or indulging in aimless, late night, television and internet obsessiveness. Both driving around in your car and late night television/computer indulgence contribute to fossil fuels going into the atmosphere and causing climate change. When you turn your electricity off, turn it all off. Don't leave those little red and green lights on your electrical outlets, computer, and stereo equipment burning all night and day. If you just can't sleep go for an evening walk or get a lite for your bicycle with a reflector and meet your friends in a lighted public place. I can tell you one thing, if you go to bed early you will get up early, unless you have a drug problem, and you will discover a whole new interesting world. Imagine the sun rising, wouldn't that be a novelty? Or what about the birds singing? Hey there is first time for everything. This is the way that people lived in previous generations before the industrial revolution and in many ways it was a lot healthier world. So do what is humanly possible within your own family unit. Text your situation and concerns and new life style to your friends or actually talk to them in person and start the withdrawal from the internet screen addiction by initiating real life contact.

Are there any more drastic recommendations I can think of? Sure there are, but remember, we are past the point of only recycling plastic and aluminum cans or using energy efficient light bulbs. We are at a point of not purchasing plastic, petroleum based products in the first place or constantly trashing them for new models. We need to use less light bulbs instead of just energy efficiency ones. All of the cell phones today are made of petroleum products and many people feel they must purchase all the yearly upgrades. Not so! My cell phones last me 5-10 years! Yours can too. All these petroleum products, including clothing other than all cotton, wool, silk, linen and hemp are driving the profits of big oil companies and contributing to global warming; polyester clothing is all petroleum derived. Because we are talking about a pending planetary disaster we need to think in terms of big drastic changes to the way we live and shop. So stop flying in commercial airlines, right now! Commercial airlines burning fossil fuels pump out 2 to 3 times more global warming chemicals per passenger per mile than automobiles. The commercial airlines industry is a big contributor to the bank accounts of big oil companies because they purchase huge amounts of fossil fuels. If everyone could stop flying for an indefinite time it would make a big difference in carbon emissions and really hurt the sales and profits of the fossil fuel industry. Again we can't let job concerns take precedence over basic human survival. There are more _planned_ job losses through Capitalist automation in all industries than will result from job losses in the fossil fuel and related industries. Besides many of the jobs lost by reduced use of fossil fuels will be replaced by clean energy jobs. The world environmental movement would be far better off if people never set foot in a Walmart super store. In addition to the way they treat their employees they pretty much specialize in petroleum plastic products imported from China and 90% of their clothing is made of synthetic petroleum products. The next time you see a film clip of the unbelievable air polluted industrial centers in China be aware that this terrible pollution is created by American buying habits and Walmart is their biggest customer.

In my experience of boycotting I am convinced that the consumer boycott is a very effective tool of direct action. Years ago I helped organize a secondary boycott of the old Mervyns store because they were selling a line of bath towels produced by one of the old garment industries, J.P. Stevens, in the South. The J. P. Stevens workers were organizing a union and were requesting a boycott of the J.P. Stevens line of towels and wash cloths. Mervyns was one of the main distributors of the product line on the West Coast and we organized a boycott of the Mervyns stores in the Bay Area. As a result of the boycott of Mervyns, which involved several marches and demonstrations outside their stores, Mervyns threatened to drop the product line if J.P. Stevens didn't settle with their workers. Within a few months, J. P. Stevens became a union shop with better benefits for everyone. So give the boycott a try in your own buying habits. It is a very effective tool that doesn't need the support of the politicians. If you are an activist, organizing type of individual then by all means organize a boycott effort outside your family setting. There currently is a movement on the University campuses by students to get the Universities to divest their investments from the big oil companies all around the issue of climate change. If you are able to contribute money I would recommend organizations like the National Resources Defense Council and the Sierra Club, all of whom have climate change at or near the top of their priorities. We are, for better or worse, a consumer society under Capitalism, so in the interest of fighting climate change, let's turn this consumer society against the system that is causing it. So many of the technical gadgets that are dependent on the electrical grid are not actually needed, but are driven by the relentless advertising of our consumer society under Capitalism which makes us *want* things so bad that we feel we *need* them. So many of the things that Americans spend their money on, they really don't need. Consumers can buy and consumers can refuse to buy. Remember, all of the digital gadgets including televisions, computer games, trash cans, plastic bags, as well as much of the clothing are all made of petroleum products which are products of the smoke stack polluters and the big oil companies. So re-evaluate your consumer habits and cut back on plastic products as well as synthetic clothing products. There are alternatives to petroleum products. Become a smart, environmental shopper and help save the planet. Boycott!

I usually get up around 5 am, but this morning I woke at 4am to the rain. Rain in the high desert of California is becoming rarer every year, as California is witnessing its worst drought in 50 years. Global warming is reducing the level of the water tables all over the world, and water shortages will grow as climate change progresses. If your normal weather patterns are for hot summers and mild winters, with climate change it will probably get hotter and less snow and rain. If you live in areas where you have mild summers and severe winters with lots of rain and snow, then under climate change you will get more extremes of the same pattern. I guess that's why they started calling it climate change, because although the overall temperature of the planet is rising, the effects are different depending on where you live. Listening to the news last night they were reporting on an early snow storm in Buffalo, New York. They have gotten 7 feet of snow in two days, which is equal to the average total snow fall for the entire season and it has come very early and all at once. A half a dozen people were caught out in the blizzards and died. The roofs of homes were caving in due to the weight. A school bus with a girls' basketball team was completely buried but was located and dug out in time. I understand all the cell phone calls from the students helped locate the bus. I guess that as long as the towers remain intact cell phones may save a lot of lives in the future and probably already have, unless people run down their batteries with senseless, compulsive texting.

I went to bed last night wondering if the extreme actions I was suggesting, like stop driving cars and going to bed early in a frantic effort to reduce electrical use and hurt the fossil fuel industry were unrealistic. My feelings were that although they require sacrifices and changes in living habits, they are not an overkill and that is exactly the level of action that is needed. I woke up this morning in the hopes that the scientific community was wrong in its assessment of climate change. I understood at that moment why some people won't accept it, they just can't. They don't want to and in some cases just can't accept that fact that the planet is dying. A lot of people will die without having ever understood what the planet is about and our role and dependency on nature. That to me is very sad and is becoming one of the negative characteristics of the current generations; their isolation from nature. The inability of some of us to accept the facts of climate change is similar to the acceptance that we are mortal. I feel this myself and just don't want it to be true, although on second thought I realize, that like it or not, it is true. So as I go on throughout the day my hope is that we can still save enough of the life supporting abilities of the planet to continue on in life, although under different circumstances and life styles than before. In these moments of weakness and sadness my human emotions take hold and my hope changes to wishing that it just isn't true and can't be happening. But those moments help me to understand why so many others are outwardly in denial, but inside must be filled with the fear, sadness and the realization that it is really happening. We are all different. My life has been one of candidly and brazenly facing the injustices of the world. I am a confronter, and not one for sticking my head in the sand, which has caused me a lot of frustration and made my life a lot harder than it could have been. But that is the way I am, and I have never been inclined to change that part of my personality. Although I have learned that some things are clearly out of our control, many things are not. The question of climate change is something that we caused so, therefore, it should be something we can correct. Although I have hopes, I don't have a lot of confidence in people taking the necessary action. I feel that if we all immediately changed our life styles we could turn things around but whether we will is another question. When it comes to nature we have come to believe that we are above nature and can control and manipulate it, when in reality we are a part of nature, we were born out of nature, just like all the other living species. We need to give more thought to how we can fit into our role and respect rather than change our environment. But maybe we have strayed too far, because it appears that nature is taking charge of the situation. The traditional Native Americans, as well as other nature based religions, viewed the world more along these lines. On the other hand, Christianity encourages the view that humans are above the other creatures and has contributed to an arrogant view towards nature. If we can somehow survive this current crisis we can learn from our mistakes and become more aware of our place in the natural environment.

I can't let my discussion of climate change end without commenting on the "fracking" process in oil and gas exploration. We all should be aware now how this process is polluting our ground water supply with the chemicals used in the process as well as the nasty pools of toxic fluids left on the surface. The fracking process itself has created new sources of oil and gas which has extended the life of fossil fuels. This could slow down the conversion to renewable and clean energy. Many of these fracking operations are located near residential neighborhoods. Recently a community in Texas with concerns over fracking have initiated legal procedures to stop the process near their neighborhood. The oil companies are fighting the legal suit on the grounds that it interferes with their "private property rights." You would think that the health concerns of the public would be more important than the companies' private property rights. Ethical and moral grounds would certainly support the communities concerns. But Capitalist laws based on private property do not consider moral and ethical issues. Again we see how the concept of private property continues to serve mostly the interest of a wealthy few.

I have attempted to encourage other ways to fight climate change in addition to the necessary confrontation with politicians and corporations head on through demonstrations and marches of peaceful civil disobedience. Although this has proven to be a successful approach, not everyone will be willing to take to the streets over something like climate change, where the worst effects are yet to come. People are more likely to march over social and economic issues which strike closer to home and leave them no choice. This being said there are growing demonstrations around the world to force our leaders to take more immediate steps to eliminate fossil fuel based energy sources. My above suggestions offer an alternative, and are also a very effective way, of combating climate change. Boycotts have been a highly successful form of political free speech under Capitalism. It's a method of direct action that corporate American cannot ignore.

I don't presume that everyone will be able to change their life styles in all of the ways I have suggested. Young people and single people may be able to eliminate automobiles completely from their lives. Many have already turned to bicycling and public transportation. But everyone should be able to pick two or three items from my boycotting ideas and change their habits to one extent or another. I am sure there are other ways to reduce the use of fossil fuels once you start brainstorming. I have only mentioned some of the more obvious ways. So whether you get rid of your car, reduce your driving, change your buying habits, cutback of your use of electricity, or take to the streets in protest against the "corporate state" and demand change, it is your choice. But to remain in a state of complacency and escape is not an option. The clock is ticking on global warming and the hour is running late.

America has been slow to embrace the reality of climate change. Those lost years during the George W. Bush Administration will continue to haunt us. The year 2000 was the time for environmental leadership. Al Gore was the environmental leader that history needed. Instead we got a President who promoted false science. In the past we were misled. Today we know the truth. The question is what are we going to do about it? But now let's leave the sad issue of climate change and return to the struggle in the workplace.

CHAPTER SIXTEEN

The Garage Gang and Local 1440
of the United Steel Workers Union

There once was a general foreman that worked at the U.S. Steel Plant in Pittsburg California. Let's just call him Nick Nasty. Nick was not just a shift foreman, he was a manager foreman who had many foremen working for him. His next promotion would have been department superintendent: a promotion he never received. I don't know why I have changed his name but I decided, with few exceptions, not to use anyone's real name in this book. That decision is mostly to protect the innocent and the good guys who may still have some lingering government files from an ever increasing intrusive government. But even with the bad guys, like Nick Nasty, I still changed his name. No sense in giving the jerk any notoriety, even if of an unfavorable nature. All the government security agencies are nowadays mostly concerned with the violence of terrorism but they will always be on the watch for anyone of Socialist leaning because that is where the long term threat to the status quo is. So why help them compile or update information on people, which is no more than an infringement of privacy? Let them review this book and update my files if they care to, but not on other people I have associated with. The one exception to not using real names was Joe Navaro, the president of the Molders Union. His role in leading the Molders in the 70s was public knowledge and he deserves the same positive recognition in working class history as he received in the Bay Area from the community of political activists and union members at the time.

But I digress. Let's get back to Nick Nasty. Nick represented the epitome of a self-interest driven foreman who delighted in making life miserable for the hard working employees he supervised. In my widely diversified working career, I have only met a couple of supervisors who even came close to the degenerate lack of ethics he displayed. The first day I came to work at U.S. Steel, hired as a mobile equipment mechanic, I started hearing all the complaints about foreman Nick: how he took pleasure in messing with people; how he was a crook who was stealing from the company; and just about every despicable characteristic you can imagine. Immediately, I joined into the existing struggle against Nick Nasty. The company and Nick spotted me as pro-union and as an activist (or trouble maker as the company term is for anyone who challenges their authority) almost from the start, and my pay was frozen as an intermediate mechanic for nearly the full 7 years I worked there. Yes, anyone who questions company policies is subject to discrimination, similar to the discrimination towards minorities and women. There was a union representative in the shop but he was mostly interested in his own advancement and wellbeing. Specifically, he was trying to get the parts man's job which was soon to become available through attrition. It was a prized job for advancement of mechanics where you didn't have to get your hands dirty anymore. Brownie had to stay on Nick's good side because the parts man's job rested in the hands of Mr. Nasty. So union representative Brownie (for brown nose) would sit in foreman Nick Nasty's office for hours having religious and good ol' boy discussions while the rest of us worked on the equipment. Brownie's favorite response to any worker who had a complaint was "you really don't have a valid grievance and there is nothing I can do." Even though I didn't, at the time, have any union representative status I began my thing of organizing the men in defiance to Nick Nasty's authority by fanning the flames of dissent that were already there and encouraging things like slowdowns in response to Nasty's different attacks on the workers in his department.

A memorable and typical example of Nick's skullduggery was an episode he initiated with Ramon, a helper who had worked in the battery shop for many years. Foreman Nick called Ramon into his office for an ass chewing session. By this time I had received union representation status. I think Ramon had missed a couple of days of work the week before, and foremen Nasty was looking for an excuse to harass someone. Ramon had a terribly, unhealthy job switching out batteries on the mobile equipment. He breathed in toxic chemicals all day and the heat level in his work area was out of sight. Ramon was truly skilled at his job and very safety conscious. But that's the way foreman Nasty was. Messing with people was a form of pastime and amusement to Nick's demented character. By the way, Ramon was a Mexican who had clearly expressed dislike for Nick's treatment of the workforce. I am sure this influenced Nick's decision to single out Ramon on this occasion. Racially motivated prejudice varied from subtle to overt between a mostly white supervising force and the hourly minority employees. Ramon's righteous outspokenness against Nick, although in private, surely reached Nick's attention through the grapevine. Although everyone in the shop expressed some sort of resentment towards Nick, the fact that Ramon was a minority, a lower paid worker as well as a critic, probably sealed the deal in Nick's decision to pick on Ramon that day. Well he had Ramon in the office for over an hour, jacking him up and making him feel insecure about his job. When he thought he had Ramon's blood pressure elevated sufficiently he then sent him down to see the company doctor. When I say "company" doctor I mean a philosophical doctor who did the bidding of management and had long forgotten his Hippocratic Oath. The doctor was notified that Ramon was on the way to his office with a heads up opinion of the situation.   The doctor talked to Ramon for a few minutes, took his blood pressure and sent him home because he was unfit for work. The reason: his blood pressure was very high and he seemed too upset and riled to perform his job. So Nasty had done his dirty work for the day and taught Ramon a lesson about missing work by making him stay home and miss more work and pay. Nasty wanted to fire Ramon but had no contractual justification for a firing. Quite frankly, I think Nick would have missed having Ramon around to pick on. So he had gotten his satisfaction by using the "company doctor." This was the kind of guy Nick Nasty was. I decided from that day on I was committed to running Nick out of the plant and making his life miserable until he was gone.

Want to know a little more about the company doctor? Well, he had a reputation for doing stuff like this for many years and many complaints had been raised against him in the union meetings. He was notorious for giving people pain pills and sending them back on the job when they actually needed time off and additional medical attention. Several years later the company doctor's life was sadly ended by some worker he had messed with. The worker came into the doctor's office with a shot gun and shot him point blank. There was righteous shock from the plant workforce over this terrible act of terror, but a lot more sympathy for the worker's fate than tears for the deceased doctor, because everyone knew about his unethical practices for many years. I think that, along with the shock of an extremely violent act, there was a sort of cold feeling of "what goes around comes around." This terrible incident actually happened after I had left U. S. Steel, but seeing as we were on the subject of the infamous doctor it seemed now was the time to reveal his ultimate fate. This is a terrible story, but I thought people who have never worked in a factory or production atmosphere should know about the terrible oppression that the system brings down on the workforce. This has been happening on the job, and in the poor communities since day one. Many company doctors are hired for their political beliefs and are nowadays kept on retainer and used by companies for their knowledge of medical legal suits and preparing reports on employees that favor the employers, when an employee is suing an employer or even applying for workman's compensation. So the derogatory term of "company doctor" extends beyond the poor medical treatment administered to workers. When events like an actual murder in the workplace reaches the news media there never is complete coverage of what leads up to tragedies like this. It's just "another act of a worker going postal upon an innocent victim." The relationship between foreman Nick Nasty and the company doctor is just one of the many ways that the Capitalist's push for more production and profits, in this case through the overuse of pain pills and the push for forced overtime. Most foremen in the "Mill" would have ignored Ramon's absence and been glad that he was back on the job. But Nick Nasty was not in the group of most foremen. He was always looking for any excuse he could find to exercise his abuse of authority. When Ramon came to me about what had happened I went down to the doctor's office and had a talk with him regarding his role in Ramon's case. The doctor said his job was "to keep people on their job with as little pain as possible." When I told him what Ramon had gone through with an hour of grilling by Nick and it was no wonder that Ramon was upset, he said he wasn't aware of that. Ramon had witnessed Nick's call to the doctor when he suggested he might want to check Ramon's blood pressure. That was at the basis of the doctor's unpopularity: the over use of addictive pain killers and disregard as to whether they needed time off and other medical attention, along with complete cooperation with managerial agendas. Although we'll never know the motive for the above terrible act of violence against the doctor it could have been the result of the workers state of mind due to prescribed drug addiction. For many years, the union had been complaining to the company over the doctor's overuse of pain killers. The sad truth is that sometimes people just lose control and freak out, resulting in terrible acts upon innocent people. The term nowadays is just going "postal," or "terrorism" in the workplace, without any follow up on the workplace conditions that may have contributed to this kind of unforgivable action.

Getting back to the struggle against Foreman Nasty. Nick had authority over the "tractor shop" inside the mill and the "garage" outside the mill. When I got to be a nuisance to him in the tractor shop he transferred me outside to the garage. Nick spent most of his time inside the mill where he could keep an eye on anything he could steal. Oh, yes, there were many stories about flatbed trucks with rolls of steel with phony bills of lading leaving the mill to Nick's *special* customers. Apparently, Nick was padding his pockets big time. The garage, on the other hand, was run almost entirely by one of Nick's older experienced foremen who was very popular with the garage employees. So for a while it was nice not to have Nick around. The guys in the garage were well aware of Nick's anti-worker activities but were shielded somewhat from him. The older garage foreman was well liked and pretty much ran the shop including everything from managing the work force functions of equipment maintenance to the scheduling of the personnel. Soon after, I was assigned to the garage, still working as an intermediate mechanic at about a dollar less an hour, I became the new grievance man for the maintenance workforce in the plant. The maintenance department was mostly skilled and semi-skilled workers. This encompassed about 800 workers out of a workforce of around 2000 employees. The maintenance department included the tractor shop, the garage and many other departments. This gave me more legitimacy in my activist activities and a lot more freedom to move around the plant. I was kept busy with grievances regarding safety issues, unjust firings, harassment etc. throughout the plant with considerable success. The negotiated contract between U.S. Steel and the Steel Workers Union was a good contract except for the no-strike clause. But on the bright side the union, by giving up the right to strike, had gained a lot more to say about working conditions and a little more to say in the running of the workforce. The company, however, was never happy and reinterpreted the contract language to benefit their authority. Former union representative Brownie had played his role in letting this happen. But when I became the union rep (grievance man), I started reinterpreting the contract in its literal sense as it had been originally intended. I was having considerable success and was able to file more legitimate grievances on behalf of the workforce. People with problems, who were previously told by the union that they didn't have a case and there was nothing the Union could do were now being embraced. There was a new man on the job. When the old garage foreman retired, general foreman Nick Nasty decided he was going to take a more active hand in running the garage like he had done in the tractor shop. This is where the real battle against Nick Nasty began. The garage gang was ready for him and they had a leader. That would be me.

The guys in the garage were a good bunch of guys. As it turns out, they had a lot more fighting spirit than the men in the tractor shop. I think this is mostly because Brownie, the previous union grievance man, worked in the tractor shop and had essentially siphoned off the dissent with his non-combative attitude. The working conditions in the garage were like utopia compared to the tractor shop which was in the middle of the huge mill where the air reeked of chemicals and heat. It was hard to breathe in the mill, let alone see as the cloud of chemicals restricted both of these bodily functions. The companies had been able to rewrite California's OSHA laws so that OSHA could not come into a plant unannounced but had to schedule an appointment. If you ever went to work and found relatively clean air it was probably because OSHA was scheduled for that day and the production process had been curtailed. But in the garage we were out in the fresh air with the several bay doors open. I had made some close friends among the garage guys and over the course of the struggle with Nick Nasty we pretty much stuck together. There was one friend whom I'll call Miguel. Miguel was about 10 years younger than I was, he was Puerto Rican and a Viet Nam combat veteran. He had suffered his share of post-traumatic stress disorder (PTSD) from his months on a small patrol boat on the Mekong Delta River in Viet Nam, being shot at daily. We had a common base in that we had both been in the Navy but I had been far luckier and never had been in combat. He was a tremendous fighter in the garage struggle, completely trustworthy and fearless like myself. He became my best friend and he always had my back. When Nick Nasty took over, he immediately started doing his thing. He hired personal friends from the outside and denied testing and promotion from within and instead hired through nepotism. People don't like change, especially when there is no reason for change. Nick started initiating unnecessary and extremely unpopular changes, like scheduling the "garage gang" with split days off. I don't know if he couldn't schedule the workforce, of about 20 mechanics and several helpers, or if this was just another example of his liking to mess with people. Most likely it was the latter because the old garage foreman had no problem. Nick also may have been able to increase his management bonus by operating with fewer employees as a result of his work schedule changes. The bonus plan for foremen, supervisors and managers is one of the plans used in all industries, white collar and blue collar. It appeals to the selfish individualism within people to get a bigger piece of the pie and always at the expense of the workforce. In my work history I have come to the conclusion that promotions are seldom based on the result of hard work and ability but rather on whether your allegiance is to the company and if you are more selfishly concerned with your own individual financial situation. The companies call this "a proper attitude." Regardless of his motives, the effects of not having two days off in a row disrupted our personal lives big time. I jumped in Nick's face immediately on this problem and became his worst and reoccurring nightmare. I started flooding him with grievances from in the garage and back over in the tractor shop. He wouldn't settle on any of the complaints so I would immediately pursue the process and push the written grievances upward to the Superintendent of Maintenance. The superintendent's name was Sig and he didn't like having to deal with all these problems. He expected his general foreman to handle the day to day problems. I had heard from rumors that Sig didn't like Nick Nasty for whatever reason. Sig once asked me what it was going to take to get peace in the garage. By then, there was a lot of disruption in the garage. There were work slowdowns and mechanics flooding the union meeting and even incidents where some of the equipment was being sabotaged and breakdowns of needed mobile equipment necessary for the movement of the product. I told him that there would never be peace in the garage as long as Nick Nasty was there. I was playing the card of my insider knowledge that he didn't like Nick anyway and had the authority to remove him if he wanted to and could justify it. So the garage gang was giving him the justification he needed.

Anytime I sat down in a grievance meeting with the company regarding Nick Nasty, or with other company representatives in the Mill, I did my thing with the contract interpretation but I always alluded to the power of the workforce behind me, insinuating that people would take matters into their own hands, if the company wouldn't compromise and settle the issues. The company also knew I would organize this dissent if necessary. I was just a leader but the real power was the people, something I hung my belief on and still do to this day. This is what made me an effective union rep and activist. I had people behind me, especially in the garage and the company knew it and hated to go up against such a person. I couldn't be bought off or influenced by the company and they knew it. This is something they hadn't had to deal with for a long time. Workers throughout the plant knew there was a new union man on the job and they all knew of the ongoing fight in the garage against Nick Nasty. I had an old timer in another department tell me that I was the toughest grievance man he had seen since Harold Dillon, almost 20 years before my time. One day, I decided to escalate the struggle against foreman Nasty and wrote an inflammatory article for the local union paper about what was going on in the garage and specifically naming general foreman Nick Nasty. Copies of that article made it back east to U. S. Steel corporate offices. Superintendent Sig had the justification, and now the pressure was on him to handle Nick. Around that time, Nick called me into his office. He was clearly upset and had trouble holding his composure. The garage gang that was around were looking through the glass windows of the office trying to hear the conversation. He had two of his foremen with him. One of them I knew didn't like Nick either. Nick made a few derogatory remarks to me. One of his remarks was, what do I do when I go home at night, kick my dog? I told him I didn't even have a dog and if I did I wouldn't kick it and besides I had him to kick around. I turned to walk out the door and the small crowd outside scattered. Nick asked me in an almost tearful way "what did I want from him?" The arrogance in him was gone. At times, he had been cocky and intimidating, even with me, and I am not easily intimidated. He had not been an easy person to confront. With this new approach to me, I knew we had won. I turned around to him, looked him right in the eye and said "I want you gone from this Mill." I turned and walked out.

That was the last contact I had with general foreman Nick Nasty. It had been a long struggle and had taken the courage of many others like Miguel. A few days later Nick had tendered his resignation for early retirement which was accepted. I assume he was bitter about losing his job and all the perks he had manipulated out of the mill in the form of dishonest money. But I had no sympathy for him. He had dug his own grave and hurt a lot of innocent people along the way. So this ends my struggle at U.S. Steel. I was tired, I was burned out. I stuck around for about a year and cleaned up some pending grievances one of which was my own grievance about lower pay which was a discrimination issue because of my union activity. I was given a bench test for full journeyman (which was the first bench test ever given as the promotion was always automatic). I had to rebuild a small four cylinder engine. Because I had gotten a couple of mechanic helpers promoted to mechanic they then moved ahead of me on the mechanic's seniority list. So when the need for seasonal layoffs came, I was laid off. I knew this would probably happen when I fought for their promotion, so I guess I would be considered to be too self-sacrificing by most people and a little too altruistic, but that's the way I am. I live by my Marxist principles of "sharing and community" as opposed to the Capitalist philosophy of "individualism and looking out solely for yourself (selfishness)." I don't expect every person to hold these same values. Indeed, most don't. The economic situations demands that we be more practical due to the necessities of struggling to survive in an unforgiving atmosphere. Sometimes a person has to turn a blind side to workplace oppression in order to look out for their families. Sometimes my altruism works against my own interests which I guess is what altruism is all about. But it's one of my values and I have no trouble looking in the mirror in the morning while some others might. Anyway I had been laid off before but this time I applied for my severance package which the company was glad to give me just to get rid of me. I think about U. S. Steel from time to time. I worked longer at U.S. Steel than any job I ever had. I keep in touch with my old buddy Miguel who lives hundreds of miles away. He still suffers from his time on the front lines in View Nam which will always be a struggle for him as it is for most combat veterans. I even wonder about the contract specialist that human resources hired because of me. Did they fire her after I left? Did they find another "company doctor" or did they learn from their mistakes and hire a more reasonable person as his replacement? Or could they even find a doctor to step into a situation like that? The poor guy he probably wasn't very apt at his profession. Maybe it was the only job he could find. I couldn't believe it when I heard about the shooting, and I didn't even know the worker who did it. Mostly I reflect on all the guys I worked with and struggled with and the camaraderie we had together. I feel that I really did contribute to society in that job. I also know that oppression far worse than at U.S. Steel is continuing in many workplaces throughout the world. So I made some improvements, saved a few jobs, got a few people promoted and raised the dignity of many especially the garage gang. I also gave U.S. Steel a taste of the power of the masses. But the monster is still alive and well and goes by the name of "The Free Market." Freedom to buy, freedom to sell, freedom to invest, freedom to exploit others and the freedom to be exploited

CHAPTER SEVENTEEN

The Code Names Are the Free Market and the Private Sector

The terms "Capitalism" and "Private Property" even today are not widely used by Journalists, politicians and economists through the news media. These terms are too straightforward and to the point, and often bring to mind their opposites which are "Socialism" and "public property." The spokespeople and the owners of the media would rather avoid drawing attention to the two main economic systems: Capitalism and Socialism, especially when discussing economic problems in the United States. So instead they use **code names** such as the *"free market"* when referring to Capitalism and the *"private sector"* when referring to private property interests. These code names have a more friendly sound and are also somewhat misleading.

My use of the term "code names" is similar to the term "doublespeak" which grew out of a central theme from George Orwell's book *1984*. The central concept of the book was "doublethink," Orwell's own term. Parallels have also been drawn between doublespeak and Orwell's classic essay Politics and the English Language which discusses the distortion of language for political purposes. So doublespeak and code names deliberately disguise the nature of the truth and are used particularly in regard to politics. In fact code names and doublespeak are a shrewd form of mind control. They are meant to distort the meaning in order to win approval or disapproval of key political issues.

The Free Market

Let's look a little closer at the term "free market." What does it actually mean, and what are the intended implications of using the term "free" in relation to the market economy of Capitalism? First, when referring to the market as "free" we are not only referring to the Capitalist market, we are promoting a particular approach to the Capitalist market. Of course all varieties of market Capitalism have their roots in private property interests, but the "free market" term has more specific implications. It implies the unrestricted, unregulated or laissez-faire sort of Capitalist market: a government hands-off form of Capitalism. The Marxist term for a laissez-faire unregulated economy is "unbridled Capitalism." That is truly the American brand of Capitalism; deregulated, hands off, laissez-faire Capitalism.

Secondly the word "free" when used to describe the market has strong, intended, political implications as well. Keep in mind that there are two systems in the United States. There is the <u>economic system</u> of Capitalism and the <u>political system</u> of constitutional democracy and the "Bill of Rights." Within the political system, free or freedom has positive implications such as, freedom of speech, freedom of movement, freedom of religion, freedom to vote or a free country. Transferring this patriotic term over to the economic system is intended to lend a righteous, patriotic meaning to Capitalism (thus the "free market"). The spokespeople don't say "the unrestricted market of private interests" which would be a more accurate definition. Instead they say "the free market." Thus we have doublespeak or a more favorable code name.

Is this free market good for the majority of people? Political reality answers with a resounding "no!" We can see what the free market of Wall Street and the mortgage/banking practices did to the people of the country and the world in 2008. It nearly caused a total collapse of the Capitalist system. Looking at the specific history of the laissez-faire, unregulated form of the free market the realities are brought into focus. In the early 1980s Ronald Reagan turned the country away from the New Deal which had imposed far reaching regulations over the private sector as a result of the 1929 Great Depression. Reagan's philosophy of "trickle down" and "deregulation" of corporate America took hold in both major political parties. By signing the Gramm-Leach-Bliley act of 1999 the Clinton Administration repealed the Glass Steagall Act of 1933. The repealed bill had been in effect since the Great Depression and it had restricted the practices of big banks and Wall Street. It specifically prohibited the merging of commercial banking and investment banking. This repeal of the Glass Steagall Act, and other deregulations, opened the flood gates to uninhibited financial speculation in banking, Wall Street and mortgage lending which, 10 years later, resulted in the 2008 collapse. The majority of our citizens have still not regained what was economically lost during the crises and probably never will. Only the very wealthy benefited from this deregulated "free" market.

So the code name free market really implies good ol' American freedom. It also suggests that the unrestricted, government hands off, Capitalist markets are better. It further implies that a controlled or government regulated market is bad, un-patriotic and against the political idea of freedom in America. None of these assertions is correct. So the real intention of code names, such as the free market, is to confuse people and get them to approve of a concept that is against their own interests. It is the politically motivated, subtle, subliminal and deceptive form of brainwash that Orwell meant with his term doublethink.

The Private Sector

Now let's take a closer look at another closely relat-ed code name: the *private sector*. The "private *sector*" has become a vague and misleading way of referring to the economic system of private property. The use of the word "*sector*" implies that privately owned interests are a part of our <u>political system</u>. It's like saying that our <u>political system</u> of constitutional democracy has a pri-vate sector and a public sector. This is not true. There is no private sector within our governmental political system. Our government (our political system) is a completely different system from the economic system of private property Capitalism. Our political system is publically owned and supposedly run in the interest of, and by, the American public. The economic system of Capitalism, on the other hand, is owned and run in the sole interest of powerful individuals and entities within the private community. The government political sys-tem is supposed to be the overseer of all things affecting the welfare of its citizens (the public). The political sys-tem should therefore be the watchdog over the private economic system which really affects the lives of every-one like no other phenomenon. The reality is just the opposite. The privately run economic system is the tail that wags the dog and the dog is the political system of public interests. Thus we have the corporate state, or corporate interests, dictating the business of govern-ment.

The term "private sector" is commonly used by our politicians and the traditional, pro-Capitalist econo-mists. The politicians, mostly Republicans, constantly try and sway the American public to the view that the private sector, or private interests, can run government programs better than the government itself. This is the growing trend and philosophy of "privatization." The most obvious of these privatization attempts are with public programs such as Social Security and public education. The privatization of the military with private security companies like Blackwater was tried in Iraq and was not very successful. Long standing examples of privatization include the U.S Postal Service and the entire healthcare system. We all hear the right wing politicians touting the private sector for running programs more efficiently than their public or government counterparts. Hmm, do they mean the way they ran their own financial industry in the years leading up to the 2008 collapse? This is a flawed philosophy which, if carried to its extreme, would eliminate the entire system of government and just turn the entire country over to the economic system of Capitalism and private property.

The privatization movement in Congress has two approaches. One approach is when the government gets out of the picture and turns the whole function over to the private interest of the Capitalist system. The healthcare system is an example of private enterprise running the whole show with private doctors, private hospitals and private healthcare companies. But the government doesn't really get out of the picture completely, because the private healthcare industry still needs help from the government and tax payers. In our privately run healthcare system the government then supplements the profits of private industry with premium payments through Medicare, Medicaid and the Affordable Care Act. Without these government financed programs the privately run healthcare system would have failed decades ago. Such companies would never have been able to provide services to millions of retired and low income Americans, and make a profit, without these government financed subsidies. You could say that the government programs support the patient's expense of healthcare. But the high cost of healthcare that needs subsidizing is created by private run healthcare in the first place. So you could just as well say that these government run programs subsidize the profits of the private healthcare industry.

The other approach is that in which the government maintains the program but contracts out different aspects of the program to private industry. An example of the contracting out approach would be California's Cal Trans. The Cal Trans agency is responsible for state highways which has some government employees, but hires out the big projects to private companies such as Granite Construction.

When private enterprise takes over a government program, either completely or through government contracts, the bottom line immediately becomes profits for the major stockholders and executives. The original purpose and intentions of these government/social programs takes a back seat to profits. The only way to administer social programs in the interests of the public, for whom they were intended, is through the government public sector which eliminates the profit motive from the picture. Although government run programs may be more costly to tax-payers initially, with government employee payroll and benefits, they will be more responsive to the needs of the public for whom they were intended. They will provide better more efficient services and eventually they will save tax payer dollars. Government run bureaucracies also provide better paying jobs and benefits than jobs created by the private sector. This serves as a boost to the declining middle class.

So how has this privatization worked in the past? A good example again, is the privately run healthcare system in the United States which is a complicated system with many different private interests and dependent on extensive government involvement to make it minimally functional. Recent attempts to bolster it up through Obama's Affordable Care Act are valiant and necessary attempts, which are making health care more available. But it still remains a free market entity with profits as its main objective. Almost all other western countries have had better results with publically run or socialized systems. If it weren't for Medicare, Medicaid and Obama Care, probably half of the country would not be able to afford healthcare. The privately owned healthcare insurance companies do nothing but limit coverage by denying claims, and overruling doctor's attempts to bring necessary treatment to patients. They absorb about 30 cents of every healthcare dollar and provide no actual medical services. They are clearly unnecessary middlemen whose sole purpose is to skim profits out of the system. The private owned hospitals pad their bills and are the main source of corruption in the Medicare program. There are also a few unscrupulous private physicians promoting procedures that will add to their incomes and many times are unnecessary. The one exception to private healthcare is the Veterans healthcare system. It is currently under attack by politicians and is gradually being pushed into the private sector free market. What the Veterans healthcare system needs is more money for new hospitals, more doctors and healthcare workers. Instead smaller amounts of money are allocated to be used to contract out the needs of veterans to private physicians. The private sector is always lobbying congress to turn more business their way.

The code name "the private sector" is also a form of sophisticated brain wash. The use of the word "sector" implies that the private interests are a section within the government instead of the separate Capitalist economic system outside the political realm. Critics of government-run programs posit corporate management as more efficient than public bureaucracies. In practice private management can't even manage itself efficiently and constantly needs government subsides through tax payer dollars and bailouts in order to survive. We need look no further than the General Motors bailout for an example of how inefficient private enterprise manages its business and winds up turning to the government to fix things.

The push to the private sector and the deregulated free market is not solely the ideological blindness of the political system. Private interests have undermined the democratic process. The private industries actually write many of the legislative bills in their own interests. All the politicians are pressured to push these bills through Congress. All politicians are dependent on corporate funds for their campaigns and the corporations are the only entity that can afford the hundreds of millions of dollars it takes to finance the political campaigns. This makes nearly all politicians literally indebted to them. In my years of following electoral politics there have been very few politicians who did not take some corporate campaign contributions. The Bernie Sanders campaign for the Presidency, for one, accepted no corporate money.

The code names or doublespeak such as "free market" and "private sector" come from the same Wall Street ad agencies that design the campaign rhetoric. These are just a couple of the terms and catch phrases used by the media. The propaganda is psychologically sophisticated, and sometimes even uses subliminal forms of brain wash. It keeps all but very astute individuals confused or supportive of ideas and policies that are against their own interests. It is part of the Capitalist propaganda that prevails, unrestricted, throughout society. People must learn to "read between the lines" and question the rhetoric of the ruling elite. We must take a stand to open up our minds and recognize the negative, routine use of language so predominant in a society slanted towards wealthy interests. We must clear the mindset that has been put upon us by the doublespeak or as Orwell labels it, doublethink.

In addition to the above code names which are intended to confuse and influence public opinion there are many other little clichés and phrases which make up the American Capitalist propaganda. Below are just a few:

- *"What's good for the company is good for the worker"* - Like layoffs to cut expenses and keep profits up?
- *"The police are just working people like the rest of us"* - True, they are working people, but they aren't necessarily working for us. They're out there mostly protecting private property and stopping outright revolts against capital by breaking up strikes and peaceful protests against political, social and economic injustices. Yes, they can help innocent people, and on occasion they do. But these cases are incidental to their main function of enforcing class rule.
- *"I made my money the old fashioned way, I earned it"* - I recently saw this familiar expression on a television commercial promot-

ed by one of the Wall Street investment firms. It was an elderly gentlemen who had supposedly gotten wealthy off his investments. Sorry, he didn't earn it. He made profits like all profits are made in corporate America. Profits come from unpaid wages, pure and simple. It would be more appropriate to say that others earned it for him.

- *"Anyone can succeed in America if they just work hard"* - Certainly, this is not even true of entrepreneurs starting up new businesses. The mortality rate of a new business is now closer to 9 out of 10 than 7 out of 10 in the 1960s. If everyone was out there starting up new businesses there wouldn't be any workers to exploit. There are also millions of people who work hard all their lives with little or no progress in upward mobility.

- *"We're all in this together"* - This one is aimed at denying that we have a class society. Sure we are all in this together, *but not equally*. We live on the same planet so we're all in the same boat alright, but the 1% are up in the tourist section and the 99% are down below manning the oars.

- *"You're still better off in America than anywhere in the world"* - Well, yes we do have more freedoms here in America than under some dictatorial regimes. But our standard of living is way down on the list in rankings among western nations. We also have more people incarcerated as a percentage of the population than any country in the world and there are homeless encampments in every major city. So it depends on who you are and what country you're referring to whether or not you have it better than people in other countries. But certainly as a blanket statement it is not true. Even our civil liberties like the right to privacy and the freedom of speech are under attack. Free speech also depends on who you are and what you say.

- "*National Security Interests*" - A deceptive term used constantly by the government. Its implication is to protect America from military attacks and secure the protection of American citizens. But too often it means the economic security of American corporate interests abroad or to blow a fog of secrecy over anything that the government doesn't want Americans to know.

- "*Voter Fraud*"- has been used by several Republican states to justify the voter I.D. laws which are intended to restrict minorities from voting. Voter fraud alleges that people are voting twice and unregistered people are voting. Multiple investigations have revealed that this alleged voter fraud is practically non-existent. These voter I.D. requirements are politically motivated racial discrimination. The code word "voter fraud" is no more than an untruthful catch phrase used to justify voter I.D laws and disguise the true discriminatory nature behind them.

- "*Make America Great Again*"- this is the campaign slogan of presidential hopeful Donald Trump. In view of Mr. Trump's hate campaign against Mexicans, Muslims and his plans to deport millions of immigrants, what

Mr. Trumps "code" phrase really is implying is "Make America *White* Again." Knowingly or not, Trump has borrowed this term from the German "Nazi" party where the term "make Germany great again" was a central theme to Nazi propaganda. With Hitler the term included extermination of the Jews. With Trump it reflects his anti-Islam, anti-Mexican mindset. In view of Trump receiving the endorsement of the past head of the American Ku Klux Clan, the parallel of Donald Trump to Adolph Hitler would appear to be more than just negative campaigning by his political adversaries.

The following clichés I agree with:

- *"If you tell a lie enough times eventually people will start believing it"* (sounds like the Republican politicians of today)

- *"You can fool all the people some of the time and some of the people all of the time but you can't fool all of the people all of the time."* (Abraham Lincoln)

- *"If a deal sounds too good to be true, then it most assuredly is not true."*

- *"Nothing in life is free"* especially under Capitalism which promotes free this and free that all the time in their advertising.

- *"The American dream only occurs when you are asleep"* George Carlin hit the nail on the head with that one.

The next time you hear a catchy little phrase or advertising slogan, or just familiar statements by anyone
in society, that has a social or political meaning, stop
and reflect on it a little instead of just embracing it. If it
doesn't sound right or true to your own life experiences
then question it, even if you have heard it a million
times before. Repetition is highly effective in political
propaganda and advertising. Also, how does the statement make you feel? Does it give you strong urges or
feelings about the world that may or may not be related
to the context in which it was used? It may have a subliminal meaning. Something being triggered in your
mind that you are not consciously aware of. Subliminal
advertising used to be illegal but nowadays advertisers
are unrestrained and they use subtle forms of psycholo-
gy all the time in their advertising. Political propaganda
and advertising are pretty much the same. It's just the
product that is different. In advertising, the product is
something they want you to buy. In propaganda, you
are being sold an idea they want you to believe. Sometimes the advertising slogans have a deeper political,
subliminal, meaning in addition to selling a product. So
they serve two purposes. You will find these little bits
of status quo propaganda on the T.V., in the media, in
Hollywood movie productions and from politicians and
political pundits. But you may also hear them in discussions with your friends who have already accepted
them and are helping to spread the falsehoods whether
they are conscious of it or not.

     We hear so much about the use of Communist
propaganda in other countries and societies, especially
societies leaning more towards Socialism than Capitalism. But there is plenty of propaganda right here in
Capitalist America. Every society has its own propaganda which reflects the views of the class in power.

The class in power in the United States is the Capitalist ruling class. And the propaganda in the United States is no different than the propaganda in the so called Communist countries. It is all directed at getting people to believe that their culture, their economic system and their political structure is the best for everyone, meanwhile disguising who in society it best serves. I am sure there are many people who would view this whole book as baseless Communist propaganda. I would view these people as victims of the Capitalist propaganda I have been discussing. Well we are nearing the end of my book, what do you think? <u>The following is fictional political satire, a humorous test of sorts, to see where you fall on the political scale from left to right:</u>

> If you agree that this book is just baseless Communist propaganda that should not be taken seriously then you may be eligible for the *Patriotic American Citizens Award.* This award is sponsored by the Republican Party Policy Committee on the curtailment of free thought and the non-profit organization "Common Sense Is All You Need" which are currently involved in challenging the theory that the earth is rotating and the sun is not actually circling the earth. Previous winners of the *Patriotic American Citizens Award* were Senator Joe McCarthy, Sarah Palin, Bill O'Reilly, Rush Limbaugh, Governor Scott Walker of Wisconsin, and Senator Ted Cruz of Texas. Current nominees for the award are Donald Trump, President George W. Bush and Rupert Murdoch owner of Fox News. Donald Trump said he thought there might be something to the theory that the earth is rotating, but wasn't sure because when he sees the morning sun rise it seems as though the sun is really moving and the ground is standing still. This statement immediately raised him to the top of the list of current nominees. George W. Bush said he was honored by the

nomination but would have to check with Dick Cheney before actually accepting any award. After a long struggle with "<u>Fact Check</u>", the Republican Party Policy Committee and the Common Sense Is All You Need organization reluctantly conceded that Rupert Murdock was not an American citizen and therefore ineligible for the award. Both of these organizations still have not conceded that President Obama is an American citizen.

On the other hand if you feel this book raises serious concerns about Capitalist propaganda in America you will automatically become eligible for the "National Security Agencies" college scholarship with the "Underground College of Indefinite Detention." Funding for this scholarship is made possible by the 2012 revision to the National Defense Authorization Act. Rumors have it that thousands of Americans who express political dissent or have questioned government policies have received this scholarship. Unfortunately, none of the recipients could be located for their comments. ***

***   In case you are not familiar with the NDAA (National Defense Authorization Act) The NDAA has been around for many years but in 2012 it was modified under sections 1021-1022 to allow for indefinite detention of American citizens with no rights to challenge their detention in the courts. It essential denies the constitutional rights of Habeas Corpus. <u>It also gives the NSA (National Security Agency) very broad powers of interpretation in its application, especially around activities of "*political dissent*" that could be seen as "*potentially terroristic.*"</u>   It has been viewed by political critics as a further extension to the Patriot Act which has trampled on the civil liberties of Americans. The act has been challenged by Occupy Wall Street, individual state legislators and PANDA the "people against the NDAA." So far federal courts have ruled against challenges to the Act. I view the Act as an example of the growing trend towards Fascism in America.

In the above spoof if you have political unity with the past winners and present nominees of the Patriotic American Citizens Award then the Capitalist propaganda has already affected you profoundly. In this case nothing short of a miracle will change your irretrievable mindset. Welcome to the reactionary far right. But if you are among the majority of Americans who are open minded and feel that this book has raised some serious concerns regarding Capitalism, including American propaganda, then I welcome you to the debate over Socialism versus Capitalism. If you agree with almost all of my political viewpoints then you are probably a Socialist whether you are consciously aware of it or not. In any event the above little bit of attempted satire is intended to look on the humorous side of a serious issue. Whether or not the "indefinite detention" has actually been applied to innocent Americans who exercise their free speech and speak out against the system is unknown. So I don't mean to encourage a conspiracy theory that political activists are being held in permanent isolation in secret underground bunkers. That is why my concerns are expressed in satire rather than unsubstantiated open allegations. The point is that if they were we wouldn't know about it and the legal ability of our government now exists for them to do so if they desire, which in itself is a movement towards Fascism. The idea of indefinite detention has been practiced in Guantanamo where prisoners are slowly beginning to receive legal representation. But everyone knows about Guantanamo whereas we probably wouldn't know if secret detention is taking place. Leaders of the Occupy movement felt that the NSA was at least starting to view some of their leaders as potential terrorists under the law changes. Senator Diane Feinstein originally had strong reservations against the extension of the patriot act to American citizens especially with the broad interpretation of terrorism possible under the Act. The California legislature is one of the states that has passed laws restricting the federal law changes of 2012 to the NDAA. So the existence of the NDAA revisions and its potential to implement Orwellian measures is certainly not a conspiracy theory and should be a frightening phenomenon to all Americans.

CHAPTER EIGHTEEN

Some After Thoughts

Immigration

In September of 2015 I was listening to a public radio report about all the refugees fleeing to Europe from
Syria and to a lesser extent from Afghanistan and Iraq.
The numbers of people involved in this mass migration
is expected to number into the millions. I had earlier
seen their images and their stories on the television. I
could feel their pain on how their lives had been disrupted and all the misery they were going through. A
part of this misery was the inhuman way they were being treated by some of the governments of the European
nations. Although most of the people in the receiving
countries were sympathetic and reaching out to the refugees, not all of the leaders of the countries, the governments, were so sympathetic. Along with my feelings
of heartache for the people was the feeling of anger towards the United States Government, namely the Bush
administration, who years earlier had been the cause of
the current migration crises as a result of the U.S. invasion of Iraq. That event, now 13 years past, had been
the biggest foreign policy disaster in the history of the
United States. It upset the balance of power in the Mideast, been a shot of adrenalin in the arm of world terrorism, turned the whole area into a war zone, and now
this! As I reflected on this current refugee crisis it also
made me think of the way many people in the United
States have come to view immigrants so negatively.
Then there are the right wing politicians who fan the
flames of the anti-immigrant sentiment. The Republi-

cans have been on the wrong side of immigration policy change in the U.S. for many years and are now using the Patriot Act and the fear mongering of terrorism as an excuse for rejecting any meaningful numbers of Syrian migrants into the United States. They turn their back on the history of our country. We are a country of immigrants. Immigrants built America, and have always been a vital and positive part of the country's prosperity. So the European community gets the refugees while we turn our back on the situation we caused. My emotions involved sorrow for the Syrians and anger towards this right wing influence which prevents American leaders from acting with compassion and instead turn a cold shoulder. But we are heading into the 2016 presidential elections and anti-immigration is a political issue that Republicans have used for a long time to consolidate their support with the fringes of American society. The fringes have come to believe that immigrants are their enemies. Even though this tragic uprooting of innocent people is unprecedented in modern times, I feel that something positive could come out of this forced migration in the long run.

The ethnicity of countries around the world is changing. Even here in the United States, whites of European decent will soon be a minority with the combined populations of Blacks, Asians and Latinos and people of mid-eastern decent comprising a majority. The world is getting smaller. The national borders are bending and the national make up of cultures and languages within individual countries are melding. This is a good thing for the human race. People can only break down their prejudices, stereotypes and fears of other nationalities in a limited way through travel, education and occasional contact with other cultures through the internet. Marxism stresses that people will develop their political and social views and class consciousness based on the material conditions of life. This includes where and with whom they live, work and socialize. Attitudes of the younger generations of Americans towards people of different ethnic backgrounds is already changing society. Their attitudes towards marriage and relationships are different than many people in my generation, many of whom had less contact with other nationalities. We are gradually discovering that people are people. We all have similar hopes, dreams, emotional feelings and problems. All people have differences but the only irreconcilable differences are "class differences": The small super rich 1% versus the multiethnic working classes.

The huge migration we are seeing today in Europe as middle class and working people flee from the war zone in Syria, although painful in the transition, will in the long run bring Europeans closer together. Also, the continued trend in immigration to the United States and other countries will bring all of us closer together. The international working class will not be separated as much by borders. Because the world is growing smaller this immigration process has been happening anyway. Actually, international Capitalism or monopoly Capitalism plays a large role in increased immigration amongst all countries. Factories, corporate headquarters, suppliers and customer services are located around the world for all international companies. The workers of the world follow the job market wherever the needs arise. The national identities of the world corporations is becoming a moot point. This is part of the new global economy. As the job market requirements demand more education, and as technology eliminates more unskilled jobs, international Capitalism is fostering a world-wide pool of unemployed workers. One of the aspects of Capitalism is that it does not create enough jobs for everyone who needs a job. This is the inevitable nature of a Capitalist unplanned economy whether local or internationally. It's the *anarchy of production* term referred to earlier. This is the new world order that politicians talked about near the end of the 20th century. Immigration is a vital requirement in this new world order of corporate consumerism. The aging populations in some countries such as China, Japan, Germany and the United States need influxes of younger generations to compensate for lower birth rates. We need a young vibrant workforce of tax payers to support the programs like Social Security and Medicare.

It is also incorrect to say that immigration takes jobs away from the citizens of countries like the United States where high rates of immigration occur. Millions of Americans in the United States are working for foreign companies who have moved to the U.S. In the new economic world order we have international workplaces with an international workforce irrespective of the country where the jobs are located. An American worker for a Honda plant in the United States has no more right to that job than the Japanese worker in Japan who lost their job when Honda re-located their plant to the United States. The immigrant worker from Mexico who comes to the U.S. looking for work has just as much right to look for work in the U. S. as the American citizen whose job may have been exported to Mexico. <u>Jobs are no longer the exclusive right of citizens in the countries where international corporations locate to and from, depending on market conditions.</u> That's just the cold hard facts of international Capitalism, the global economy, and the emergence of the international workforce. If anything immigration will create new jobs in the United States, not eliminate them. Immigrants comprise a larger portion of entrepreneurs than Americans in general. These entrepreneurs start up small businesses and create jobs. They also spend money and create the need for more products and services and subsequently more jobs. The jobs being lost by American workers are many times the result of the job market shifting to more high tech jobs. American workers are becoming less educated and trained to fill these positions. If the United States doesn't revitalize its higher education system to provide an affordable education for Americans, this technical job void will be filled more and more by immigrants educated in Europe and other countries that put more emphasis on free higher education. But, of course it is easier for companies to bring qualified immigrant workers into the country to fill these jobs than it is to get corporate America to pay the more taxes necessary to improve higher education; another example where the bottom line of profits puts American citizens out of work, permanently! The larger the unemployed labor force the easier it is to reduce wages for everyone. So, the Capitalists win again. Capitalism is definitely a rigged system in the interest of the owning class. But it's not immigrants who are creating lower wages. They may be more hard pressed to accept sub-standard wages, but it is our economic system that causes lower wages and eliminates jobs. With the exception of the highly educated immigrants, most immigrants wind up in the worst jobs which nobody really wants. Many disgruntled unemployed Americans blame their situation on the immigrants they see with jobs. They don't blame their situation on other Americans who are fortunate enough to be working. This selective blame is a mindset of racial prejudice and it is encouraged by politicians such as Donald Trump and many others who point the finger at immigrants as responsible for taking American jobs. It encourages racial hatred, nationalism and isolationism which leads to war. This in turn diverts attention away from the root of the problem, which is the system of Capitalism that does everything it can to eliminate jobs and lower the wages of those still working.

So although growing immigration will gradually bring us closer together socially and politically it will not solve the unemployment problems inherent under Capitalism. It will supply a more available workforce to the international Capitalist job market and it will help some economies to grow. It cannot solve the problem of a growing surplus labor force and the lack of sufficient jobs. The unplanned economy of Capitalism will continue to create unemployment, homelessness and despair which contributes to the growing violence in society and leaves behind a growing number of otherwise productive working people. The contradictions between the haves and the have nots will continue to grow until the conditions will eventually reach a revolutionary situation. But with growing immigration the working class will become more united for the final struggle against capital. When the world's multi-nationalities are living together within the same countries the importance of national borders will become blurred and nationalism less of an issue. Who knows it might even reduce the effectiveness of the cry "defense of the fatherland" or "national security" to rally the people behind imperialist wars. The causes of these wars will continue to be economics but racially biased nationalism has always been the driving appeal to the masses to support the wars.

Technology and Jobs

Much has been said about the disappearance of the

middle class in America. It's not just the middle class that is disappearing. The working class in general is becoming an unemployed working class. Job eliminating technology is the main cause behind this. Technology doesn't necessarily have to be aimed at job elimination. Technology has been guided by the private property interests of Capitalism to concentrate on eliminating jobs and on increasing weapons of warfare. The current blow to the middle class is the technology that replaced high paying blue collar factory workers. These jobs didn't just solely go overseas they were replaced right here in America by robotic assembly lines. Also for several decades good paying middle management jobs have been replaced by clerks using management computer applications. If there is one positive aspect in the otherwise shrinking middle class it is in high tech computer science jobs. Some young college graduates are starting out with companies like Google and Facebook at middle class salaries of $100K or more. But in my opinion eventually computer technology will approach artificial intelligence where these jobs will no longer be necessary. We are getting close to quantum computing which will be a huge qualitative leap in the ability of computers to program and design themselves and essentially run the world with very little human input and maintenance. Just as the blue collar workers saw their jobs disappear at the height of their potential earning years I believe that the millennia generation of computer designers, engineers, programmers etc. will suffer the same fate. It is no longer a fantasy, science fiction notion, that computers may literally run the world with as many as 90% of the population unemployed. So the rush of young people to get an education in computer technology and revitalize the American dream may be short lived. The ones who already have these jobs may be ironically working to eliminate their own jobs. Others coming up through the education ladder may find that the jobs no longer exist when they complete their education and enter the workforce. Once it got started in the late 70s to early 80s it took about 30 years for manufacturing technology to eliminate high paying blue collar jobs. But based on the Moore's Law of technology advancement, even though revised downward recently, it sure won't take even 20 years before high tech jobs begin disappearing as well.

The declining conditions of Capitalism and its inability to provide for society is not a straight pathway downward. It is filled with little bumps up and down on its eventual way to the bottom. We recovered somewhat from the 2008/2009 depression but not back to where we were before. A small segment of the population benefiting from these middle class high tech jobs more than likely represent false hope for the generations with their goals set on acquiring similar jobs. The inability of Capitalism to provide the necessary level of employment will continue downward in the long run. That is because the drive for profits include technology specifically aimed at eliminating jobs not creating them.

The 2016 Presidential Campaign

As the 2016 presidential primary campaigns of the two main parties has come to a close, a billionaire outsider, Donald Trump has been elected as the Republican Party nominee for president. If it wasn't for his hatefulness and ignorance on almost all issues his candidacy would be a humorous spectacle defining the Republican Party's race to the bottom. After George W. Bush left office with the American economy in shambles and the Mideast in turmoil I felt that I would probably never

have to see another Republican President in my lifetime. I still believe that Donald Trump will have less of
a chance on winning the presidency than the two previous candidates who lost against President Obama. It is
just that Donald Trump is a whole lot more terrifying
than any candidate in U.S. history. His victory in the
primaries was possible for two main reasons. One, a
misdirected anger brought about by the growing inequities of a Capitalist world. This anger resulted in the
right wing fringe of the Republican Party ready to throw
the baby out with the bathwater. The other reason is
the growing illiteracy of most Republican voters who
truly don't understand the politics of Mr. Trump and
unfortunately don't care. If Donald Trump becomes
President of the United States, the gradual move to Fascism will proceed with leaps and bounds. A prospect I
do not look forward to.

A far more interesting and unusual aspect of the
campaign is the popularity of Bernie Sanders, the self-
proclaimed *Democratic Socialist* and Independent senator who unsuccessfully challenged Hillary Clinton in the
Democratic primaries. Not since Hubert Humphrey has
a Socialist of any sort made a serious run for the White
House. Bernie centers his attention on the big corporations, Wall Street and the overall plight of working people. He speaks of a *revolutionary movement* for change,
which implies motivating the masses to direct action
which is something that is rarely expressed by politicians including Hillary Clinton. Of course, Bernie Sanders isn't a real Socialist because he believes in the Capitalist system. If he didn't he wouldn't have spent his
whole life working for reforms within the system. But
he certainly believes in the necessity for strong oversight of the Capitalist economic system and the expansion and protection for Socialist entitlement programs.

This view is a breath of fresh air in a political environment of callousness towards working people. Despite his age he has mobilized huge support from younger millennium voters. The fact that he is a self-proclaimed Socialist, of whatever version, has not bothered his supporters in any way. This shows how Americans are becoming open to and curious about Socialism and also see the systemic and problematic nature of Capitalism. It is also a shift within the Democratic Party beginning to move away from years under the influence of Reaganomics that has overwhelmed the Republican Party. Elizabeth Warren was one of the first to speak out strongly against corporate America and Sanders is elevating that sentiment in the context of a Presidential bid. Whether the Democratic Party will continue this return to the left and reclaim their long lost history of the working man and women's party remains to be seen. I was not surprised that Bernie Sanders was unable to wrestle away the nomination from Hillary Clinton, who has spent years acquiring the support of the Democratic Party machine. But unlike the clown prince Donald Trump, Bernie Sanders could have been elected had he received the Party nomination. As a Marxist, I no longer get overly enthusiastic about elections although I have never missed voting in a national election. As I have said before, voting is not a right people should give up simply because of its growing ineffectiveness. Although in time Bernie Sanders may be forgotten, I find it encouraging that anyone who claims to be a Socialist can mobilize such enthusiastic and widespread support.

Donald Trump's nomination represents the decadent and stubborn philosophy that the Republican Party has been pursuing for a long time. The party of Reagan has pursued incorrect economics philosophy, anti-immigrant, anti-woman and anti-LGBT rights for a long time. Many in the Republican Party establishment have refused to endorse him even after he received the nomination. This is because of his openly expressed hatred and foul mouthed rhetoric that insults even some Republicans. The nasty things that Donald Trump says outright are what many Republican politicians and voters, have been expressing, but less overtly, for a long time. Donald Trump is not changing the Republican Party. He is the outgrowth of the race to the bottom of Republican politics that started with Reagan and has been hell bent on self-destruction for decades. The Republican Party philosophy has created Donald Trump and he may be the final blow that literally destroys the party.

On the other hand Sander's popularity is representative of the open and growing awareness of the failure of Capitalism. So thank you Bernie. You too have captured the media spotlight, in a positive way, and are adding to the education process of Americans against the ingrained anti-Communist/anti-Socialist mindset. This election year is unique like none I've ever witnessed. There is big change in the air for American electoral politics. What that change will be remains to be seen. It could be a new major party that would challenge or replace the old Republican Party.

The Subtle Merger of Subsidizing Profits

The continuous corporate mergers have been around for decades and are part and parcel of monopoly Capitalism. Each merger is bigger than the last and there is always a loss of American jobs with each merger. But the destructive nature of mergers is not limited to the corporate economic environment. The merger between the economic system and the political system, between Capitalism and democracy is at least as damaging because it undermines the entire political process. A particular method of this merger is government subsidizing the profits of corporations. This method warrants a closer look as it is sometimes very subtle. It reflects the increasing inability of the so-called free market to accomplish its inherent purpose of making profits without government assistance. The subsidies are also an aspect of the growing "corporate state" which is really in charge of our country's priorities.

Here are just a few of the ways the government _subsidizes corporate profits_ and props up the failing ability of Capitalism to stand on its own. These examples are representative of the merger between the economic and political systems:

- The _military budget_ which helps corporations to establish and hold economic positions around the world far more than it brings peace and security to Americans and the rest of the world.
- _Tax breaks and loopholes_ which gives corporations free handouts.
- Private run charter schools for profit which rely on government subsidies to parents used in the tuition costs which diverts more taxes to private enterprise and takes money away from the starving public education system.
- Government subsidies to start up clean energy companies is environmentally correct, but accentuates the fact that these new industries wouldn't have a chance to compete against the status quo fossil fuel industries without government assistance. This type of subsidy is unfortunately needed to facilitate

the competitive nature and entrepreneur-
ship of the Capitalist system which is *alleged*
to occur naturally in the free market.

- <u>Medicare, Medicaid and the Affordable Care
Act</u>, which, although helpful and necessary
for Americans, actually subsidizes the completely privately run healthcare industry
which would never be able to make a profit
and provide even minimum services to a
large portion of Americans.

- <u>Government financed technology research</u>
which is then turned over to the private sector for product development and the marketing of profitable commodities. Government
support of technology development too
many times subsidizes profits rather than
taxpayer interests.

- <u>Through tax breaks and direct subsidies to
the huge pharmaceutical industry for prescription drug development.</u> After the drugs
reach the market, there is absolutely no control over the pricing of these drugs to the
American public. To make matters worse,
Medicare and other government programs
(with the exception of the Veterans Administration) are not even allowed to negotiate
the prices of the drugs with the American
drug manufacturers. These same American
pharmaceutical companies can and do sell
their products much more cheaply to foreign
markets. Medicare recipients are forced to
give up their Medicare drug benefits and
purchase many expensive drugs on their
own from Canada and around the world because it is against the law for the private

Medicare health plans to purchase prescription drugs outside the United States. The American pharmaceutical industry has a death grip on the U.S. legislatures who pass and uphold these laws insuring uncontrolled pricing and has become a glaring example of our political system subsidizing private property profits. All of this results in many Americans going without their medication. It is the epitome of the corporate/government merger process.

- <u>Government backed mortgage lending</u> through agencies such as Fannie Mae and Freddie Mac which guarantee hundreds of billions of government backed loans with taxpayer dollars. Without these subsidies to private lenders, which guarantees their profits, the home lending market would be reduced to a fraction of its current activity and home ownership would never have existed. Even with these subsidies, the American dream of home ownership is still disappearing.

- <u>Attacks on unions through right to work laws</u> which subsidizes company profits and lowers living standards for Americans (see Chapter Four).

This money flow of hard earned taxpayer dollars onto the balance sheets of American corporations accentuates their dependency on the government to maintain their survival and the survival of the system based on private ownership in general. It clearly refutes the position of conservatives about the virtues of free market Capitalism. Capitalism has never responded to the needs of the vast majority of Americans without exten-

sive government subsidies, regulation and social programs and it's only getting more dependent on tax payer dollars as the Capitalist system becomes increasingly
unable to stand on its own. The corporate state, the
Capitalist economic system, is dragging down our entire
political system, and its strength and power continues
to grow.

The power of the economic system of private ownership over our political system of constitutional democracy is inevitable, but it has really gotten out of
hand in the last 30 plus years. The gullibility and lack of
education of the American public, as voters, is in part
responsible for this failure of the democratic process. A
lot of people don't know who or what they are voting
for. But American citizens are not the cause of the problem. The massive amount of misinformation and propaganda in society is what has confused voters, especially
uneducated voters. When I was in college back in the
60s I wrote a paper in an international relations class
that put forward the position that democracy cannot
function without an educated population. It was a new
idea to the class professor at the time. Today I still hold
to that belief as I see uneducated and uninformed voters
voting for candidates who clearly do not reflect their
economic interests or the ideals of what we have stood
for as Americans. Too many voters have fallen victim to
the single issue appeals of politicians and are blinded to
the more important ideologies of these candidates. As
higher education slips away from the grasp of more and
more Americans we are slowly becoming a nation of il-
literates. That is exactly what the ruling class, the corporate state and the benefactors of private property desire: a nation of misinformed, confused and disenchanted voters who are righteously angered and easily
manipulated.

The mergers within the corporate world are obvious and in general contribute to the growth of monopoly Capitalism. But the many ways the government has been subsidizing the free market represents a silent merger between the corporate state and the democratic political system. It represents the growing power of the corporate state over the political system, but also reflects the fact that the Capitalist free market cannot stand on its own without huge tax payer assistance. The claims of free market advocates are bogus. The whole corporate state is dependent on corporate welfare in its many forms. A completely free market environment without government financial help would have collapsed into economic anarchy a long time ago.

Reflections and Projections

The aging process is many times characterized by the tendency to grow more conservative and more tolerant of things that in our youth were seen as unacceptable. There are anti-establishment activists who turn to electoral politics or completely away from politics; doubters who turn to religion in moments of desperation, and unsuccessful risk-taking entrepreneurs who come to grips with varying degrees of poverty. In the world of politics not all older people fall into this category. Many of us are still quite young in spirit and hold on to the sentiments of dissatisfaction with the world and continue to visualize systemic change. My views on politics and religion haven't changed much throughout my adult life. I remain dedicated to the struggle for Socialism and view myself as a true agnostic when it comes to religion. I view the arrogance of both atheists and the Christian faithful as naïve and full of unprovable arguments. I was never inclined to entrepreneurial high risk taking in my economic planning, and always felt that Social Security would be my best bet for economic survival in old age. So I just went with the odds and my values and attempted to live within my limited means. The most positive thing I got from my parents was a strong work ethic. Everyone had to work in my family and the value of always doing the best job you could was the golden rule. I wind up better off than many of the people I see at my age. I have the necessities of life, and for this I am very grateful. But nothing is necessarily permanent and when I see the never ending attempts by the Republican Party politicians, in particular, to attack social programs I view with concern my tenuous economic situation. Then again the whole country, if not the world, is in a tenuous situation. So I don't worry about it. Instead I speak out against it, vote against it and take direct action when I can to preserve what we have and fight for more. But I know in my heart and my mind where we are headed.

One of the biggest failures of western philosophy, according to the Buddhists, is that people don't recognize the impermanence of the world and are stubbornly resisting inevitable change. That is the difference between progressive liberals, and Socialists as compared to conservatives who cling to the status quo. We progressives know that you can't have progress without change and that change is inevitable. The constantly changing nature of the universe in which we live will derail "the *best laid plans of mice and men*" (Robert Burns). This quotation rings true especially to men and women who cling to the past, the present and refuse to embrace the future. We liberals see the changing world and struggle to influence the direction of the change. Conservatives struggle against any change and in many cases try to roll the clock back. By the time many people are old enough to experience and possibly understand this inconsistency of life they will be very close to pushing up daisies. The wealthy successful Capitalists will eventually see their financial empires disappear as nothing in the universe is permanent. Wisdom can come with aging but aging does not guarantee wisdom.

The extent of education through academic studies and learning through experience and contact with different cultures is a strong determinant on whether you turn out as a liberal progressive or a head in the sand die-hard conservative. Statistics show that the higher your education level the more likely you are to vote Democratic. Other poles indicate that "white" uneducated males are the most likely to embrace Republican conservatism and the wild conspiracy theories put forward on talk radio and through other media forms. One of the many disgusting, and ironic, one liners of Donald Trump is that "he loves the uneducated voters." The education process starts at a very young age in the family. I recently read a quote, I forget where, that "parents *should teach their children how to think and not what to think.*" This is a philosophy of raising your children to be open minded rather than growing up to mimic the beliefs of their parents. Unfortunately, teaching your children how to think is not nearly as widely practiced in parenting as it should be. The trickle-down theory of brainwash can start in early family life.

During my childhood I was exposed to mostly conservative Republican politics and traditional Christian beliefs. I am the only sibling that later rejected these ideas. I am also the only one who went to college and traveled the world and observed other cultures. I left the rural setting that I was raised in and experienced inner-city life. I remember when I first started to embrace beliefs different from my parents, while in college, the shock and raised eyebrow reaction I received. I was even encouraged to leave college when previously I had been encouraged towards higher education. But somehow I had learned to think for myself. It's not easy to step outside your familiar comfort zone but if you want to learn and grow you must at least experience the world from different viewpoints. Following your heart and values in life is not always easy. It sometimes means going against the grain of your loved ones and standing firm for your beliefs. On the upside I have no problems when I brush my teeth in the morning and view my reflection in the mirror.

I know that the majority of Americans are not in agreement with my anti-Capitalist political views, not even the disenchanted Americans. But I am just as certain that eventually the majority of society will reach this conclusion and the option of Socialism will be there waiting. When it comes to people unable to accept the need for an economic revolution, many highly educated intellectuals and the uneducated working class, appear frozen in their beliefs. I am neither a highly educated intellectual nor an uneducated working class person. I am in the middle. I am part of the *educated* working class. My perspective helps me to see the pitfalls of both the successful intellectuals and the masses of struggling uneducated working class. On the one hand it is the *classless* intellectual liberals with the economic security of their professional affluence who turn a blind eye to the constant examples of class struggle. They instead cling to the hope for changes to political policy as the solution to the growing chaos in the national and world order. On the other hand the uneducated working class clearly see the *class* nature of their economic interests and interests of the 1%. Yet they become easily influenced by the demagoguery of right wing rhetoric and turn on each other rather than uniting against the very rich. Both these different segments of society are groomed to look with condescension upon the concept of Socialism, Marxism and revolutionary philosophy. Both are held back by misguided patriotism, peer pressure and political smugness. The liberal intellectuals, articulate traditionally acceptable means of change and cling to what economic security they still have. The uneducated working class have given up on politics they don't understand and continue to strive for social mobility which is always just beyond their reach. And neither is able to reach beyond their respective mindsets and embrace revolutionary politics. But stubbornness and misguided confusion will not change the unavoidable systemic dynamics that will eventually create an intolerable reality for everyone. Revolution will come. The question is will we be together and ready for it.

CHAPTER NINETEEN

Looking Forward
The future is in our hands

Some books sum up an otherwise negative analysis of the world with a rose colored ending. To me that is a hypocritical approach and can be confusing to the reader regarding the authors message. I'm not going to do that. I leave the question of hope out there but not false hope. The purpose of my political persuasion is to convince people that Capitalism is the elephant in the room, which is being ignored, and is at the basis of the world's problems. I don't want to encourage false hope that things will just get better on their own, or that others will resolve the injustices for us. It will take all of us, or a majority of the people, to force the economic and political changes necessary. In addition to identifying the cause of social, economic and political injustice, I have attempted to change common held beliefs that Communists are a bunch of atheists who lurk in the corners waiting to steal the minds of our children. The minds of children have already been tainted, and not by Communists. The ideology of Capitalism and free market individualism has flooded their minds for generations. And any objective review of history shows that Marxists, Socialists/Communists have been the most ardent supporters and consistent allies of all progressive social movements. We have always had a dedicated commitment to working class people.

I feel that we are moving into a protracted era of public protest and civil disobedience. The current level of the direct action is still within the confines of class struggle but as the sometimes violent attacks of the rul-

ing class on our civil liberties, and on our material conditions of life increases, the struggle will approach class
warfare. The recent internal meltdown of the Capitalist
system (2008) has done permanent damage to the
American way of life. The middle class was probably a
short run illusion anyway and it's not going to come
back to the level it was before the 2008 melt down.
Every aspect of society is falling apart as far as the poor
and working poor are concerned. But for government
programs (which are always being threatened) we
would have anarchy in the streets. Children would go to
school hungry and many do anyway. The meager wages
we are paid are hardly enough to feed an individual let
alone a family. Our prisons are literally overflowing.
Close to 2 million full time jobs have been permanently
lost in the last few years. Home equity for the middle
class has taken a blow and the first time home buyer
market has all but disappeared. The only thing that is
keeping our people afloat are credit cards and what is
left of public assistance programs. For all practical purposes, Capitalism has already failed for a growing number of working people. Can you imagine what it would
have been like if the Republicans had been successful in
privatizing Social Security prior to the stock market
crash? We haven't heard the last of that yet, or the
many other cutbacks to public assistance programs
planned by the Republican Congress members. The
sooner we stand up together, the sooner we can slow
down the attacks on our hard won reforms and possibly
regain and expand some of the lost benefits. In the
course of this struggle, people will become more comfortable with the direct action it will take to effect any
systemic change. I don't know when a more systemic
revolutionary change will occur. Marxism says that
most people can only learn and become more class con-

scious based on the material conditions of their lives. This means that for millions of Americans things will have to get far worse before they are motivated to take direct action. I am convinced that things will continue to get progressively worse. Marxism implies that the ruling class will not give up their power peacefully. Every indication from the history of class struggle confirms this prediction is correct as there has been a lot of violence and bloodshed created by the ruling class whenever people demand big changes. Replacing Capitalism and private property with a form of Socialism and collective ownership would be a huge change. I guess I still hold out the hope that a violent revolution will not be necessary. Most Marxists feel that a Socialist revolution will need to occur on a world scale at about the same time. This view is probably right as the Russian revolution was unable to survive in an otherwise Capitalist world. But Marx's critique of private property and Capitalism has certainly proven to be correct in defining the problem. This is the nature of the current revolutionary struggle for justice in America: to educate people on the systemic nature of the problem and to encourage direct action in the struggle for political and economic reforms.

I would like to share with you some statistics from Chris Hedges 2012 book entitled "Days of Destruction Days of Revolt." Chris Hedges was part of the New York Times team that won a Pulitzer Prize for their coverage of global terrorism. He was an early outspoken critic of the Iraq invasion. Chris also participated in some "Occupy Wall Street" events. If you really want to know how the bottom half of the economically deprived live in the United States this book is for you. At the beginning of his book he has included some startling statistics about the United States as compared to the other industrialized nations of the world. I wish to share some of these statistics with you now. Following are excerpts from those statistics. Many Americans may find these facts surprising, if not shocking, depending on your frame of reference: your position in the economic strata of society.

Among industrialized nations, the United States has the

- highest poverty rate, both generally and for children;
- greatest inequality of incomes;
- lowest government spending as a percentage of GDP on social programs for the disadvantaged;
- lowest average number of days for paid holiday, annual leaves, and maternity leaves;
- lowest score on the United Nations index of "material well-being of children";
- worst score on the United Nations gender inequality index;
- lowest social mobility;
- highest public and private expenditure on health care as a percentage of GDP.

These trends are accompanied by

- highest infant mortality rate;
- highest prevalence of mental-health problems;
- highest obesity rate;
- highest proportion of population going without health care due to cost;
- second-lowest birth-weight for children per capita, behind only Japan;
- highest consumption of antidepressants per capita;

- third-shortest life expectancy at birth, behind only Denmark and Portugal;
- highest carbon dioxide emissions and water consumption per capita;
- second-lowest score on the World Economic Forum's environmental performance index, behind only Belgium;
- third largest ecological footprint per capita, behind only Belgium and Denmark;
- highest rate of failure to ratify international agreements;
- lowest spending on international development and humanitarian assistance as a percentage of GDP;
- highest military spending as a portion of GDP;
- largest international arms sales;
- fourth-worst balance of payments, behind only New Zealand, Spain, and Portugal;
- third-lowest scores for student performance in math, behind only Portugal and Italy, and far from the top in both science and reading;
- second-highest high-school dropout rate, behind only Spain;
- highest homicide rate;
- largest prison population per capita.

What is it about the United States compared to other advanced Capitalist countries that is responsible for the above negative statistics? Even in regards to living standards, the U.S. lags far behind most Capitalist/western nations. The last analysis I read was that we rank 18th among 20 western Capitalist countries in living standards. The statistics above reveal part of the facts behind the low ranking plus a whole lot more of where our national priorities and shortcomings are. As a percentage of GNP, we spend more by far on our military than any industrialized nation in the world, and that includes China. China's military budget is 25% of the U.S. military budget. This huge military budget is used mostly to promote American Corporate economic expansion far more than providing for national defense. National security has come to mean national economic security for the wealthy minority. The president of the United States is the commander and chief of our military, but in this role the office of the President has been referred to as the *"Chief International Marketing Officer"* for corporate America. This somewhat slanderous term was not created by Socialists such as myself, but originated from traditional political satirists and represents a grass roots understanding of the economic interests represented through an endless cycle of American invasions and occupations. This huge American military budget could easily be characterized as another form of subsidies to corporate profits for the nation's wealthiest families. The nation's poor and working poor suffer the most as this Pentagon spending sucks up the money for much needed social programs which the free market cannot provide and in turn lowers the standard of living for Americans compared to other European countries with far smaller military budgets and more public benefits.

When we talk about the declining standards of living in the United States the question of our declining infrastructure reigns high on the list of ignored priorities by both government and corporations. Our sewer systems, water delivery systems, the energy grid, our highways and mass transits systems are all decaying or falling behind even the emerging nations of the world.

Our internet system is one of the slowest in the western world. We are moving very slowly and reluctantly into renewable clean energy while other countries like China have taken the lead in, for example, the manufacturing of solar panels. So it's not just social programs that are in need of financing that is being wasted on costly military expenditures. The whole face of America is deteriorating. Yes we have a strong military and that is supposed to make America great? It seems clearer that our military has caused more problems in the world and damaged this false sense of *greatness* that our leaders indulge in. Just as corporations have a single priority of profits our politicians indulge in the arrogant puffing of America being the greatest nation in the world. Of course our military is unmatched in the world but the way we flaunt our military muscle has discredited our role as a world leader and created poverty and decay at home.

The United States has a unique form of laissez-faire (unregulated and less government involvement) Capitalism compared to other Capitalist countries around the world. We have, for many decades, adopted a political environment of deregulation, corporate subsidies and loopholes, and a top down attitude toward social programs. Instead, the *trickle-down* theory that the free market, left alone, will ensure economic justice and domestic tranquility has been influential in American politics and is an extension of Libertarian, Reaganomics free market Capitalism. As discussed in Chapter Two, any attempts by liberals in Congress to implement additional needed social programs or expand existing ones have been met on the right with accusations of moving towards Socialism. These accusations are an absurd notion. Americans have very little social benefits compared to the Capitalist countries practicing *Keynes eco-*

nomics. The main reason that other Capitalist countries have more social benefits, which add greatly to the standard of living and wellbeing of its citizens, is because the people of these countries fought for these benefits, in the streets, through mass action just as we did in America. They also, to a certain extent, embraced Socialistic programs. European Capitalism has been referred to as Democratic Socialism. The European countries are still taking to the streets with direct action and Americans for the most part are not. People all over Europe are used to coming out and demonstrating and marching over issues that are dear to them. The people of these countries, in Western Europe, know that it takes aggressive action for the Capitalists to open their wallets and share with the people. Americans seem oblivious to their own history of direct action such as the labor movement, the civil rights movement, the Anti-Viet Nam war movement, women's suffrage, and against child labor. Even Social Security and the New Deal was in response to marches by Socialists / Communists and other Americans responding to the economic conditions brought about by the "Great Depression." But for the last half century we Americans have forgotten the need to struggle. We have fallen to sleep on the couch in a state of political complacency. Even today when the great recession has taken its toll on the middle class and others only a small, but growing, portion of the population is taking to the streets. As a nation we seem to complain and recognize the dwindling condition of working people, we are all aware of it, but then we take the "oh well, it's out of my control" attitude and go back to our world of escape. I don't understand why this is so except that the American media plays a role in promoting any political action other than voting being somehow undignified and at the same time plays down the wide spread reality of growing poverty. In fact the media doesn't even cover marches and rallies in advance so unless you are on other forms of social media you don't even know about planned events. But if we want to improve standards of living and be able to make our voices heard on other issues we need to get over the stigma and join the rest of the world in direct action. Voting is only a small part of the democratic process and is becoming increasingly ineffective. The Democratic Party encourages false hope in the future and is no longer seen as the party of the working class, a status it held for several decades after the New Deal. The Republican Party is even worse and continues its discredited philosophy of "trickle down Reaganomics" while at the same time it actually attacks existing programs that benefit working and middle class people. The racist overtone of the Republicans also keeps us divided and further acts against political direct action. It is time to stop listening to these political pundits and the news media and Hollywood's portrayal of American life. It's time to turn off your T.V's, put away your video games, flush your "pot" down the toilet, stop listening to the religious hypocrisy of ministers who tell you to leave it up to God and just pray, and instead take to the streets in peaceful protest. There is nothing wrong with praying, but praying alone is pure escape. Jesus didn't just pray, he was an outspoken religious and political activist who followed the view that "God helps those who help themselves." Too many Americans have chosen escape over facing up to the fact that they need to act. Drugs and alcohol are a big part of this escape. America is the biggest drug culture in the world. We would prefer to sit around "toasted" than act in our own interests. Drug addiction is part of the decadency of declining Capitalism. The complacency and false hope that important issues will work things out themselves or someone else will do it for us has got to end. That is my appeal: for people to get off that sofa, employ their free will, unite with others for strength, and fight. If we just give up without a fight then we probably deserve the continuing misery that is in store for us.

I am not a cynic, nor a pessimist. A pessimist is someone who holds a negative or cynical view as part of their personality and sees everything in the world as a result of that pessimism. I study the world, examine in detail the problems, study the history of struggle, view the actual conditions objectively and come up, unfortunately, with a negative analysis of the direction of the human race as pertaining to social and economic problems. I refuse to see the glass half full when it is clearly half empty and for many people, more than half empty. I am sorry if this analysis will eventually require such a huge task as another revolution, but I won't water down my view to give some appeasement to the notion that we just need to get better politicians or send a few greedy Capitalists to prison, actions in themselves that I clearly support. If I were a pessimist, and had no hope I wouldn't have spent a good portion of my life fighting for change. I have great confidence in the ability of the masses of the people to effect change. I feel that united people power can overcome anything that the benefactors of the current system can throw at us. I just don't see this united effort happening, especially and I emphasis especially, in the United State of America. Instead I see us fighting each other, black against white, citizens against immigrants, Republicans against Democrats, Marxists against Capitalists, men against women, straights against gays, nation against nation, religions against religions, Socialists against Fascists and the United States of America against a growing majority of the world. What makes me angry is that I truly believe that these differences are intentionally fostered, encouraged and sustained by the dominant ruling class who benefit from these attempts to keep us divided.

I have been testing Marx's theory throughout my life, as others have done before me. I have observed the growing injustices of Capitalism and its effects on society: the shifting of wealth, the disappearing middle class and the growing unemployed working class. I can see the endless wars, driven by imperialist economic interests. I watch our cities being engulfed by poverty and homelessness and minorities rising up against racism and police brutality. I see students who are indebted for life with the burden of student loans who still cannot find good paying jobs. There is violence and terrorism everywhere. I see the infrastructures of America falling behind some 3rd world countries. America is filled with mental disorders and dysfunctional families and drug and alcohol addiction is everywhere. It is this observed protracted downward trend throughout history and my lifetime that brings me to the conclusion that life is going to get progressively tougher for us all until we take the initiative to change it. And changing it will most likely take an all-out revolution. I really hope that I am wrong. No one wants to have another revolution. I hope that somehow there can be a peaceful transition to a more equitable society. The one thing that I am sure of is that even a peaceful transition to social and economic justice will still require a huge movement of Americans in direct action and civil disobedience. The history of struggle for reforms throughout the world has absolutely proven this to be the case. Unforeseen events of the future can also play a big role in history. Unforeseen events can have either positive or negative effects and sometimes negative events can turn out to have overall positive effects and vice versa. Therefore unforeseen events, although grasping for straws, can still provide some hope.

Speaking of unforeseen events brings us back to climate change. Climate change was obviously one of the events that was unforeseen by Karl Marx. If climate change runs its worst case scenario then none of the other problems will matter. The worst case scenario is that the planet will no longer be able to support life. But before that happens the radical weather patterns will only aggravate the economic and social problems, causing yet more unforeseen events. So although I carry the anger that the Capitalist led industrial revolution caused the problem, I can't obsess on the past. We have to address the problem, and quickly. It is elevating itself to the highest priority. It is the biggest problem for the whole world, all nations and all peoples. Because the U.S. is one of the top three users of fossil fuels we Americans have a special obligation to ourselves and the rest of humanity, and to nature to act. The reality is that we are acting less than other countries in response to climate change. I realize that some of the measures I advocated in Chapter Eighteen are probably unrealistic for many people, but they were meant to highlight the seriousness and urgency of the issue. A lot of people especially young and single people might actually be able to accomplish most of these extreme lifestyle changes. From the list of actions I listed in Chapter Eighteen everyone should be able to make some of the necessary changes. Because if this approaching Armageddon, created by humans, doesn't encourage people to take to the streets and sacrifice some of their habits and toys then nothing will. In the coming years some of the life style changes will be forced on society anyway because of growing poverty or the effects of climate change. By then the options will be fewer and the situation much more pressing.

Organizing the struggle for justice has been changing and will keep changing much more with the advent of the digital age and social networking. There will still be a need for physical bodies of protest but the call to action will be much easier than before the advent of hand held devices and social internet access. This is mostly a good thing where much organizing can be done via the virtual world and people will have access to others around the country and the world instantaneously. The drawback is lack of privacy. The powers in charge, the various arms of the government (the FBI, the NSA, etc.) will know a lot more about what the struggle is undertaking and it will be harder to protect individual leaders. But in general it will be a huge advantage to organizing and democratic actions will take on a whole new face. It is actually happening now and with the exponential change in technology advances, there is no telling what doors it will open to people. The establishment will have the same technology but with unlimited resources giving them an edge in undermining the growing resistance. But surveillance by the government works both ways and organizers will have hackers and computer experts as well, so the people will have a heads up on government activities and files as well. There will be many more exposés of the government and it will be harder for the strong arm of the government, the security agencies, to hide their covert and many times lawless actions. The transparency and exposure of government and corporations will grow which will add more vigor to the struggle. In the world of organizing one of the problems has always been to prevent individual acts of misguided people, sometimes violent in nature. These acts are sometimes initiated by government undercover agents who attempt to undermine otherwise peaceful democratic actions. But sometimes these individual acts come from within the movement by "impatient individualism" in disregard for the need to keep all actions as peaceful and democratic as possible. In the digital age, these same individual acts of cyber warfare will have to be monitored and criticized by the majorities and the leadership of the struggle. The small group "Anonymous" comes to mind. Their hacking the websites of MasterCard and Pay Pal in response to these companies suspending payments to the whistle blower WikiLeaks seem initially as a justified action if you support the exposure of government activity by WikiLeaks. MasterCard and PayPal said the U.S. Government put pressure on them to prevent payments to WikiLeaks. The interference with the ability to donate to a cause (which is a form of free speech) by the U.S. Government makes the action by MasterCard and PayPal more than just a private sector issue but rather another example of the Government interfering with free speech as well. But the resulting negative effects by Anonymous on millions of credit card holders, working people, speak for itself. Individual acts like this, which are not well thought out, can bring the Government security organizations down on everyone as they attempt to label the whole movement as cyber terrorists. So these individual acts discredit and take away from the overall positive nature of the struggle. In the old days, before terrorism, the FBI would try to label all of the anti-war demonstrators as Communists or Communist sympathizers. But as the resistance of the people grows and law enforcement agencies adopt more aggressive tactics, any unthoughtful individual acts, whether cyber or otherwise will make matters worse. It will give the government an excuse to invoke the charge of terrorism against the class struggle. Some of you may question whether Federal and local law enforcement are really the bad guys that I portray them to be. That's because you have never been involved in social protest against the establishment. But once you do get involved in any social, political struggle it won't take long to understand whose side the laws favor. The different branches of law enforcement are not flexible or sympathetic to pro-testors and neither are the laws that they are out there enforcing.

Law enforcement will be at the forefront of society in the future with "police brutality" becoming a central major issue. The role of the "*State*" in any society is to represent the dominant class. Not the largest class, which are the different economic levels of the working class, but the *dominant,* ruling class, the owners of the wealth including the means of production. The "State" consists of the government branches: The Congress, the Executive and Judicial branches, and Law Enforcement (the strong arm of the State). The Judicial branch is, in my estimate, a failed body of government in the U.S. from the top down, from the current Supreme Court to the local municipal courts. They have failed to repre-sent the interests of the majority of our citizens on far too many occasions. For decades the courts attempted to handle the breaking down of society by mass incar-ceration, of mostly minorities, through laws like the "three strikes and you're out." But now our prisons overflow and we are beginning to release the multi-tudes back into society out of necessity. Congress has nearly failed to function at all and has resisted legislat-ing any positive laws or programs in the interest of working people. When we do get a small step forward, such as "The Affordable Care Act," then the Republicans immediately attack it and pick it apart piece by piece.

The presidency seems to have its hands tied and remains preoccupied with military adventures and international issues. In the meantime, the domestic economic situation gets progressively worse for struggling working people. People, slowly but surely, take to the streets in protest and righteous anger. In order for the ruling elite to maintain order and protect the establishment which serves their economic interests, they will turn more and more to the police force which becomes more militarized and brutal. It is the beginning signs of a revolutionary atmosphere and a movement towards Fascism.

So the growing role of law enforcement and police brutality will become a glaring political issue in the United States as society continues to deteriorate and civil disobedience grows. The police brutality currently centers mostly on minorities, mainly blacks and Hispanics and a few poor whites. The concentration of attacks on minorities clearly reflects blatant racism on behalf of the police and city governments. But minorities make up a disproportionate part of the poor working class. So the attacks by police in minority communities reflects the growing class struggle. There has always been police brutality against minorities even when there was widespread good economic times for many white people. Today these attacks are far worse, and in many instances, are willful murder. As the crisis of monopoly Capitalism grows the police brutality will spread to the white population as well, as it works its way up the class ladder. Police officers are people who come out of the working class like all of us. But the fact is they are not really working for us. They are basically working for the affluent and the rich even though they might see their role differently. They are caught in the middle and eventually they too will have to take sides. As I write these words, the murder of unarmed black victims such as Eric Garner of New York City and Michael Brown of Ferguson, MO. and hundreds of other instances around the country have caused demonstrations that even the mainstream media cannot ignore. With all of the violence and murders by the nation's police forces of blacks and Hispanics, still to my knowledge not one single police officer has gone to jail. With all the Grand Jury investigations and trials, one by one they are exonerated. The corrupted justice system is leaving the people no choice except to take to the streets. The entire system; the judicial system, the incarceration process, and the police forces selective harassment against blacks and other minorities have clearly demonstrated that to the system "<u>black lives don't matter</u>." That is why the Black Lives Matter movement gets so upset when politicians, and others, simplistically respond to their slogan with "all lives matter." The statement "*all lives matter*" has a pearly white implication to it and has become another, racist, *code term.*

In the future there will be more poor people on the streets begging for food and handouts and involved in various acts viewed as socially unacceptable by local businesses and policemen. As the level of oppression rises there are bound to be more outbreaks of violent acts. There just isn't any avoiding that, just like individual acts of terrorism are realistically impossible to stop. But the level of peaceful, non-violent protest could be so large that people will just be herded into certain areas of the city and quarantined much like the ghettos of major cities and the homeless communities of today. Society won't be able to jail them all because, as even today, there will be too many in proportion to the available jails. The failed judicial system will not be able to handle them and the police will become more and more the judge and jury. If it gets bad enough temporary prisons or holding pens may arise in and around the cities and the National Guard or our standing armies may get involved. The above scenarios already are a part of our history from the struggles of the 60s and 70s and earlier in American history but on a smaller scale than I anticipate for the future. So the growing inability of monopoly Capitalism to deal with society's problems will result more and more in the wealthy relying on the police force and the military in an attempt to maintain law and order. If through direct action we demand and achieve more programs of public assistance ahead of time we may be able to keep the injustices to the level of class struggle instead of escalating into all out class warfare and fascism. This will allow time for society to accept Socialism as the goal.

The struggle for reforms within the system is both morally and objectively necessary. Through the mass struggle for reforms, and the realization of the impermanency of past gains, the country will eventually see the necessity for more systemic changes and hopefully come to realize that private property has always been the driving force of class inequality. It is possible that Capitalism could collapse, beyond bailouts, on its own before the country has realized the need for Socialism and an organizing effort towards a system of public property is underway. An internal economic, and resulting political collapse, would be a disastrous scenario that could result in anarchy and reversion to a tribal society. This is not what a conscientious Socialist with democratic principles, like myself, wants to see (the collapse of Capitalism). Marxists want to build a movement against capital before such an event happens. This will result in a truly democratic revolution once the economic conditions have deteriorated to the point of unacceptability. That's the difference between truly educated Marxists and pseudo revolutionaries who always feel that *now* is the time for revolution. The extreme of this individualistic approach are the crazies of the private militia mindset. They're like the "tea party" on steroids! Many of them hope for the collapse of the political system and stand ready to accelerate the collapse. They have acquired a blind hatred for the government and anything it does. They have been educated by conspiracy theories and are mostly an uneducated white male movement filled with racism and anti-Semitism. These armed militia vigilantes are endemic to rural communities and are often filled with white supremacy ideology. They are the sad reality of Capitalist propaganda that diverts political dissent away from the true enemy of Capitalism and private property and instead fosters distrust and ignorance about Socialism and public property.

When the declining economic conditions will come together with the political awareness is hard to foresee, but it is probably several generations to a century or so off in the future. The Capitalists will have an option. They can decide to support a widespread welfare state and extend their power and privilege or they can stubbornly hoard their riches and force a revolution sooner than later. One thing is for sure. Nothing lasts forever, and Capitalism with all its obvious inequalities is certainly no exception. But the time of struggle for reforms, including more public assistance programs, and the political education of society is now.

The success and moral indicator of any society is no better than the poorest element within it. In the United States the homeless population represent the most impoverished. This is where the attention of government economic policy should be primarily directed. The Capitalist free market will never address the poorest of the poor. In fact it creates them. Too much political rhetoric is directed at the struggling middle class. You can't correct dire poverty and homelessness by improving or reinvigorating the disappearing middle class. We need to start at the very bottom of the social/economic ladder. This is the economic priority that only government programs can address. I don't see many politicians, at least on the national level, speaking to the needs of the bottom 5%. These are the people that Socialism recognizes, and that both Capitalism and our political system, disregard.

So this is what I see in looking forward. No one knows precisely where the struggle against economic, social and political injustice will take us. But wherever the resistance and whatever the issue the Socialists, the Marxists, and the Communists, will be involved with other activists. We will be offering leadership and insight and many times just in the background supporting the grass root uprisings. Because that is what we do, "Educate, Motivate and Participate."

EPILOGUE

It was May 1, 2012. May Day or "International Workers Day." I had driven into downtown Los Angeles to participate in the celebrations and marches. There was a rally/march planned by Occupy Los Angeles and, later in the afternoon, there was a march planned by coalitions within the Latino community. It was also an election year and the immigrant community was becoming quite frustrated and impatient with the Obama administration making no progress on a new immigration bill. The deportations had reached record levels under Obama despite the overwhelming support by the Latino community for Obama in the 2008 election. I stayed in L. A. all day and attended both events. They were both spirited political and cultural events with live music, food and leftist poets. The Occupy march stands out in my mind as one of the most effective actions of "peaceful civil disobedience" that I can remember.

The Occupy march was about 7,000 people strong. The Los Angeles police department always attempts to keep the demonstrators/marchers off the streets and onto the sidewalks. This is never completely effective depending on the number of people and the mood of the crowd. One of the favorite "chants" of the Occupy movement was "Whose streets? Our streets!" So sometimes when the police bull horns order people onto the sidewalks and off the streets there is temporary compliance then people go right back to the streets. This march had too many people to even fit on the sidewalks and it was the streets all the way. The march started in Pershing Square in downtown L.A. It snaked all over the downtown area and was planned to finish back in Pershing Square. The city had been notified of this plan ahead of time. In most of the "Occupy" events the march planners do not notify the city of what course the march will take or where it will end up. This is a precaution to prevent the police misusing the information. Many times the police will use this information to plan their tactics and to break up the march or allocate their forces to corner the marches, and entrap them for mass arrests. Most of the times the marchers themselves don't know exactly where the march is going. So the secrecy of the planners is for the safety of the marchers. At least this is the reasoning behind most Occupy Los Angeles events that I have attended.

I am reminded of an incident in the city of Oakland, California, where the police, knowing the plans of the marchers cornered several thousand marchers, and then ordered them to disperse. There was no way for the marchers to disperse and the Oakland police knew this full well. They had consciously trapped them. The police then moved in with violence causing many injuries and mass arrests. Some of the marches escaped, running into a business and out through the back doors only to find a chain link fence in the back. These lucky few were able to break through the fence and escape. The whole episode was a terrible unethical act by the Oakland police department which resulted in unnecessary violence and injuries.

Situations like the above Oakland incident are in part why Occupy Los Angeles event details are usually not shared with the establishment. Many of the protest details are completely impromptu. But in this case they did notify the City of Los Angeles and the Police department knew that the rally would start at Pershing Square and end up at Persian Square for final speeches and festivities. In hindsight this notification was a big mistake. The march went well, no incidence of violence or anything other than high spirited people with their demands and chants. Then near the end of the march within 2 or 3 blocks of Pershing Square the leaders of the march came running back to the marchers to inform us that the police had set up a barricade to prevent the march from returning to Pershing Square and that we were going to break through the barricades. We were further advised to tighten up our ranks. I was near the front of the march. When I arrived at the barricades, there were still thousands behind me. The wooden barricades were there and maybe 50 or more police officers behind them with their clubs ready. Then from the crowd came 10 or 12 marchers carrying what looked like Roman Shields. Carrying these shields they went to the front of the march pressing these shields up against the wooden barricades with the police on the other side. They then started slowly pushing their shields up against the barricades with all the rest of us closely packed behind them. The barricades were slowly being pushed aside and all the time the crowd was chanting "we are peaceful, we are peaceful." The police were not so peaceful. They were whaling away with their batons, trying to beat the protesters, but all they could do was beat against a wall of shields that eventually pushed a portion of the barricades aside. It broke an opening in the barricade, and then 7000 people slowly, but with persistence, made their way through the barricades and the police line. We completed removing the rest of the barricades as we passed through. The police were forced upon the sidewalks in a humiliating, thwarted attempt to prevent thousands of protestors from returning to Pershing Square and divert us, instead, towards the civic center area. This civic center area had currently been deemed off limits for Occupy activities. I stopped for a moment and spoke to a police captain or lieutenant who was overseeing this provocative and completely unnecessary operation. I just said, "you guys made a big mistake here." He responded, "I would have to agree with you." No one knows what the intentions of the police were had they been successful in steering us into the no-no land of the civic center area. It could have been a whole lot worse. No one was hurt except for the pride of a few red faced police officers. So this is what peaceful, civil disobedience is all about. No bottle or rock throwing, no weapons, no mobbing and trampling the police lines. Just bravery and resolve and tactical organizing among the protestors. The continuing chant "we are peaceful" throughout this whole episode helped to remind ourselves not to let anger interfere. The chant was also to tell the police not to get out of control because we were peaceful, but we were coming through.

I was 70 years old at the time of this inspiring event. Every time I reflect on the experience it sends chills down my spine and makes me proud to have been a part of this peaceful act of determination demonstrated by the marchers. I am not through with protests, but it is unlikely that I personally will witness a more aggressive, yet peaceful and well organized demonstration. My personal experience has been that it is the police, and not the working class, who are usually responsible for initiating and provoking violence, and this situation was no exception. But as the intensity of the struggle against American Capitalism progresses in the coming decades, not all spirited rallies, protests and marches will be as successful in preventing violence as May Day, 2012 in Los Angeles California.

AUTHOR'S SUGGESTED READING LIST

- An Inconvenient Truth: By Al Gore, published in 2006 by Rodale Press.

- Capitalism and After, The Rise and Fall of Commodity Production: By George
Thomson, copyright 1973. Published by the China Policy Study Group, London. Printed in Great Britain, by The Garden City Press Ltd.

- Confession of a Union Buster: By Martin Jay Levitt with Terry Conrow. Copyright 1993 – Crown Publishing Inc. New York.

- Days of Destruction, Days of Revolt: By Chris Hedges and Joe Sacco, Published by Nation Books, 2012

- ILL Fares the Land: By Tony Judt, 2010, The Penguin Press, New York.

- Labor's Untold Story: By Richard O. Boyer and Herbert M. Morais, 3rd Edition, Tenth printing 1976, Published by United Electrical, Radio and Machine Workers of America.

- Nickel and Dimed: On not getting by in American. By Barbara Ehrenreich. Copyright 2001 - By Metropolitan Books. Written from the author's perspective as an undercover journalist. It investigates the impact of the 1996 Welfare Reform Act on the working poor in the United States.

- Political Economy – A Beginner's Course: By A. Leontiev, Proletarian Publishers, P.O. Box 40273, San Francisco, Ca. 94140.

- Solidarity Forever – An Original History of the IWW: By Stewart Bird, Dan Georgakas and Deborah Shaffer. Copyright 1985, Lakeview Press, Chicago.

- The Origin of the Family, Private Property and the State: By Frederick Engels, 3rd printing 1975 by International Publishers Company, Library of Congress card number 79-184309.

- Who Killed the Electric Car? Available only on DVD.

www.ingramcontent.com/pod-product-compliance
Lightning Source LLC
Chambersburg PA
CBHW060235290526
45789CB00001B/57